Legal Pluralism Explained

Legal Pluralism Explained

History, Theory, Consequences

BRIAN Z. TAMANAHA

OXFORD
UNIVERSITY PRESS

OXFORD
UNIVERSITY PRESS

Oxford University Press is a department of the University of Oxford. It furthers
the University's objective of excellence in research, scholarship, and education
by publishing worldwide. Oxford is a registered trade mark of Oxford University Press
in the UK and certain other countries.

Published in the United States of America by Oxford University Press
198 Madison Avenue, New York, NY 10016, United States of America.

Library of Congress Cataloging-in-Publication Data
Names: Tamanaha, Brian Z., author.
Title: Legal pluralism explained : history, theory, consequences / Brian Z. Tamanaha.
Description: New York, NY : Oxford University Press, [2021] | Includes index.
Identifiers: LCCN 2020036082 | ISBN 9780190861551 (hardback) |
    ISBN 9780190861568 (paperback) | ISBN 9780190861575 | ISBN 9780190861582 |
    ISBN 9780190861599
Subjects: LCSH: Legal polycentricity. | Legal polycentricity—History.
Classification: LCC K236 .T36 2021 | DDC 340.9—dc23
LC record available at https://lccn.loc.gov/2020036082

DOI: 10.1093/oso/9780190861551.001.0001

3 5 7 9 8 6 4 2

Paperback printed by Marquis, Canada
Hardback printed by Bridgeport National Bindery, Inc., United States of America

Note to Readers
This publication is designed to provide accurate and authoritative information in regard to the subject
matter covered. It is based upon sources believed to be accurate and reliable and is intended to be
current as of the time it was written. It is sold with the understanding that the publisher is not engaged
in rendering legal, accounting, or other professional services. If legal advice or other expert assistance is
required, the services of a competent professional person should be sought. Also, to confirm that the
information has not been affected or changed by recent developments, traditional legal research
techniques should be used, including checking primary sources where appropriate.

*(Based on the Declaration of Principles jointly adopted by a Committee of the
American Bar Association and a Committee of Publishers and Associations.)*

You may order this or any other Oxford University Press publication
by visiting the Oxford University Press website at www.oup.com.

For Lani Tamanaha Broadbent

Table of Contents

Preface and Acknowledgments

This book has been over three decades in the making. In 1986, as a young Assistant Attorney General in Yap, Micronesia, I was confronted with an effective system of customary law that operated largely outside the state legal system. This experience upended my basic assumptions about law, which I had previously assumed was the monopoly of the state. At the time I had not heard of legal pluralism. Thereafter, when I undertook graduate studies in legal theory, I learned not only that legal pluralism was a common phenomenon around the world, but also that most jurists and legal theorists were completely oblivious to it. I then wrote a series of articles to try to make sense of legal pluralism: "The Folly of the Social Scientific Concept of Legal Pluralism" (1993), "A Non-Essentialist Concept of Legal Pluralism" (2001), "Understanding Legal Pluralism" (2008), "The Rule of Law and Legal Pluralism in Development" (2011), and "The Promise and Conundrums of Pluralist Jurisprudence" (2019). When writing this book I set these articles aside to develop a deeper and broader understanding.

My goal is to provide an explanatory guide to anyone interested in legal pluralism. I also hope to make theoretical contributions to our understanding of law. It turns out that centering on legal pluralism across the course of history and today tells us a great deal about law and society.

Apart from my experiences as a lawyer and training as a legal theorist, for personal reasons I am well situated to write about this topic. Sally Falk Moore was my master's thesis advisor at Harvard Law School. John Griffiths and I developed mutual respect over time, notwithstanding our initial clash of ideas. I had engaging conversations about legal pluralism with Gordon Woodman and Simon Roberts. Sally Engle Merry and I have discussed our mutual interest in Hawaii, legal pluralism, and other matters on multiple occasions over the years. Roger Cotterrell has been my tutor in legal sociology from the outset of my scholarly career. Marc Galanter and William Twining are old friends with whom I have shared experiences and discussions on various topics personal and professional. These preeminent scholars in legal anthropology, legal sociology, and legal theory are leading thinkers of the first generation of legal pluralists. I have learned a great deal from their ideas and this book is indebted to all of them.

I thank Jamie Berezin, my editor at Oxford University Press, for his support for this book and his patience at my missed deadlines.

This book is dedicated to my sister, Lani Tamanaha Broadbent. I am deeply grateful to Lani for the sacrifices she made in caring for our parents in the last stage of their lives. While I cannot repay her, I can express my heartfelt gratitude through this dedication. Thank you, Lani.

Introduction: Three Themes

Legal pluralism is everywhere. In every social arena one examines, a seeming multiplicity of legal orders exists. There are village, municipal, and county laws of various types; there are state, district, or regional laws of various types; there are national, transnational, and international laws of various types. In many societies there are additional forms of law, like indigenous law, customary law, religious law, and the law of distinct ethnic or cultural communities. The contemporary period has witnessed a vast increase in public and private regulatory regimes on various matters at all levels. Coexisting forms of law may be similar in orientation, coordinated with one another, and mutually supportive or complementary; they may make competing claims of authority, impose conflicting norms, and operate through contrasting processes; they may exist wholly apart or thoroughly intertwined. Legal pluralism creates uncertainty because people may not know which legal regime will apply to their situation, and it also creates opportunities for people to opportunistically select from among legal regimes, or to pit one form of law against another in pursuit of their goals. Legal officials in situations of legal pluralism face potential rivals, compete for power and resources, and can be mutually cooperative or antagonistic.

Legal pluralism is everywhere in another sense. First mentioned in the 1960s, references to legal pluralism exploded in ensuing decades as the notion propagated across academic fields from anthropology, to sociology, legal history, comparative law, international law, transnational law, and jurisprudence.[1] Two decades after its initial introduction in legal anthropology, in a 1988 overview that significantly boosted its visibility, Sally Engle Merry declared: "Legal pluralism is a central theme in the reconceptualization of the

---

[1] A search in Heinonline reveals very few uses of the phrase "legal pluralism" prior to the 1970s, followed by a rapid increase in the 1980s, 1990s, and thereafter. A Google Ngram of "Legal Pluralism" likewise exhibits a sharp increase in references to legal pluralism in books commencing in the mid-1970s in both relative and absolute numbers. https://books.google.com/ngrams/graph?content=%22legal+pluralism%22&year_start=1800&year_end=2008&corpus=15&smoothing=3&share=&direct_url=t1%3B%2C%22%20legal%20pluralism%20%22%3B%2Cc0#t1%3B%2C%22%20legal%20pluralism%20%22%3B%2Cc0.

Legal Pluralism Explained. Brian Z. Tamanaha, Oxford University Press (2021). © Brian Z. Tamanaha.
DOI: 10.1093/oso/9780190861551.003.0001

law/society relation."[2] More recently, "legal pluralism has become a standard fare in international and comparative law circles."[3] A collection on "pluralist jurisprudence" declared that legal theorists must move beyond their state-centered focus to take account of coexisting forms of law.[4]

Interest in legal pluralism extends beyond academia. Governments and development agencies have spent several billion dollars to develop state legal systems across the Global South with disappointing results.[5] Law and development theory and practice emphasize the importance of the rule of law and economic development. Customary and religious systems of law were seen as parochial, backwards, regressive, and antithetical to women's rights and human rights. World Bank development experts observed, "Development theorists and practitioners have tended to either blindly ignore the ubiquitous phenomena of legal pluralism or regard it as a constraint on development, a defective condition that must be overcome in the name of modernizing, state building, and enhancing 'the rule of law.' "[6] Recently, however, development practitioners "have begun to reexamine some of the underlying assumptions about legal pluralism and to explore the opportunities that might exist in contexts where legal pluralism is a pervasive reality."[7] An international relations theorist focusing on post-conflict situations observed that "Understanding legal pluralism is important for any legal or policy intervention, including but by no means limited to state building."[8]

Even as it has secured the attention of growing numbers of scholars and development practitioners, however, the notion of legal pluralism remains mired in complexity, confusion, and disagreement. After reviewing two decades of proliferating literature on legal pluralism jurisprudent William Twining remarked, "I have come away feeling that it is little better than a

---

[2] Sally Engle Merry, "Legal Pluralism," 22 Law & Society Review 869 (1988).

[3] C. Valcke, "Three Perils of Legal Pluralism," in S.P. Donlan and L. Heckendorn Urscheler, eds., *Concepts of Law: Comparative, Jurisprudential, and Social Scientific Perspectives* (Farnham: Ashgate, 2015) 123.

[4] Andrew Halpin and Nicole Roughan, eds., *In Pursuit of Pluralist Jurisprudence* (Cambridge: Cambridge University Press 2017).

[5] See Stephen Humphreys, *Theatre of the Rule of Law: Transnational Legal Intervention in Theory and Practice* (Cambridge: Cambridge University Press 2010) 128–32. Brian Z. Tamanaha, "The Primacy of Society and Failures of Law and Development," 44 Cornell International Law Journal 209 (2011).

[6] Caroline Sage and Michael Woolcock, "Introduction: Legal Pluralism and Development Policy: Scholars and Practitioners in Dialogue," in Brian Z. Tamanaha, Caroline Sage, and Michael Woolcock, eds., *Legal Pluralism and Development: Scholars and Practitioners in Dialogue* (New York: Cambridge University Press 2012) 1.

[7] *Id.* at 2.

[8] Geoffrey Swenson, "Legal Pluralism in Theory and Practice," 20 International Studies Review 438, 458 (2018).

morass."[9] A factor contributing to the confusion is that scholars from multiple disciplines have invoked the notion of legal pluralism. Each discipline is internally divided into various schools of thought, and academic disciplines differ from one another in their bodies of knowledge, concepts, and objectives. While on the surface it might appear that a single notion of legal pluralism is applied across fields, an impression perpetuated by shared references to the same cluster of theorists (John Griffiths, Eugen Ehrlich, Sally Falk Moore, etc.), different meanings of legal pluralism are being utilized, often unrecognized as such.

Adding to the confusion is the thin meaning and capaciousness of the term *pluralism*. Pluralism simply means more than one, which can be applied to anything and framed at various levels of specificity and generality. The label legal pluralism has been used to refer to a plurality of interpretations of a single set of laws; to subsystems of law within a single system; to the same tribunals applying distinct bodies of law and separate tribunals applying different bodies of law within a system; to hybrid legal systems that grew out of the interaction between distinct bodies of law; to the coexistence of separate forms of law within a single society; to the coexistence of different subject matter regimes within international law; to the coexistence of multiple legal systems between and across states; and other variations. Each of these examples has been discussed in the literature on legal pluralism, though they are very different.

Complexities and disagreement about the meaning of "law" is another source of confusion. A core proposition across most versions of legal pluralism is that state law is not the only form of law. This assertion requires a definition or concept of law or some way to identify what counts as law as well as to distinguish law from non-law. Legal pluralists have grappled with these threshold issues for five decades now, with multiple concepts of law proposed in the literature, and no end in sight. This struggle is understandable. "What is law?" has never been resolved despite a multitude of attempts by theorists going back centuries. Since each version of legal pluralism is shaped by how law is conceived, there are multiple versions of legal pluralism, each built around a different view of law. The consequence is "a pluralism of legal pluralisms."[10] Legal pluralism is a conceptual mess.

---

[9] William Twining, "Normative and Legal Pluralism: A Global Perspective," 20 Duke Journal of Comparative and International Law 473, 487 (2010).

[10] See Emmanuel Melissaris and Mariano Croce, "A Pluralism of Legal Pluralisms," Oxford Handbooks Online, April 2017, https://www.oxfordhandbooks.com/view/10.1093/oxfordhb/

This book explains legal pluralism in two senses. First, drawing from history and theory, I explain why and how legal pluralism is a common phenomenon across societies past and present, and I show its consequences. Second, I explain what is involved in theoretical disputes surrounding legal pluralism, and I articulate a way to frame legal pluralism that works for development practitioners, scholars, and theorists. This undertaking poses a formidable challenge. The topic crosses over multiple disciplines and audiences with different interests and concerns, and the literature addressing legal pluralism is enormous and expanding too rapidly to stay abreast of. This book is not a comprehensive review of every situation of legal pluralism and everything written about it in every field, which would fill a never-completed set of volumes. Because legal pluralism is literally everywhere, it is impossible to cover comprehensively. Instead, using illustrative examples, I present legal pluralism in broad strokes that convey the most salient empirical, theoretical, and normative issues and consequences involved, in clear prose aimed at a general audience.

To set up this exploration, in this Introduction I first identify what legal pluralism is framed in opposition to: the image of monistic state law. Next I set forth two streams of legal pluralism: abstract legal pluralism constructed by theorists versus folk legal pluralism understood in social-historical terms. Then I outline three categories of law that appear throughout the book: community law, regime law, and cross-polity law. These are preliminary clarifications of major themes that arise time and again in discussions of legal pluralism, filled out in the course of the book. I close with a brief illustration of legal pluralism.

Monistic State Law

Pluralism can be applied to anything involving more than one. In academic settings it is usually applied by way of contrast to a unity of some sort. "The conceptual logic of pluralism thus pits it dialectically against 'monism,' whatever field of human investigation we care to consider."[11] Legal pluralism stands in opposition to the widely held image of monistic state law. "What

9780199935352.001.0001/oxfordhb-9780199935352-e-22; Margaret Davies, "Plural Pluralities of Law," Halpin and Roughan, *supra* note 4, at 239.

[11] Gregor McLennan, *Pluralism* (Minneapolis: University of Minnesota Press 1995) 25.

Is Legal Pluralism?" (1986) by John Griffiths, which significantly shaped academic understandings of the topic, identifies this target (though he substitutes the typical label "monism" with "centralism"):

> According to what I shall call the ideology of legal centralism, law is and should be the law of the state, uniform for all persons, exclusive of all other law, and administered by a single set of state institutions. . . .In the legal centralist conception, law is an exclusive, systematic and unified hierarchical ordering of normative propositions, which can be looked at either from the top downwards as depending from a sovereign command (Bodin, Hobbes, Austin) or from the bottom upwards as deriving their validity from ever more general layers of norms until one reaches some ultimate norm(s) (Kelsen, Hart).[12]

"Legal centralism is a myth, an ideal, a claim, an illusion."[13] "A central objective of a descriptive concept of legal pluralism," Griffiths declared, "is therefore destructive: to break the stranglehold of the idea that what law is, is a single, unified and exclusive hierarchical normative ordering depending from the power of the state, and of the illusion that the legal world actually looks the way such a conception requires it to look."[14]

The origins of the monist view of law trace back to two main theorists. Jean Bodin articulated an account of absolutist sovereignty in 1576 that claimed the exclusive power to make law: "It is only sovereign princes who can make law for all subjects without exception, both collectively and individually."[15] Thomas Hobbes's famous *Leviathan*,[16] published in the mid-seventeenth century, likewise articulates a supreme, indivisible, lawgiving sovereign located in the abstract state. Both accounts were theoretical abstractions and political advocacy, not consistent with actual arrangements at the time. Multiple sources of law existed in their day and the notion of the state was still in early stages of crystallization.[17]

---

[12] J. Griffiths, "What Is Legal Pluralism?," 24 Journal of Legal Pluralism 1, 3 (1986). I have omitted his citations to the theorists listed.

[13] *Id.* at 4.

[14] *Id.* at 4.

[15] Quoting Bodin, in Jens Bartelson, "On the Indivisibility of Sovereignty," 2 Republic of Letters: A Journal for the Study of Knowledge, Politics, and the Arts 85, 87–88 (2011).

[16] Thomas Hobbes, *Leviathan* (Oxford: Oxford University Press 1996).

[17] Quentin Skinner, "The State," in Terence Ball, James Farr, and Russell L. Hanson, eds., *Political Innovation and Conceptual Change* (Cambridge: Cambridge University Press 1989) 120.

As the state system solidified in ensuing centuries, what originally was an abstract vision of the state monopoly over law became an implicitly held understanding shared by many theorists and the public in advanced capitalist societies. Max Weber's ideal type of the modern bureaucratic state, which he formulated in the early twentieth century, captures this understanding, as encapsulated in this passage by William Novak:

> (1) A rationalized and generalized legal and administrative order amenable to legislative change; (2) a bureaucratic apparatus of officers conducting official business with reference to an impersonal order of administrative regulations; (3) the power to bind—to rule and regulate—all persons (national citizens) and all actions within the state's official jurisdiction via its laws; and (4) the legitimate authority to use force, violence, and coercion within the prescribed territory as prescribed by the duly constituted government. Unification, centralization, rationalization, organization, administration, and bureaucratization have become the hallmarks of fully developed, essentially modern states.[18]

State law is unified, hierarchically organized, comprehensive, monopolistic, and supreme over all other orders within society. This is the monistic law state.

Prominent twentieth-century legal philosophers have identified these traits as essential features of law. "Since all legal systems claim to be supreme with respect to their subject-community," Joseph Raz asserts, "none can acknowledge any claim to supremacy over the same community which may be made by another legal system."[19] Echoing Bodin, Raz posits supremacy as a criterion for the existence of a legal system: "We would regard an institutionalized system as a legal system only if it is necessarily in some respect the most important institutionalized system which can exist in that society."[20] "In a nutshell," Raz asserts, a legal system is "a system of guidance and adjudication claiming supreme authority within a certain society and therefore, where efficacious, also enjoying such effective authority."[21]

---

[18] William J. Novak, "The Myth of the 'Weak' American State," 113 American Historical Review 752, 761 (2008).

[19] Joseph Raz, *The Authority of Law*, 2nd ed. (Oxford: Oxford University Press 2009) 119.

[20] *Id.* at 116.

[21] *Id.* at 43.

Dissenting voices over the centuries have challenged this vision of the supreme, unified, monopolistic law state on three main grounds: it is inconsistent with many historical and contemporary manifestations of law, multiple forms of law exist besides state law, and it is normatively problematic. Seventeenth-century efforts at achieving greater state uniformity provoked backlash from local communities. "If God, they argued, had created provinces that were naturally different from each other, it was important that the laws by which they were governed should conform to their distinctive character."[22] Jeremy Bentham criticized Blackstone's account of the supreme sovereign: "The people may be disposed to obey the command of one man against the world in relation to one sort of act, those of another man in relation to another sort of act, else what are we to think of the constitutional laws of the Germanic body."[23] Otto von Gierke in the late nineteenth century argued that law also exists in social associations, a position influentially reiterated by Eugen Ehrlich a generation later.[24] In the early twentieth century, political theorist Harold Laski observed, "We have to admit, so your monist philosopher tells us, that all parts of the State are woven together to make one harmonious whole . . . The unity is logically necessary. . . . Pluralism, in an ultimate sense, is therefore impossible."[25] The monist theory of the state has an affinity with absolutism, Laski warned: "Therefore all order consists in the subordination of the Plurality to Unity, and never and nowhere can a purpose that is common to many be effectual unless the One rules over the Many and directs the Many to the goal."[26] Pragmatist philosopher John Dewey criticized the monist theory of the state as an abstraction that fails to account for myriad variations within and among states.[27] Against this vision, he asserted that "temporal and local diversification is a prime mark of political organization,"[28] and he advocated "a pluralist conception of the state."[29]

Jurists have invoked the monist law state image in conjunction with sovereignty to justify a multitude of dubious assertions and actions. In the

[22] J. H. Elliot, "A Europe of Composite Monarchies," 137 Past and Present 48, 65 (1992).

[23] Jeremy Bentham, quoted in H.L.A. Hart, "Bentham on Sovereignty," 2 Irish Jurist 327, 333 (1967).

[24] See Otto Gierke, Basic Concepts of State Law and the Most Recent State Law Theories, 25 University of Wisconsin Studies in the Social Sciences and History 158, 182 (1935); George Heiman, *Otto Gierke, Associations and Law: The Classical and Early Christian Stages* (Toronto: University of Toronto Press 1977).

[25] Harold Laski, "The Sovereignty of the State," 13 Journal of Philosophy 85, 87–88 (1915).

[26] *Id.* at 87.

[27] See John Dewey, *The Public and Its Problems* (Athens, GA: Swallow Press 1954 [1927]) Chapter 2.

[28] *Id.* at 47.

[29] *Id.* at 73.

past, ideas about sovereignty and monist law provided key justifications for Western colonization, seizing land, and disregarding indigenous law in settler countries. Today the monist law state is an implicit standard widely held by jurists for what a properly constructed system of law consists of, deeming anything that departs from this image inherently flawed and in need of rectification.

One objective of this book is to dislodge the image of the monistic law state. In setting after setting throughout history and today, I show, the monistic view of the law state is descriptively inaccurate and theoretically unsound, and has been applied in normatively problematic ways. Chapter One discusses empires over the last two millennia that secured imperial rule while leaving community laws in place; the decentralized multiplicity of law in medieval Europe; the *millet* system in the Ottoman Empire under which people utilized their own religious law and institutions; extraterritorial courts that European powers created in faraway lands well into the twentieth century; and the British East India Company, which administered separate systems of laws and courts for expatriates, Hindus, and Muslims. Chapter Two examines European colonization, which created transplanted state legal systems alongside pre-existing bodies of customary and religious law, and brought workers from outside in large numbers for plantations and mining, creating a wave of legal pluralism across the Global South that remains entrenched today. These two chapters demonstrate that the monist law state is a recent invention inconsistent with many manifestations of law.

Legal theorists are wont to dismiss counter-examples like these as exceptions, deviations, or corruptions that do not challenge their image of the monist law state, which they take for granted as the central case of law. "It is part of the very idea of a central case that there still might be cases (even statistically preponderant cases) that do not exhibit all the features that make the central case the central case," wrote legal philosopher John Gardner.[30] Similarly, Dennis Galligan observed, "Theorists ought to direct their minds to corrupt, defective, exceptional, or marginal legal systems, but having done so, are likely to conclude . . . that they make no difference to the concept."[31] Historical instances of legal pluralism and law in the Global South are exotic and interesting, a legal theorist might conclude, but can be adjudged defective or corrupt, not sufficient grounds to question the image of the monist

---

[30] John Gardner, *Law as a Leap of Faith* (Oxford: Oxford University Press 2012) 152.
[31] Denis J. Galligan, "Concepts in the Currency of Social Understanding of Law: A Review Essay on the Later Work of William Twining," 35 Oxford Journal of Legal Studies 373, 392 (2015).

law state. What legal theorists project, however, is a highly idealized image of law that does not comport with reality.

Bringing the examination closer to home, making it harder to dismiss, Chapters Three and Four shift to Western legal systems to expose a variety of legally pluralistic contexts contrary to the monist law state. Chapter Three describes legal institutions of Romani (Gypsy) communities across Europe; indigenous law in New Zealand, Canada, Australia, and the United States; and Rabbinical Courts and Sharia Tribunals in the United States and United Kingdom. Chapter Four examines state law within the United States legal system(s), showing that law is not fully unified and hierarchically organized, a condition that also exists within highly developed national legal systems across Europe. European Union law, applied in the Court of Justice of the European Union as well as in national courts, exists alongside the laws and constitution of each nation, applied by national constitutional and high courts, and added to the pluralistic mix is the European Convention on Human Rights applied by the European Court of Human Rights. Thereafter, I convey the contemporary proliferation of transnational law and regulation in public, private, and hybrid forms, many of which are neither wholly national law nor international law.

These various legal arrangements, I show again and again, are incompatible with the monist law state image in two fundamental respects: state law does not have a monopoly over law within society and state law is not organized as unified hierarchical wholes. My positive account of law replaces the monist image in both respects: showing that state law coexists with other forms of collectively recognized law, and offering a descriptive account of state legal regimes as complexes of innumerable distributed legal institutions throughout society that work in the aggregate, with various interconnections, though not as unified wholes.

These examples and varieties of legal pluralism—external to, internal to, and intermingled with state law—are presented to persuade jurists, theorists, and law and development practitioners to set aside the vision of the monist law state and be open to new ways of conceiving of law that recognizes the pervasiveness of legal pluralism and the variety of ways law exists within, across, and outside of state systems. Legal institutions of various types exhibit varying extents of coordination, cohesion, competition, and conflict.

Discarding the monistic image of law is important not just for theoretical purposes, and to improve our understanding of law as a social phenomenon, but it also has policy implications. Jurists engaged in law and development activities have long assumed that law across the Global South will, and should, one day evolve toward unified state legal systems. This study offers abundant reasons to believe the imagined evolution toward state law monism will not occur for many generations, if at all. To grasp these situations, law must be conceived of in more variable and pluralistic terms that exist for endemic underlying reasons, not as temporary aberrations.

Abstract Legal Pluralism versus Folk Legal Pluralism

Scholarly discussions of legal pluralism commonly use a distinction first articulated by Griffiths between "weak" and "strong" legal pluralism (relabeled "classic" and "new" by Merry[32]). When Griffiths published his programmatic essay, the term legal pluralism had been used for two decades to refer to postcolonial societies that recognized customary and religious forms of law. He argued that this "weak" legal pluralism is actually a manifestation of legal centralism because it is a product of state recognition. "'Legal pluralism' in the weak sense has little to do with the concept of legal pluralism which is the subject of this article,"[33] he declared, sharply distancing his concept from studies of postcolonial law. His essay centers on "strong" legal pluralism based on a sociological concept of law independent of the state—"an empirical state of affairs, namely the coexistence within a social group of legal orders which do not belong to a single system." As Merry noted, these two contexts of legal pluralism "make odd companions" in that they have different targets and "they come out of different scholarly traditions."[34]

The strong-weak distinction is frequently invoked by scholars, along with Griffiths's argument that only strong is genuine legal pluralism, whereas weak is not. Theorist Ralf Michaels remarked, "Griffiths's emphasis that the character of law should not depend on recognition by the state has been hugely influential within the literature on legal pluralism."[35] Despite its success, the strong-weak distinction is flawed and distorting. Many situations of legal pluralism covered in this text do not map onto his dichotomy between state recognition (weak) versus independent law

---

[32] Merry, *supra* note 2, at 872–74.

[33] Griffiths, *supra* note 12, at 8.

[34] Merry, *supra* note 2, at 874.

[35] Ralf Michaels, "Law and Recognition—Towards a Relational Concept of Law," in Nicole Roughan and Andrew Halpin, eds., *In Pursuit of Pluralist Jurisprudence* (Cambridge: Cambridge University Press 2017) 99.

(strong). Customary and religious forms of law often exist independently through ongoing cultural processes *and* the state recognizes them for various reasons, and often they are intertwined unofficially and officially. The coherence of his strong-weak distinction, furthermore, depends on his scientific conception of law, which does not work, as Griffiths himself came to acknowledge when he later repudiated legal pluralism (for reasons explained in Chapter Five).[36]

A more illuminating distinction can be drawn between what I call "abstract legal pluralism" and "folk legal pluralism," which I elaborate in Chapter Five. Abstract legal pluralism is the product of social scientists and legal theorists whose aim is to provide a scientific or philosophical theory of law;[37] folk legal pluralism understood in social-historical terms focuses on forms of law collectively recognized by people in society, which vary and change over time. Scientific and theoretical concepts of law and legal pluralism are plagued by irresolvable problems, which I detail. This book articulates and applies social-historical folk legal pluralism.

There are numerous versions of abstract legal pluralism, but they share several basic similarities. First, every theory formulates or identifies a concept or definition of law. These concepts of law can be grouped in one of two broad categories: law as normative ordering within social groups, and law as institutionalized norm enforcement. Another common trait of abstract legal pluralism is that the plurality they center on is a *multiplicity of a single form of law* theoretically defined, not a *multiplicity of different kinds of law*. Another trait is that each theory takes a ubiquitous social phenomenon (normative orders, institutionalized rule systems) and relabels it as "law," now theoretically understood. This move leads to another common trait: all versions of abstract legal pluralism suffer from over-inclusiveness by including social phenomena that do not appear to be law. Merry raised this troubling issue in her review of legal pluralism: "Where do we stop speaking of law and find ourselves simply describing social life?"[38] For reasons I explain in Chapter Five, legal pluralism is still plagued by this problem today, three decades after she flagged it.

---

[36] John Griffiths, "The Idea of Sociology of Law and its Relation to Law and to Sociology," in Michael Freeman, ed., *Law and Sociology* (Oxford: Oxford University Press 2006) 63–64.

[37] John Griffiths, "The Division of Labor in Social Control," in Donald Black, ed., *Toward A General Theory of Social Control*, vol. 1 (New York: Academic Press 1984) 39.

[38] Merry, *supra* note 2, at 878.

Folk legal pluralism proceeds in a different fashion and produces a wholly different account of legal pluralism. It does not formulate a scientific or philosophical concept of law. Law is ultimately a folk concept. Folk legal pluralism identifies law by asking what people in a given social arena collectively recognize and treat through their social practices as law (*recht, droit, lex, ius, diritto, prawo*, etc.). Sharia and Halakhah *are law* because Muslims and Jews, respectively, recognize that as law. In contrast to abstract legal pluralism, which centers on a multiplicity of a single phenomenon defined as law, folk legal pluralism is about a multiplicity of different forms of law collectively recognized by people within society (state law, customary law, religious law, etc.), as well as a multiplicity of the same kind of law. This approach does not relabel social phenomena, but instead accepts the collective identification of law by people within the community, and consequently it is not plagued by over-inclusiveness.

Another crucial set of differences arise from these contrasting presuppositions, methods, and orientations. Abstract legal pluralism abstracts from a paradigm of law to produce *a singular concept or definition with a fixed set of defining features* that purportedly provides a standard for what qualifies as law in all contexts. The social-historical theoretical perspective I apply to folk legal pluralism, in contrast, does not formulate an abstract concept of law with a single set of defining features, but instead accepts that collectively recognized manifestations of law vary widely and change over time in connection with surrounding social, cultural, economic, political, technological, and ecological circumstances.[39] Sharia takes a different form in an Islamic theocracy than it does in liberal democracies. Contrary to the abstract monist theory of the law state, John Dewey observed, this perspective entails "a consistently empirical or *historical* treatment of the changes in political forms and arrangements, free from any overriding conceptual domination such as is inevitable when a 'true' state is postulated."[40]

One of the objectives of this book is to expose the irresolvable problems thrown up by abstract legal pluralism and to demonstrate the soundness of folk legal pluralism understood in social-historical terms. Illustrating its usefulness, the first four chapters utilize folk legal pluralism without stumbling over theoretical difficulties. The conceptual issues revolving around abstract legal pluralism and folk legal pluralism will be elaborated in detail in Chapter

---

[39] For an account of this view of law, see Brian Z. Tamanaha, *A Realistic Theory of Law* (New York: Cambridge University Press 2017).

[40] Dewey, *supra* note 27, at 46.

Five. Suffice it to say here that much of the morass surrounding legal pluralism is created by abstract legal pluralism.

Community Law, Regime Law, Cross-Polity Law

Three categories are useful in tracking law across the many different situations addressed in the course of this book: (1) basic laws and institutions of social intercourse within communities addressing property, personal injuries, marriage, divorce, sexual restrictions, inheritance, debts and obligations, and others; the body of rules people utilize in their daily social interaction; (2) regime laws that constitute, support, and enforce the power of the governing regime, including taxation and customs fees, forced labor and military service, laws against sedition, border controls, and much more, with governing regimes frequently nested within or encompassing in whole or part other sub-regimes; (3) laws that deal with matters between and across organized polities, including national law, international law, and transnational law. These categories are based on rough distinctions that emerge from the observation of folk law phenomena across contexts and over time. For ease of reference, I descriptively label these categories, respectively, *community law*, *regime law*, and *cross-polity law*.

Many manifestations of legal pluralism past and present involve juxtapositions among and between manifestations of these three categories of law. The consolidation of the state system across Europe that began to accelerate in the sixteenth century involved a concerted push by state legal officials to encompass community, regime, and cross-polity laws within the unified territorial state. Ruling regimes over homogeneous societies find it easier to enact comprehensive, uniform bodies of administrative, criminal, and civil law applicable to everyone. Ruling regimes over heterogeneous societies with significant populations of different cultural and religious communities must somehow accommodate, officially or unofficially, legal differences across these communities.

An especially fecund source of legal pluralism, which appears time and again in this text, is the resilience of the basic laws and institutions of social intercourse within the community that exist alongside regime law. Empires throughout history have enforced laws that furthered the objectives of the ruling regime while not interfering with community law. Versions of this occurred with European colonization of Africa, the Middle East, Asia, and the Pacific. This legacy still exists today, as described in a report issued by the World Bank legal department:

> In many developing countries, customary systems operating outside of the state regime are often the dominant form of regulation and dispute resolution, covering up to 90% of the population in parts of Africa. In Sierra Leone, for example, approximately 85% of the population falls under the jurisdiction of customary law, defined under the Constitution as "the rules which, by custom, are applicable to particular communities in Sierra Leone." Customary tenure covers 75% of land in most African countries, affecting 90% of land transactions in countries like Mozambique and Ghana. . . . In many of these countries, systems of justice seem to operate almost completely independently of the official state system.[41]

These situations are pluralistic in two senses: multiple communities exist side by side within the territory of a state each following their own customary or religious (community) laws; and state (regime) law enacts its own set of laws on the same matters, from which customary and religious law often diverges.

Recognizing that manifestations of law can vary in connection with surrounding factors makes it possible to observe continuities in bodies of law even as they undergo changes. Consider that customary law in small-scale hunter-gatherer societies often did not involve institutionalized enforcement; in more populous organized societies, like chiefdoms and early states, community laws were enforced by institutions established by the ruling regime. The former situation is community law with no regime law; the latter is regime law that encompasses community law. Cross-polity law has changed over time as well: what began several millennia ago as specific covenants between two polities on matters like treatment of emissaries and foreign merchants, today involves a profusion of regulatory activities between and across polities. Continuity and change also occur in particular bodies of law in relation to surrounding circumstances. For over two millennia, Jewish community law—Halakhah enforced by rabbinical courts—has been subjected to a range of treatment by the governing polity: from repression to ignored to recognition and enforcement. Across these divergent treatments and institutional arrangements, whether underground or with official

---

[41] Leila Chirayath, Caroline Sage, and Michael Woolcock, Customary Law and Policy Reform: Engaging with the Plurality of Justice Systems (World Bank Legal Department Paper 2005) 3.

regime support, many Jewish communities have continued to live in accordance with Halakhah.

Forms of community law, regime law, and cross-polity law are rooted in traditions, manifested in ongoing institutions, and continuously change subject to surrounding influences. Folk legal pluralism takes each form of law on its own terms, follows their historical development, and examines their interconnections (or disjunctions) with surrounding cultural, social, economic, ecological, technological, and political aspects of society as well as their interaction with other forms of law within the same social arena. This lens enables a rich understanding of legal pluralism.

A Snapshot of Legal Pluralism

This brief snapshot helps set the stage for the exploration of legal pluralism that follows. Thirty-five years ago I moved to Yap in the Federated States of Micronesia to assume an Assistant Attorney General position in a newly independent country carved out of the former Trust Territories of the Pacific Islands administered by the United States. The state laws and legal system were transplanted from the United States, including nearly all of the lawyers and high court judges working within the system, who were occupied mainly with government matters and commercial activities, as well as occasional major crimes. In daily social intercourse in the villages people largely followed customary law administered by chiefs, including matters of property, marriage and divorce, and personal injuries, often on terms not reflected in state law. The populace had little knowledge about state law, which was written in American legalese they did not understand, and on the outer islands the state legal system had virtually no presence. The state and national constitutions officially recognized custom and tradition, but had limited interaction with it. A de facto bifurcation (albeit not sharp or fixed) existed between customary law followed within the community and a state legal system mainly occupied with government affairs and major commercial transactions. The arrangement worked cohesively for the most part, each dealing with its own matters, though occasions arose when the two systems came into direct clash.

In two separate incidents a month apart a teenage boy raped a girl. Thereafter, the community of each of the victims met in a customary gathering to discuss what should be done in response. The traditional leaders at these gatherings decided that the boys must be punished—whereupon the victim's relatives and others in the community severely beat the boys.[42] One boy had a bloodied face and broken arm; the other was beaten unconscious and hospitalized for five days (the latter received a more severe punishment because his victim was from a higher caste, which magnifies the offense). A traditional reconciliation ceremony held thereafter resolved the matter within the community.

Following these events, a national prosecutor brought rape charges against the two boys. They admitted their guilt and proceeded to sentencing. State legal officials ordinarily did not file criminal charges when customary punishments were administered because that resolved the matter within the community, but charges were brought in this instance because it was a serious crime under the criminal code that required prosecution. The family of the victims took the side of the defendants in the state proceedings, asserting that the boys had already been appropriately punished. The attorney for a defendant argued that "as a matter of customary law, the beating may have restored [him] fully to the community."[43] Judge Richard Benson (an American expatriate) sentenced the boys to two years in jail. He refused to consider the customary punishment because he did not want to send the message that people could "take the law into their own hands."[44] This language suggests they were acting as vigilantes, not people carrying out legitimate customary punishment on behalf of the community.

On appeal, the Supreme Court ruled that owing to the constitutional clause recognizing custom and tradition, the customary punishment should be considered as a mitigating factor to reduce the punishment. More telling than the outcome is how Judge Edward King (an American expatriate) construed events. Judge King skeptically and disapprovingly described the conduct of the villagers: "Both defendants suffered substantial, even brutal, beatings perpetrated by people who saw themselves as somehow representing the victims and their communities."[45] He asserted the monist view that state law is supreme and exclusive:

---

[42] An account of this case is provided in Brian Z. Tamanaha, "A Battle Between Law and Society in Micronesia: An Example of Originalism Gone Awry," 21 Pacific Rim Law & Policy Journal 295 (2012). These events are described in the consolidated reported case Tammed v. FSM, Tamangrow v. FSM, App. No. Y1-1988 (July 17, 1990), 4 Intrm. 266 (App. 1990).

[43] *Id.* at 5.

[44] *Id.* at 5–6.

[45] *Id.* at 6.

In adopting the Declaration of Rights as part of the Constitution of the Federated States of Micronesia and therefore the supreme law of the land, the people of Micronesia subscribed to various principles which place upon the judiciary the obligation, among others, to assure that arrests are based upon probable cause, the determinations are arrived at fairly, and that punishments for wrongdoing are proportionate to the crime and meet prescribed standards.[46]

Judge King condemned the policy of state legal officials of not bringing charges after customary punishment and reconciliation had taken place:

This practice of course amounts to a substitution of the customary punishment in place of the judicial proceedings and punishment contemplated by the Constitution and state statutes. Under the policy of the Yap attorney general's office, beating is no longer just a customary punishment, but also serves as the entire official state trial and punishment for that specific offense. The traditional leaders who authorized the punishment, and the village members who carried it out, may well be transformed through this ratification into government agents or officials.[47]

State law is the only form of law in Micronesia (in his mind), so therefore, Judge King reasoned, if state legal officials recognize customary punishments by the community, in effect this constitutes *the state's* legal actions. The judge issued a thinly veiled warning that the state could be sued for civil rights violations if they continued to defer to customary punishments.[48]

From the perspective of the community, including the victims and defendants, the punishment was an appropriate customary law response that directly resolved the situation independent of the state legal system. Yapese customary law did not owe its existence to the fact that a clause was included in the written constitution recognizing custom and tradition (drafted by a staff of American lawyers), but rather because as far back as they could remember they carried out their daily social intercourse through this law. It was *their* law literally, which they collectively created through their

---

[46] *Id.* at 24-25.

[47] *Id.* at 39.

[48] In an article addressing this case he wrote after retiring, King acknowledged that his purpose was to threaten state officials with liability to pressure them to stop their practice of deferring to customary punishments. Edward C. King, "Custom and Constitutionalism in the Federated States of Micronesia," 3 Asian-Pacific Law & Policy Journal 249, 278 (2002).

understandings and actions—unlike the transplanted state legal system that administered laws they did not live by run by officials from another society using technical legal language and procedures they did not understand.

Legal pluralism is complicated and messy and challenges basic assumptions about law perpetuated by the widely held monist law state image. Jurists and judges frequently hold and express monist assumptions about law, while members of the community may collectively recognize other legitimate forms of law functioning alongside state law. Just because state legal officials declare their monopoly over law, this does not make it necessarily so. Jurists sometimes have difficulty seeing beyond their own image and construction of law. Readers must be open to the unfamiliar to appreciate the extraordinary range of manifestations of coexisting forms of law and their implications presented in the course of this book.

One
Legal Pluralism in Historical Context

Until a half century ago there was little mention of "legal pluralism" as a concept despite the fact that the phenomenon has existed in many settings for millennia. Historians Jane Burbank and Frederick Cooper explain: "The normality of legal pluralism in many forms—different rules for different groups, devolved authority to interpret and enforce them, sustenance of multiple and sometimes conflicting jurisdictions—explains in part why rulers, legal theorists, politically minded explorers, theologians, and other writers at that time do not seem to have needed a concept for it, or considered it worthy of debate."[1] Not only was the coexistence of multiple forms of law a normal state of affairs, but also prior to the consolidation of law in the territorial state there was no alternative position against which to frame legal pluralism. It's like a fish that lacks a sense of water as a medium unless it breaches the surface to encounter air for the first time.

This chapter attempts to recover a sense of the historical normalcy of legal pluralism. A pivotal shift of the past several centuries has been from law attached to a person's community toward territorial states that claim a monopoly over law—a long-term project that has always been marked by major exceptions and has never been fully accomplished. This chapter traces the course of this shift. Prior to this shift, the widely held view, now largely forgotten, is that everyone was entitled to be judged by the law of their community, called "personal law" at the time because it attaches to each person, though I descriptively label this "community law" to enable comparisons to other contexts. The first step is to understand empires, which are cauldrons of legal pluralism, using the Roman Empire as an example. Then I cover legal pluralism during the High Middle Ages, followed by the slow process by which the state gradually crystallized, absorbing other forms of law within its ambit, though not entirely. Then I address, in order, three legally plural contexts in the early modern period: *millets* in the Ottoman Empire,

---

[1] Jane Burbank and Frederick Cooper, "Rules of Law, Politics of Empire," in Lauren Benton and Richard Ross, eds., *Legal Pluralism and Empires, 1500–1850* (New York: NYU Press 2013) 279.

Legal Pluralism Explained. Brian Z. Tamanaha, Oxford University Press (2021). © Brian Z. Tamanaha.
DOI: 10.1093/oso/9780190861551.003.0002

extraterritoriality, and the plural legal system entrenched in India by the British East India Company.

How Empires Create Legal Pluralism

Empires have shaped human societies for millennia. An empire is a polity with an imperial center or metropole that dominates polities at the periphery.[2] They span large territories across land or sea, consisting of congeries of populations with multiple languages, ethnicities, religions, levels of technology, ecological systems, forms of political organization, and ways of life. Empires extract wealth and resources from subordinate polities through imposing taxes, tributes, forced labor (military conscription, corvee, slavery) and customs fees on trade conducted on terms favorable to the dominant polity, and generally utilizing or seizing what they desire. The initial extension of imperial authority frequently occurs through violent military conquest, aided by securing local allies and dynastic marital unions, followed by pacification and regularized imperial control.

Each empire constructs its own unique arrangement, but they share certain patterns owing to common challenges. They must create effective systems for extracting resources, implement an administrative structure, establish transportation and communication infrastructures that tie the periphery to the imperial center, and maintain authority across great distances over diverse populations that numerically outstrip the imperial center.[3] At its peak the British Empire—"on which the sun never sets"—encompassed substantial parts of Africa, large regions of the Middle and Near East, the Indian subcontinent, the Malaysian Peninsula, Hong Kong, Australia and New Zealand, Canada, and various island groups in the Pacific and Caribbean. On the Indian subcontinent alone, in the mid-nineteenth century, fewer than 50,000 British ruled 150 million people,[4] on top of many millions of people in others areas under British dominion.

---

[2] See Susan Reynolds, "Empires: A Problem of Comparative History," 79 Historical Research 151, 152 (2006).

[3] The literature on empires is extensive. My analysis is indebted particularly to Jane Burbank and Frederick Cooper, *Empires in World History: Power and Politics of Difference* (Princeton: Princeton University Press 2010); Heather Streets-Salter and Trevor R. Getz, *Empires and Colonies in the Modern World: A Global Perspective* (New York: Oxford University Press 2016).

[4] Streets-Salter and Getz, *supra* note 3, at, 278.

Empires commonly effectuate rule through an administrative apparatus staffed by imperial representatives, utilizing native elites (pre-existing or newly put in place) and their networks of rule, and exploiting or reinforcing existing divisions and rivalries (language, ethnic, religious, caste, class, etc.) to prevent unified opposition. Imperial administrative approaches range from direct rule to indirect rule.[5] Direct rule is costly and requires significant manpower. The imperial power sweeps away existing political elites and replaces them with imperial administrators establishing and enforcing newly imposed economic, political, and legal regimes. Empires with assimilationist ambitions that seek to fully absorb the periphery use direct rule—erecting a comprehensive governing and legal structure, resettling people from the metropole in substantial numbers to dominate the population at the periphery, as well as killing, marginalizing, or pushing out pre-existing residents.

Rather than fully absorb the periphery, which is costly and requires substantial manpower and sustained effort, many empires instead use indirect rule and concentrate their efforts on political control and economic exploitation. This approach relies on coopting and rewarding local leaders while keeping intact much of the existing political substructure and prevailing laws. Imperial regimes enlist the service of local elites for the mutual benefit of both parties. After observing successful historical empires, Machiavelli in *The Prince* (1513) proposed indirect rule for taking control of vast dominions, enlisting second-level powers to work for the imperial state, who would be happy with their enhanced status.[6] "[A]llow them to live with their own laws, forcing them to pay a tribute and creating an oligarchy there that will keep the state friendly toward you."[7]

Personal (Community) Law During and After
the Roman Empire

"In ancient law the personality principle was dominant."[8] "In the first place the law of the tribe was personal. It followed the person wherever he traveled

[5] *See id.* at 272–75. Streets-Salter and Getz identify four modes of governance: direct rule, indirect rule, responsible governance (settler societies), and proxy rule (private companies).

[6] Niccolo Machiavelli, *The Prince*, translated and edited by Peter Bondanella (Oxford: Oxford University Press 2005) 11–12.

[7] *Id.* at 19.

[8] G.C.J.J. van den Bergh, "Legal Pluralism in Roman Law," 4 Irish Jurist 338, 343 (1969).

or resided . . . Law, like religion, was a personal possession."[9] Under this view, "every man was entitled everywhere to be judged by that tribal law by which he 'professed to live.' "[10] This is what I call community law.

The Roman Empire encompassed parts of Britain, much of the continent of Western Europe, Greece and the Middle East, as well as Northern Africa, completely surrounding the Mediterranean Sea. As the Roman Empire wore on it became more assimilationist, engaging in direct rule and expanding the grant of Roman citizenship "in a tremendous effort to transform the personal law of citizens into a universal law for the whole empire."[11] The *ius civil* of Roman law applied only to Roman citizens; *ius gentium* was considered law common to all peoples (a part of natural law), primarily concerning commercial law and aspects of international law.[12] Aside from these forms of law, "In principle, the Romans did not interfere with local communities if they could avoid it; everybody was left to live in his own traditional way by his own law."[13]

In distant provinces Roman courts were few in number, so in many locations the only available venue was a local tribunal applying local law. But even Roman courts in the provinces recognized and applied local law, relying on local legal experts to attest to the applicable law; in Egypt, where local courts were abolished, Roman courts applied existing bodies of Greek and Egyptian law to basic matters, including family, inheritance, property, contracts, and some pre-existing procedures and legislation, even in instances that were contrary to Roman law.[14] Produced by professional jurists, Roman law initially treated custom as a fact that carried authority through the weight of tradition, and later came to recognize it as a form of law. As large numbers of Germans moved into Roman territories to serve the Roman military, they were allowed to arrange their affairs according to their own community law rather than Roman law, consistent with the personality principle.[15] "Foreign legal practice confronted them [Roman authorities] as

<hr>

[9] Simeon L. Guterman, "The Principle of Personality of Law in the Early Middle Ages: A Chapter in the Evolution of Western Legal Institutions and Ideas," 21 University of Miami Law Review 259, 271–72 (1966).

[10] Max Weber, *Economy and Society*, vol. 2, edited by Guenther Roth and Clause Wittich (Berkeley: University of California Press 1978).

[11] Guterman, *supra* note 9, at 259, 273.

[12] Ernest Barker, "Translator's Introduction," in Otto Gierke, *Natural Law and the Theory of Society 1500–1800* (Boston: Beacon Press 1957) xxxvi–xxxvii.

[13] Van den Bergh, *supra* note 8, at 343; Guterman, *supra* note 9, at 295.

[14] See Jose Luis Alonso, "Customary Law and Legal Pluralism in the Roman Empire: The Status of Peregrine Law in Egypt," 43 Journal of Juristic Papyrology 351 (2013).

[15] Guterman, *supra* note 9, at 273.

a matter of colonial administration and they treated it as such in their usual manner, that is, purely pragmatically and extremely liberally, so long as no threat to their political power was involved."[16]

An instructive example of changing relations between community law and regime law is Roman treatment of Jewish law. Following the takeover of Palestine, Judea was recognized as a Roman province, and "the governor maintained the principle of leaving civil justice to the local Jewish institutions,"[17] which furthered Rome's desire to not provoke resistance to their rule. When early Jewish revolts were defeated, they forfeited official recognition as a civic entity, but under the personality principle they continued to be recognized as people entitled to Jewish law in civil cases between Jews, applied in Roman courts or Jewish courts (which had concurrent jurisdiction).[18] This same treatment occurred in the Roman provinces of Greece, Egypt, and Syria. Even after Roman citizenship was extended by imperial decree to all free male inhabitants of the empire in 212 A.D., Jews continued to be subject to Jewish courts applying Jewish law. After the early fourth-century Christianization of the Roman Empire, official Roman recognition of Jewish courts was withdrawn, though rabbinical courts still decided religious matters. Roman courts took jurisdiction over criminal and civil matters, although Jews could voluntarily bring their cases to Jewish courts acting as arbitrators.[19] Through a number of changes in the political relationship between the Roman state and Jews, the personality principle tied to the law of the Jewish community continued to be adhered to in substance, even when it was officially restricted.

The Roman Empire succumbed in the fifth century to successive waves of invasions by various Germanic tribes, but the personality principle continued. Shorn of its territorial authority, Roman law remained as personal law after collapse.[20] Under Visigoth rule, courts would apply Roman law in cases between Romans (including certain aspects of criminal law), while Gothic law was applied in cases between Goths or between Romans and Goths.[21] Eighth-century Frankish (Ripuarian) instructions to officials made this explicit: "to the entire population there residing, Franks, Roman, Burgundians

---

[16] Van den Bergh, *supra* note 8, at 345.

[17] Alfredo Mordechai Rabello, "Jewish and Roman Jurisdiction," in N.S. Hecht, ed., *Introduction to the Sources and History of Jewish Law* (Oxford: Oxford University Press 1996) 144.

[18] *Id.* at 145–47.

[19] *Id.* at 153–54.

[20] See Guterman, *supra* note 9, at 271–72.

[21] *Id.* at 277–81.

as well as other nations, should live and conduct themselves well under your rule and government, and may you direct them in the right path according to their law and custom."[22] In the early medieval period "the first question that defendants had to answer when they were sued in courts" was "Quale lege vivis? What is your law?"[23] Recognition of personal law even included criminal law: "If he is condemned he shall suffer the penalty which is indicated in the law of his country and not what is prescribed by the law of the Ripuarians."[24]

Whether under Roman or German rule, and through the Middle Ages thereafter, there was no notion of a monopoly of law by the state and no notion that the law must be uniform within a territory. Except when contrary to interests of the ruling regime, people continued to live according to their existing customary and religious legal regimes, including substantive laws of marriage, divorce, inheritance, property, personal injuries, debt and agreements. No single system addressed all matters—administrative, criminal, and civil—as modern legal systems purport to. Law was compartmentalized by authorities (imperial, royal, religious, feudal, municipal, village), by groups (ethnic, cultural, religious) and associations (merchants, guilds), and by subject matter. This continued for centuries, as new forms of political-legal authority became entrenched across Europe, including the newly constructed Holy Roman Empire and the universal Roman Catholic Church, adding to the legal pluralism.

Legal Pluralism of the High Middle Ages

Throughout the medieval period law was seen as the product of social groups and associations that formed legal orders, as Max Weber elaborates, "either constituted in its membership by such objective characteristics of birth, political, ethnic, or religious denomination, mode of life or occupation, or arose through the process of explicit fraternization."[25] During the second half of the Middle Ages, roughly the tenth through fifteenth centuries,[26] there were

---

[22] Quoting a Frankish edict. *Id.* at 286.

[23] Claudia Storti, "Ascertainment of Customs and Personal Law in Medieval Italy from the Lombard Kingdom to the Communes," 24 Journal of the Max Plank Institute for Legal History 257, 259 (2016).

[24] Guterman, *supra* note 9, at 287.

[25] Weber, *supra* note 10, at 695.

[26] A concise summary of developments leading up to this period is Frederick M. Maitland, "A Prologue to a History of English Law," 14 Law and Quarterly Review 13 (1898).

"several distinct types of law, sometimes competing, occasionally overlapping, invariably invoking different traditions, jurisdictions and modes of operation."[27] Types of law included imperial and royal edicts and statutes, canon law, unwritten customary law of tribes and localities, written Germanic law, residual Roman law, municipal statutes, the law of merchants and of guilds, and in England the common law, on the continent the Roman law of jurists after the twelfth-century revival of the Justinian Code. The types of courts included various imperial and royal courts, ecclesiastical courts, manorial or seigniorial courts, village courts, municipal courts in cities, merchant courts, and guild courts. Serving as judges in these courts, respectively, were emperors and kings or their appointees, bishops and abbots, barons or lords of the manor or their appointees, local lay leaders, leading burghers, merchants, and members of the guild. These various positions were not wholly separate—many high government officials were in religious orders, while churches held landed estates that came with local judicial responsibilities. "Bishops, abbots and prioresses, as lords of temporal possessions, controlled manorial or honorial courts at which they sometimes, though not generally, presided in person, exercising responsibility for criminal and customary law."[28]

"The result was the existence of numerous law communities," Weber wrote, "the autonomous jurisdictions of which overlapped, the compulsory, political association being only one such autonomous jurisdiction in so far as it existed at all."[29] Jurisdictional rules for judicial tribunals and the laws to be applied related to the persons involved and the subject matter at issue. The personality principle linked law to a person's community or association, and under feudalism property ownership came wrapped together with the right to judge those tied to the property. "Demarcation disputes between these laws and courts were numerous."[30] Jurisdictional conflicts arose especially in relation to ecclesiastical courts, which claimed broad jurisdiction over personal status laws (marriage, divorce, inheritance) and moral crimes, as well as church property and personnel, matters which regularly overlapped with the jurisdiction of other courts. Furthermore, different bodies of law could

---

[27] Anthony Musson, *Medieval Law in Context: The Growth of Legal Consciousness from Magna Carta to the Peasant's Revolt* (Manchester: Manchester University Press 1981). A detailed account of medieval law and the state is Alan Harding, *Medieval Law and the Foundations of the State* (Oxford: Oxford University Press 2002).

[28] Musson, *supra* note 27, at14.

[29] Weber, *supra* note 10, at 697.

[30] Raoul van Caenegem, *Legal History: A European Perspective* (London: Bloomsbury 1991) 119.

be applicable in a given court in a given case. "It was common to find many different codes of customary law in force in the same kingdom, town or village, even in the same house, if the ninth century bishop Agobard of Lyons is to be believed when he says, 'It often happened that five men were present or sitting together, and not one of them had the same law as another.' "[31] In long-settled areas, the personal law of communities became local customary law.[32] People living within cities were subject to municipal statutes and customary law on certain matters (penal law, procedural), and the community law to which they were attached.[33]

Thus legal pluralism was a normal aspect of medieval life. The legal authority of separate sources was accepted on their own terms: law of kings and emperors, customary law of the community, feudal law of the landowning class, law of the Church, law of municipalities, and law of associations (guilds, merchants). No single source of law was comprehensive and superior to all others on all matters. Royal law was important but rivaled by ecclesiastical law and could not unilaterally alter feudal and customary law. Legal historian Frederick Maitland observed about the law-issuing power of ninth-century kings and emperors: "Within a sphere which can not be readily defined he exercised the power of laying commands upon all his subjects, and so of making new territorial law for his whole realm or any part thereof; but in principle any change in the law of one of the folks would require that folk's consent."[34]

Crystallization of the Law State

Medieval political and legal structures were thoroughly decentralized.[35] The consolidation of law in the state would take place over the course of centuries across Europe, at different paces along different paths.[36] A fundamental change entailed transitioning from medieval political and legal arrangements based on networks of relationships toward bureaucratic administration

---

[31] John Morrall, *Political Thought in Medieval Times* (Toronto: University of Toronto Press 1980) 17.

[32] Maitland, *supra* note 26, at 23.

[33] Storti, *supra* note 23, at 260.

[34] Maitland, *supra* note 26, at 26.

[35] Charles Tilly, "Reflections on the History of European State-Making," in Charles Tilly, ed., *The Formation of National States in Europe* (Princeton: Princeton University Press 1975) 21–25.

[36] A concise overview is Joseph R. Strayer, *On the Medieval Origins of the Modern State* (Princeton: Princeton University Press 1970).

comprised of officeholders carrying out prescribed roles and responsibilities. Feudal law was constructed on ties of fealty that ran from the nobility and their vassals with substantial landholdings, further subdivided through the practice of subinfeudation among subordinate vassals, and so forth, down to serfs who worked the land. This created multilayered networks of relationships, nobles at the pinnacle, with everyone linked in descending hierarchies of mutual obligations in which services or rents were owed by persons lower in the rung to those above in exchange for use or control of the land and its fruits. These networks of relationships formed sinews within the polity since kings were themselves major landowners (the king of England was titular owner of all land), with relationship ties to barons, who were formidable political figures. Advisors and staff to kings and barons, furthermore, were members of the household staff paid from personal streams of landholding income and other sources of revenues they were due. Relations with external powers involved "far-flung systems of relations forged by interstate ties between leading families and noble or princely houses as they sought to further their interests, and to the interaction between these strategies and internal political arrangements."[37]

Institutions of government in the medieval period, to put the point in contemporary terms, did not constitute a distinct "public" sphere. "The state was, in short, a system of institutions, of powers and practices, that had as one of its defining features a sort of programmatic permeability to extraneous (or, if one prefers, 'private') powers and purposes while retaining an overall unity of political organization."[38] The fully constituted law-state, centuries in the making, would require well-developed bureaucratic offices funded by the government fisc, and legal institutions staffed by trained officials who carried out the law.

Consolidation of law in the state involved the elimination, absorption, or ejection of four rival sources of legal power: empires, the Church, nobles, and cities.[39] The Holy Roman Empire, in 1500, centered around Germanic-speaking lands covering much of central Europe, extending from the Baltic Sea to Northern Italy, consisting of a multitude of political entities, including kingdoms, duchies, principalities, and independent cities, each with their

[37] Giogio Chittolini, "The 'Private,' the 'Public,' the State," 67 Journal of Modern History S34, S42 (1995).

[38] *Id.* at S46.

[39] See Martin van Creveld, *The Rise and Decline of the State* (Cambridge: Cambridge University Press 1999) 59–117.

own authorities. Europe had about 500 "independent political units" at the time.[40] There was no fixed imperial capitol. Emperors ruled hereditary lands directly as king, and over the rest of the empire—areas ruled by their own kings, princes, and dukes—the emperor exercised powers to hold court, issue legal edits, veto acts, collect taxes, appoint dukes and other heads, and wage wars, among other powers.[41] In the early sixteenth century, Charles V simultaneously headed *two* overlapping but distinct empires: as Holy Roman Emperor and as monarch of the Habsburg Empire, which included Austria, the Netherlands and Belgium, Spain and its American territories, and much of southern Italy.

The Church and its clergy were separate from but also intertwined with royal and manorial courts in various ways. Catholic doctrine distinguished two spheres—the spiritual governed by the Church and temporal governed by the secular state—with the Church the higher of the two.[42] The legal powers of the Church were extensive: "apart from the power to lay down and interpret divine law, the right to nominate and promote its own officials; the right to judge and punish both its own personnel and, in cases involving the care of souls, laymen; the right to offer asylum to fugitives from secular justice; the right to absolve subjects from their oaths to their rulers; and, to support the lot, immense landed estates, a separate system of taxation, and, here and there, the right to strike money as well."[43] With a central role in the community on matters of marriage, wills, defamation, and religious and moral conduct, the Church had court hierarchies separate from the state, though assistance from the king's officers was required to arrest people avoiding its jurisdiction.[44] In addition, as mentioned, church magnates with substantial landholdings exercised legal powers held by lords, and church officials regularly resorted to royal courts in land disputes. Finally, since they were the educated class in society, "to a large extent the clergy staffed the king's household administration and the central courts which crystallized from it."[45]

The Reformation and the devastating religious wars that ensued shattered the grip of both Empire and Church. The Empire and the Church were directly at odds when troops of Emperor Charles V sacked Rome in 1527,

---

[40] *Id.* at 25.

[41] On the significant powers of the emperor, see Andreas Osiander, "Sovereignty, International Relations, and the Westphalian Myth," 55 International Organization 251 (2001).

[42] Gierke, *supra* note 12, at 87–88.

[43] van Creveld, *supra* note 39, at 60.

[44] Harding, *supra* note 27, at 137.

[45] *Id.* at 137.

temporarily imprisoning Pope Clement VII, wounding the prestige and power of the Church. Protestant rulers confiscated Church property, restricted Church legal functions, and rejected the authority of the emperor.[46] Protestant views maintained the dualism of spiritual and temporal, but discarded the claim of church sovereignty[47]—setting off a long-term shift in the West that ultimately would remove public legal powers of the institutional church, relegating it to the private realm. The Holy Roman Empire and Habsburg Monarchy spanned Catholic and Protestant areas and consequently were internally riven by the Reformation. The Thirty Years War (1618–1648), initiated by Emperor Ferdinand II against Protestant rulers to restore his right to establish Catholicism in his domains, resulted in millions of deaths. "The Peace of Westphalia which, in 1648, concluded the war marked the monarch's triumph over both the Empire and the church."[48] Thereafter, Europe was partitioned among states and smaller polities ruled by kings, princes, and dukes with the power to determine internal matters within their territories (though significant imperial legal powers continued, as explained shortly). The treaty of Westphalia, for this reason, is widely identified as a key marker in the establishment of Europe as a collection of independent states and the birth of the international system of states.[49]

Nobles were formidable figures within medieval society: wealthy landowners; political rivals to monarchs; and local magnates with administrative, policing, and judicial authority. Their legal powers included the exercise of civil and criminal jurisdiction—not a sharp distinction at the time—involving their lands, tenants, and serfs that attached to ownership of the land as "the customary rights of lords."[50] Barons or their designees dealt with disputes related to land tenancy on their estates, including rents, title and transfer issues, inheritance, contracts and debts, as well as homicide, injuries, arson, robbery, rape, and public disturbances. In villages within their domain, nobles appointed laypeople to preside in village courts "in which the peasants themselves did the judging, spent their time exacting fines for their lords for offenses against local by-laws, awarding damages for 'civil' injuries

---

[46] van Creveld, *supra* note 39, at 66–70, 84–85.

[47] Gierke, *supra* note 12, at 88–90.

[48] van Creveld, *supra* note 39, at 86.

[49] An influential critique of this view is Stephen D. Krasner, "Compromising Westphalia," 20 International Security 115 (1995). Krasner points out that states were not independent sovereigns as a result of the Peace of Westphalia, and states since has never been consistent with the image projected by the theory of sovereignty.

[50] Harding, *supra* note 27, at 50.

inflicted by one householder on another, and settling disputes concerning peasant land-tenure."[51] These tribunals applied by-laws and local customary law; in civil cases their orientation was to come to a just result "based upon factual equities rather than on substantive law."[52] Kings in England during the latter part of this period appointed local notables (gentry and leading burghers) to unpaid positions as Justice of the Peace exercising policing and judicial authority and collecting taxes; in France, seigniorial judicial offices were owned by major landowners and could be bought and sold.[53]

Towns (or "communes") and cities were corporations with free residents enjoying substantial rights of self-governance, often with charters of recognition issued by kings.[54] They enacted regulations, collected municipal dues and royal taxes, had fortifications and militias, and were centers of manufacturing and trade. The most successful became independent city states engaged in long distance trade, like Venice and Genoa, and the Hanseatic League of cities that dominated commerce in the Baltic and North Seas. Towns and cities were scattered across Europe, usually with the support of monarchs, who financially benefited from their economic activities and tax collection. They exercised policing and judicial authority over a full range of civil and criminal matters, which potentially overlapped with the judicial rights of manorial, ecclesiastical, and royal courts.[55] As a consequence, during this period there were "long-running disputes and short-lived compromises about [overlapping jurisdiction] between churches, lay lords, communes, and royal officials."[56]

In understandings of the time monarchs were dispensers of justice in the realm based on their position as monarch and ultimate lord over the domain. They established royal courts that heard major cases, often involving land, including disputes among and against lords and bishops. Land disputes with potential volatility were often resolved through negotiations backed by the king.[57] While royal courts occupied an essential place in the system, they handled relatively few cases—evidenced by the fact that in the thirteenth century no more than twenty to twenty-five royal judges operated across

---

[51] *Id.* at 53.

[52] Lloyd Bonfield, "The Nature of Customary Law in the Manor Courts of Medieval England," 31 Comparative Studies in Society and History 514, 531 (1989).

[53] David Parker, "Sovereignty, Absolutism, and the Function of the Law in Seventeenth-Century France," 122 Past & Present 36, 51–54 (1989)

[54] See van Creveld, *supra* note 39, at 104–17.

[55] Harding, *supra* note 27, at 5–60.

[56] *Id.* at 61.

[57] *Id* at 67.

England, which had the most developed system of royal courts at the time.[58] The vast bulk of legal activities involved decentralized policing and adjudication carried out by local actors (knights, squires, abbots, mayors, village leaders) without economic support from royal coffers. The process of incorporating law within the state involved the gradual absorption of these local institutions. "In cases like the state's seizure of control over justice from manorial lords, churches and communities, the right itself was continued in more or less the same form, but under new management."[59]

A significant early step in unifying law in the state was the thirteenth-century creation by monarchs of assemblies with judicial and political responsibilities that in various ways knitted together institutional components of law.[60] In France, a *parlement* staffed by jurists was created by the king in his royal household to remove from seigniorial courts major cases involving the nobility, church officials, and royal officers; *parlements* were created for each large region, in the aggregate constituting a high court system of royal justice that spanned the country.[61] Evolving over time, kings came to consult the *parlement* on treaties and it acquired an official role in registering new laws. English parliaments, consisting of lay and church nobles from across the nation (and later a commons with squires and wealthy burghers), were initially called together by the king to render final judgments in cases of great political importance, but they soon took on significant additional roles, sitting as a permanent high court in Westminster above various king's courts, proposing legislation, approving taxes, and receiving petitions from people, ultimately leading to a significant increase in legislation addressing a wide range of matters.[62] With the creation of the parliament, "statute making as the essential and continuous activity of the king was recognized to have begun in England."[63] By the fifteenth century representative bodies existed in Poland, Hungary, Spain (Castile), Sweden, Germany, and the Low Countries.

Another element in the creation a unified system was a substantial increase in people trained in law who would collectively build the law of the realm. Medievalist Marc Bloch observed, "The consolidation of societies into great states or principalities favored not only the revival of legislation but also

---

[58] Strayer, *supra* note 36, at 48.
[59] Tilly, *supra* note 35.
[60] *Id.* at 22–23.
[61] Harding, *supra* note 27, at 160–70.
[62] See Musson, *supra* note 27, at 184–211.
[63] Harding, *supra* note 27, at 186.

the extension of a unifying jurisprudence over vast territories."[64] *The Treatise on the Laws and Customs of the Kingdom of England*, attributed to Glanvill, circulated in the 1180s, followed a half century later by *Bracton's On the Laws and Customs of England*. The thirteenth century also saw the publication of treatises on Norman, French, Castilian, and Saxon customary law.[65] This outpouring of juristic work coincided with the twelfth-century revival and teaching of Roman law in Bologna, Paris, and Oxford, which drew students from across Europe; and it coincided with the flowering of systematic analyses of canon law (following Gratian's *Decretum*). Jurists trained at universities brought Roman law concepts, categories, procedures, and modes of legal analysis to courts across Europe, contributing to a shared *ius commune* consisting of a mix of canon law and Roman law.[66] Clergy were trained in canon law, which drew heavily on Roman law, enabling them to work in ecclesiastical or secular courts. For English common law, training took place by observing court proceedings, attending lectures by judges, using manuals based on the work of Glanville and Bracton, and reading case reports—instruction that was formalized in the Inns of Court in the early fourteenth century.[67] The common training, knowledge, practices, and socialization of lawyers and judges in the building legal tradition helped bring greater uniformity to law, though significant lay participation as judges and juries would continue for centuries.

Through the cumulative effect of this combination of changing ideas, institutions, and actions a gradual cultural shift was taking place from perceiving community and associations as the basis of society and law toward territorial-based polities: "This shift—from a political landscape in which territory was identified through *society* to one in which society was ordered through *territory*—lies at the heart of the state making process."[68]

The final piece in the consolidation of the law state was the notion of the state as the supreme legal sovereign with a monopoly over law. Medievalist Walter Ullmann observed that "the historical landscape of the Middle Ages

---

[64] Marc Bloch, "The Feudal World," in Norman Cantor and Michael Wertham, eds., *Medieval Society: 400–1500* (1967) 43

[65] Harding, *supra* note 27, at 191.

[66] A.D.E. Lewis and D.J. Ibbetson, "The Roman Law Tradition," in A.D.E. Lewis and D.J. Ibbetson, eds., *The Roman Law Tradition* (Cambridge: Cambridge University Press 1994); Peter Stein, *Roman Law in European History* (Cambridge: Cambridge University Press 1999).

[67] Musson, *supra* note 27, at 39–40.

[68] Rhys Jones, "Mann and Men in a Medieval State: the Geographies of Power in the Middle Ages," 24 Transactions of the Institute of British Geographers 65, 65 (1999).

[was] unadorned with, and wholly devoid of, the concept of the state."[69] Medieval kings and emperors ruled as overlords of the lands of their dominions with bonds of loyalty owed to them personally. There was no understanding of the state as an abstract entity and no conception of the separation of the individual person from the office. Sixteenth-century kings were still expected "to ensure that their personal revenues remain sufficient to uphold both their own kingly state and the good state of their government."[70]

In an essay tracing the emergence of the concept of the state, political theorist Quentin Skinner shows that up through the fifteenth century the phrase "state of the realm" referred to its condition and *stato* was commonly used to refer to the ruling regime.[71] Machiavelli, writing in the early sixteenth century, was the first prominent theorist to begin using the notion of state in an abstract sense. "He thinks of *stati* as having their own foundations and speaks in particular of each *stato* as having its own particular laws, customs, and ordinances."[72] Italian city-state republics of the day, prominently Venice and Florence, developed the idea that temporary holders of government offices operate within a structure of law to administer for the common good of the community.[73] It was not until the sixteenth century when an abstract notion of a state apart from a sovereign came into focus.

Jean Bodin, writing in the latter half of the sixteenth century, offered the first influential conception of the sovereign law-state.[74] He described sovereignty in terms of supreme lawmaking power, evident in this sampling of quotes: "persons who are sovereign must not be subject in any way to the commands of someone else and must be able to give law to subjects"; "it is only sovereign princes who can make law for all subjects without exception, both collectively and individually"; "the entire force of civil law and custom lies in the power of the sovereign prince."[75] This was the birth announcement of the supreme, monistic, unified law state. "His doctrine fits in perfectly with the efforts by the great princes of his age to monopolise the most

---

[69] Walter Ullman, "Juristic Obstacles to the Emergence of the Concept of the State in the Middle Ages," 12–13 Annali di Storia del Diritto 43, 44 (1968–69).

[70] Quentin Skinner, "The State," in Terence Ball, James Farr, and Russell L. Hanson, eds., *Political Innovation and Conceptual Change* (Cambridge: Cambridge University Press 1989) 103.

[71] *Id.* at 92–99.

[72] *Id.* at 102.

[73] *Id.* 107–109.

[74] *Id.* at 120.

[75] Jens Bartelson, "On the Indivisibility of Sovereignty," 2 Republic of Letters: A Journal for the Study of Knowledge, Politics, and the Arts, 85, 87–88 (2011). Citations to Bodin's text have been omitted. See also Nicholas Greenwood Onuf, 16 Alternatives: Global, Local, Political 425 (1991).

important powers of state and to eliminate the independent power of the church, the great vassals and the cities in key areas of foreign policy and domestic administration."[76]

Hobbes's famous *Leviathan*, published in the next century, likewise articulates a supreme, indivisible, lawgiving sovereign located in the abstract state. State is used in the Introduction in the fully modern sense: "For by art is created that great LEVIATHAN called a COMMONWEALTH, or STATE, (in Latin CIVITAS) which is but an artificial man."[77] Bodin and Hobbes wrote during periods of great turmoil, seeking to articulate political theories that established an enduring order. As Skinner points out, their theories were (respectively) a "reaction against the ideologies of popular sovereignty developed in the course of the French religious wars, and, subsequently, in the English Revolution of the seventeenth century."[78] Otto von Gierke explained the logic of their abstract argument: "From the quality of being the 'supreme' earthly authority, there is deduced the whole of that absolute omnipotence which the modern state demands for itself."[79] "Supreme" was analytically expanded to include exclusive, comprehensive, and all powerful. Supplementing their abstract analysis, their primary justification for a supreme, indivisible sovereign was the prudential argument that otherwise "the state itself will lose its unity and dissolve into factions, divided along the lines of status or faith."[80]

What Bodin and Hobbes articulated did not descriptively match law in Europe at the time. State law had not yet supplanted the independent legal authority of the Church in Catholic lands, nor fully absorbed manorial law, customary law, municipal law, and various associations in society (like guilds). Existing decentralized legal authorities were, in effect, re-described to fit the theory by construing their legal powers as grants from the sovereign, although their legal authority had long been grounded in tradition and usage (except for cities with royal charters).[81] Nor was their theory of supreme sovereignty subject to no higher legal power consistent with the significant presence of the Holy Roman Empire that persisted through the end of the eighteenth century. The Imperial Cameral Tribunal in Wetzlar and the

---

[76] Randall Lesaffer, *European Legal History: A Cultural and Political Perspective* (Cambridge: Cambridge University Press 2009) 315.

[77] Thomas Hobbes, *Leviathan* (Oxford: Oxford University Press 1996) 7.

[78] Skinner, *supra* note 70, at 121–23.

[79] Gierke, *supra* note 12, at 41.

[80] Bartelson, *supra* note 75, at 90.

[81] See George H. Sabine, *A History of Political Theory*, 3rd ed. (New York: Holt Rinehart Winston 1961) 407.

Imperial Aulic Council in Vienna were courts people could appeal to from the highest courts in territories of the empire; they had original jurisdiction in disputes between estates and their rulers, or complaints by subjects against their ruler.[82] Many of the cases involved disputes over taxation. In the eighteenth century, as many as 250 cases were filed annually with the Tribunal, which issued over 100 decisions (others were settled or mediated), and the Council received over 2,000 cases annually.[83] Both courts had the authority to issue binding decisions, enforced by the emperor, which could have serious implications within territories, including the deposition of rulers by the emperor.[84] (Their supranational position exhibits certain parallels to the Court of Justice of the European Union and the European Court of Human Rights today, discussed in Chapter Four.)

"Well into the seventeenth century," Joseph Strayer observed in his classic essay on state formation, "the best-organized states were in a sense only federations of counties or provinces, and each unit of the federation adapted orders from the center to fit its own needs."[85] Legal pluralism prevailed. Church courts continued to exercise substantial independent legal authority. Private relations and interests penetrated many legal offices, most visibly the private ownership of legal and judicial positions in France, which did not cease until the Revolution.[86] A fully bureaucratized legal system with officials salaried by the state would not become a reality until well into the nineteenth century, following the implementation of regular taxation and effective government administration.

Bodin and Hobbes articulated a normative vision of what they believed law in the sovereign state *should* be. While major elements of their theories have been rejected,[87] the core vision they articulated of the unified supreme law remains powerful. One of the most prominent contemporary legal philosophers, Joseph Raz, declares that an essential feature of legal systems

---

[82] Osiander, *supra* note 41, at 273–77.

[83] *Id.* at 275–76.

[84] *Id.* at 274.

[85] Strayer, *supra* note 36, at 100.

[86] William Doyle, "The Price of Offices in Pre-Revolutionary France," 27 The Historical Journal 831 (1984).

[87] They have been widely criticized for suggesting that the sovereign cannot be subject to legal constraints (other than natural law). Hobbes argued as a practical and logical matter a sovereign cannot be bound by the law because it makes the law: "nor is it possible for any person to be bound to himself because he that can bind, can release; and therefore he that is bound to himself only, is not bound." Hobbes, *supra* note 77, at 176. Modern rule of law societies have solved this difficulty by creating disbursed law enforcing and law applying institutions within states that hold government officials and the state itself to legal requirements.

is "they claim authority to regulate any type of behavior"; and "legal systems claim to be supreme."[88] "Since all legal systems claim to be supreme with respect to their subject-community," he asserts, "none can acknowledge any claim to supremacy over the same community which may be made by another legal system."[89] "By making these claims the law claims to provide the general framework for the conduct of all aspects of social life and sets itself up as the supreme guardian of society."[90] Bodin's sixteenth-century theory is dressed by Raz in twentieth-century legal philosophy clothes. Both theories were inconsistent with the reality of law historically as well as when they were articulated.

Millets in the Ottoman Empire

The Ottoman Empire was among the wealthiest and most powerful empires in the world at its peak in the sixteenth century, a Muslim polity that controlled North Africa, Egypt, parts of Arabia and the Middle East, Greece, and Southeastern Europe. As with all empires, the challenge was to manage extraordinarily diverse groups of people across great distances.

Islamic law is a personal law that applies to believers. In the early stages of Islamic conquest Muslims were a minority that ruled majority populations of other religions, which Islamic rulers had to accommodate. Jews and Christians, "People of the Book," recognized as *dhimmi*, were allowed to live in accordance with their own laws and tribunals contingent on their loyalty to the state and payment of a poll tax, subject to restrictions in clothing, the prohibition of public displays of religious symbols, and other disabilities.[91] For centuries of Islamic rule over the Iberian Peninsula, known as Al-Andalus, Christians and Jews lived under their own laws and institutions through this arrangement. After Christian rule was progressively reestablished over Iberia during the fifteenth century, Jewish courts and Muslim *kadi* courts continued to function under royal recognition. "The Christians found that by paying a salary to qadis and other Muslim officials they would ensure

---

88 Joseph Raz, *The Authority of Law*, 2nd ed. (Oxford: Oxford University Press 2009) 116–21.
89 *Id.* at 119.
90 *Id.* at 121.
91 See C.E. Bosworth, "The Concept of *Dhimma* in Early Islam," in Benjamin Braude and Bernard Lewis, eds., *Christians and Jews in the Ottoman Empire: The Functioning of a Plural Society*, vol. 1 (New York: Holmes & Meir Publishers 1982) 37–51. The status of dhimmi was also extended to Hindus, Zoroastrians, and others.

order and support the peaceful collection of taxes and tribute."[92] This policy continued until a harsh program implemented at the turn of the sixteenth century imposed forced conversion to Christianity or expulsion, prompting many Muslims and Jews to leave, many relocating to Ottoman territories.

Within the Ottoman Empire, Islamic religious authorities and educational systems, while accorded a limited degree of independence from the state, were thoroughly subordinate to and served state purposes—including as bureaucratic officials and magistrates staffing official *kadi* courts backed by the power of the state. (They were simultaneously state and religious representatives.) In addition to the system of state courts, the Ottoman Empire created the *millet* system, providing for the legal autonomy of selected religious/ethnic communities. Initially there were three *millets*: Greek Orthodox, Armenian, and Jews. Each contained various distinct linguistic, ethnic, and religious sub-communities; by the close of the nineteenth century nine *millets* had official status, including Roman Catholics and Copts.[93] This was "not a top-down coherent system designed by Ottoman Turks," but rather a series of varying arrangements that accommodated local circumstances.[94] The Ottoman state recognized the religious leaders of these communities— prominently the Greek Orthodox Patriarchate—as well as local priests and laypeople within towns and hinterlands, serving as administrators and judges, who were intermediaries between the Ottoman state and local communities.[95] The prestige and wealth of these intermediaries was bolstered by status and revenues from fees and tax collection, and via their recognition by the state as well as the community, though they could be replaced by Ottoman authorities if tax collections were inadequate or there was unrest within the community. Members of different *millets* were not strictly segregated territorially, instead living side by side in towns or clustered together in neighborhoods and villages, interspersed and distributed in different proportions throughout the Ottoman Empire. In the *millet* system we see,

[92] Lauren Benton, *Law and Colonial Cultures: Legal Regimes in World History, 1400–1900* (New York: Cambridge University Press 2002) 41.

[93] For a detailed account of the complexity and evolution of millets, see Kemal H. Karpat, "Millets and Nationality: The Roots of the Incongruity of Nation and State in the Post-Ottoman Era," in Benjamin Braude and Bernard Lewis, eds., *supra* note 91, at 141–69.

[94] Jan Erk, "Non-Territorial Millets in Ottoman History," in Tove H. Malloy and Francesco Palermo, eds., *Minority Accommodation through Territorial and Non-Territorial Autonomy* (Oxford: Oxford University Press 2015) 119, 127.

[95] See Karen Barkley and George Gavrilis, "The Ottoman Millet System: Non-Territorial Autonomy and its Contemporary Legacy," 15 Ethnopolitics 24, 25–28 (2016).

once again, a robust manifestation of community law alongside and mixing with regime law.

The term balkanization, with its implication of fragmentation among differing neighboring groups, reflects these arrangements on the Empire's Balkan Peninsula. The magnitude of this arrangement can be appreciated through the numbers of people in the mid-nineteenth century: the total Ottoman population around 35 million included approximately 21 million Muslims, 13 million Greeks and Armenians, 900,000 Catholics, 150,000 Jews, and 300,000 other sects.[96]

Jurisdiction was based on the personality principle and issues at hand. Matters between Muslims or between Muslims and non-Muslims, as well as criminal matters, were taken to Islamic *kadi* courts. (Aspects of this arrangement would change with extraterritoriality and secular reforms discussed later.) *Kadi* judges were appointed by the Ottoman government. Their orientation was to do justice in the particulars of each case, while applying secular Ottoman law, Islamic law, and local customary law—an internal pluralism of legal sources within Ottoman law.[97] Civil matters among and between Christians and Jews were handled by their own religious tribunals applying religious law, though they could bring their cases to *kadi* courts if they wished.

While the bulk of actions involving Jews and Christians were managed within the *millet* system, people also actively engaged in forum shopping, resorting to Islamic courts in a significant proportion of cases. *Dhimmis* had several reasons to invoke Islamic courts: Islamic divorce and inheritance laws were more favorable to women than Christian and Jewish laws, prompting women to resort to *kadi* courts; people of different religious communities engaged in a dispute might prefer an Islamic court; Islamic courts rendered immediate rulings and had a reputation for doing justice (exhibiting greater flexibility than *millet* courts holding to religious doctrines); fees for *kadi* courts could be lower than religious courts; *kadi* court decisions were coercively enforced by state officials, which religious courts lacked; and legal transactions conducted through *kadi* courts were recorded in official state records, unlike religious court

---

[96] Elia H. Tuma, "The Economic Impact of the Capitulations: The Middle East and Europe: A Reinterpretation," 18 Journal of European Economic History 663, 682 (1989).

[97] An excellent overview of the kadi and millet courts, which informs this discussion, is Karen Barkley, "Aspects of Legal Pluralism in the Ottoman Empire," in Lauren Benton and Richard J. Ross, *Legal Pluralism and Empires, 1500–1850* (New York: NYU Press 2013) 83–107.

proceedings.[98] Christian and Jewish religious leaders tried to restrict access of their people to Islamic courts, which they perceived as a threat to their religious laws and community integrity, potentially bringing embarrassing issues to light outside their communities, and cutting into revenues they received from fees.[99]

The *millet* system endured for over four centuries, evolving over time, until the dismemberment of the Ottoman Empire after World War I. Remnants of the *millet* system still exist in certain former Ottoman territories. Egypt recognizes the rights of Copts and Jews to live in accordance with their own personal status laws (although separate courts have been abolished); Lebanon, with its perpetually weak state, is divided among self-administered religious communities applying their own respective laws.[100] Israel recognizes fourteen separate religious-ethnic courts with mandatory jurisdiction applying their own laws on marriage, divorce, maintenance, and succession.[101]

Capitulations and Extraterritoriality Across the World

Like the *millet* system, the Ottoman capitulary regime had historical precursors. Capitulations involved a special status held by foreigners who were subject to their own laws and tribunals under the authority of the foreign consul while exempt from Ottoman law—a legal exemption which later came to be known as extraterritoriality. The origins of this practice extend back two thousand years to legal exemptions for trade diasporas around the Mediterranean; "interregional exchange networks composed of spatially dispersed specialized merchant groups that are culturally distinct, organizationally cohesive, and socially independent from their host communities while maintaining a high level of economic and social ties with related communities" in other locations.[102] In the tenth and eleventh centuries, the Byzantine Empire had granted versions of this status to Venetians, Genoese, and others

---

98 See Timur Kuran, "The Economic Ascent of the Middle East's Religious Minorities: The Role of Islamic Legal Pluralism," 33 Journal of Legal Studies 475, 488–92 (2004); Barkley and Gavrilis, *supra* note 95, at 27; Barkley, *supra* note 97, at 94–100.

99 Barkley, *supra* note 97, at 101–103.

100 Barkley and Gavrilis, *supra* note 95, at 30–35.

101 Yuksel Sezgin, "The Israeli Millet System: Examining Legal Pluralism Through Lenses of Nation-Building an Human Rights," 43 Israel Law Review 631 (2010).

102 Gil J. Stein, "From Passive Periphery to Active Agents: Emerging Perspectives in the Archaeology of Interregional Interaction," 104 American Anthropologist 903, 908 (2003).

with colonies of traders at ports and trading towns across the Empire.[103] Muslim caliphates in twelfth- through fourteenth-century Egypt granted commercial and political privileges to Pisans, Venetians, Genoans, French, and others living in Alexandria to attract Mediterranean trade.[104] Variations of these arrangements were in place when the Ottoman Empire captured Constantinople in the mid-fifteenth century (later renamed Istanbul).

Both the *millet* system and the capitulary regime were grounded in the personality principle that people are governed by their own community law.[105] The main differences are that *millets* applied to religious communities, while capitulations applied mainly to foreign traders, though this distinction would later break down, as explained shortly. Capitulations began as permissive grants by the Ottoman government, but transformed over time into impositions by Western powers, which subsequently imposed extraterritoriality at locations around the world. The meaning and implications of capitulations changed in the course of the consolidation of the territorial state, going from unexceptional legal arrangements to deviations from theories of state legal sovereignty.

Ottoman capitulations were granted to France and England in the sixteenth century, and expanded and renewed multiple times thereafter. The core privileges granted to French and British nationals and their descendants included rights of residence, trade, and freedom from taxes (except for a fixed low customs tax); the right to apply their own laws in all civil matters, with exclusive jurisdiction to be adjudicated by their own consular officials; and the right of consular representatives to be present when citizens are subject to criminal laws, which later was extended to almost total freedom from all Ottoman legal proceedings, civil and criminal.[106] Disputes over property were heard in Ottoman courts; and, later in the nineteenth century, commercial disputes between Ottoman subjects and foreigners were heard in mixed courts (called "international courts") with panels of native judges and

---

[103] Nasim M. Soosa, "The Historical Interpretation of the Origin of the Capitulations in the Ottoman Empire," 4 Temple Law Quarterly 358 (1930);

[104] Alexander H. De Groot, "The Historical Development of the Capitulatory Regime in the Ottoman Middle East from the Fifteenth to the Nineteenth Century," *Oriente Moderno, Nuova serie,* Anno 22 (83), Nr. 3, The Ottoman Capitulations: Text and Context (2003) 577–78, 575–604.

[105] Soosa, *supra* note 103, at 371.

[106] See Edwin Pears, "Turkish Capitulations and the Status of British and Other Foreign Subjects Residing in Turkey," 21 Law Quarterly Review 408 (1905); James B. Angell, "The Turkish Capitulations," 6 American Historical Review 254 (1901); Lucius Ellsworth Thayer, "The Capitulations of the Ottoman Empire and the Question of their Abrogation as it Affects the United States," 17 American Journal of International Law 209, 217 (1923).

foreign judges applying the French commercial code.[107] France and England also exercised the power to place other foreign nationals under the protection of their respective flags. At its peak, thirteen European countries, along with the United States and Brazil, had acquired extraterritorial privileges, the bulk established in the nineteenth century through treaties;[108] though French and British insistence on exclusive jurisdiction in all suits in Egypt against their foreign nationals was "in flagrant contravention of the text of the Capitulations."[109] Typically these treaties were permanent, "confirmed now and for ever," as stated in the 1838 treaty with England.[110]

At the end of the nineteenth century, sixty-six British courts were operating across the Ottoman Empire, the most extensive presence, though other European nations had courts as well.[111] Starting out as simple hearings heard by a counsel, the British system developed civil, criminal, and procedural codes, as well as trial and appellate courts, with a British Supreme Court sitting in Istanbul.[112] The extensive, intrusive legal presence of the British in the Ottoman Empire, it should be noted, existed at the same time British jurists espoused the image of the monist law state.

The capitulation system was extravagantly abused by nations and individuals. Using their power to confer protected status on others, foreign ambassadors over time extended this status to substantial numbers of natives for economic and political reasons—creating a "protégé system" that expanded to include several hundred thousand Ottoman natives.[113] Foreign ambassadors sold the protected status (flag protection) for substantial sums to supplement their incomes;[114] native merchants and traders benefited because holders of protégé status were exempted from general taxes and paid much lower import and export duties (3–5 percent) than Ottoman merchants (9–12 percent), securing a competitive advantage and greater profits.[115] This

[107] Thayer, *supra* note 106, at 216–17; David Todd, "Beneath Sovereignty: Extraterritoriality and Imperial Internationalism in Nineteenth Century Egypt," 36 Law and History Review 105 (2018).

[108] Thayer, *supra* note 106, at 209, 211–12.

[109] Todd, *supra* note 107, at 115.

[110] *Id.* at 111.

[111] Turan Kayaoglu, *Legal Imperialism: Sovereignty and Extraterritoriality in Japan, the Ottoman Empire, and China* (Cambridge: Cambridge University Press 2010) 4.

[112] *Id.* at 6.

[113] See Salahi R. Sonyel, "The Protégé System in the Ottoman Empire," 2 Journal of Islamic Studies 56 (1991).

[114] Angell, *supra* note 106, at 257.

[115] Elias H. Tuma, "The Economic Impact of the Capitulations: The Middle East and Europe: A Reinterpretation," 18 Journal of European Economic History 663, 680 (1989); Feroz Ahmad, "Ottoman Perceptions of the Capitulations 1800–1914," 11 Journal of Islamic Studies 1 (2000).

practice intersected with the *millet* system because many of the Ottoman citizens who purchased this status were Catholic, Greek Orthodox, Armenian, or Jews, members of *millet* groups that predominated in networks of financial, trade, and professional actors.[116]

Political considerations led Russia—a rival regional empire aiming to weaken the Ottoman Empire—to make wholesale offers of protection (flag protection or easily obtained citizenship) to Greek Orthodox and Armenians in the name of protecting members of the Orthodox Church, enrolling over 100,000 Greeks as protected persons.[117] Austria, another regional rival empire, extended protection to 200,000 Moldavians.[118] Other European powers followed suit. A British jurist appointed to the British Supreme Court in Istanbul observed: "These protected Ottoman subjects were looked upon as the subjects of Russia, if they were of the Greek faith; of Italy, France, and Austria, if they were of the Roman faith; and of England and Germany, if Protestants."[119]

Whether for economic or political reasons, the total number of people who came under the capitulations in the nineteenth century was substantial, many of whom were not foreigners by birth—securing a highly beneficial economic and legal position that generated resentment among Muslims. Alexandria had nearly 50,000 people with protected status (many not foreign born) out of a total population of 230,000 in the 1880s.[120] "In fact, many Alexandrians acquired legal protection from multiple consulates, shifting their legal identities in order to maximize their immediate social and economic interests."[121] Istanbul had 50,000 people with foreigner status in the mid-nineteenth century.[122] Large numbers of people, foreigners and natives, were thereby exempted from law applicable to the general population. The Ottoman government repeatedly protested these abuses, and restricted the protégé system by issuing an order in 1869 that prohibited subjects from being naturalized by a foreign government.[123] Although it repeatedly

---

[116] Charles Issawi, "The Transformation of the Economic Position of the Millets in the Nineteenth Century," in Benjamin Braude and Bernard Lewis, eds., *supra* note 91, at 261–85.

[117] Ahmad, *supra* note 115, at 5; Sonyel, *supra* note 113, at 60–61.

[118] Angell, *supra* note 106, at 257.

[119] Quoted in Sonyel, *supra* note 113, at 62.

[120] Ziad Fahmy, "Jurisdictional Borderlands: Extraterritoriality and 'Legal Chameleons' in Precolonial Alexandria, 1840–1870," 55 Comparative Studies in Society and History 305, 312–13 (2013).

[121] *Id.* at 306.

[122] Sonyel, *supra* note 113, at 64.

[123] Thayer, *supra* note 106, at 218.

demanded that the capitulations be canceled, European powers adamantly refused, united in their opposition.

What originated as benefits unilaterally conferred by the powerful Ottoman state to encourage trade with Europeans had transformed by the nineteenth century, following the rise of European economic and military might, into shackles the weakened Ottoman government ("the sick man of Europe") could not escape. In a mid-nineteenth-century legal reform effort (*Tanzimat*), the Ottoman government enacted a number of codes to create a modern system of secular law, including a criminal code and a commercial code based on the French model, as well as a maritime code and several procedural codes; along with criminal and commercial courts, with mixed panels of judges in cases between Muslims and non-Muslims.[124] The result was a hybrid system with European and Islamic elements. "Two bodies of law of different origin, reflecting the rules and principles of two of the major legal families in the world, the civilian and the Islamic, were in effect operative together, with the same force and independent of each other, applicable to the same body of people."[125]

Public resentment at extraterritoriality as an unfair humiliation was widespread. Undeterred, Europeans insisted on maintaining extraterritoriality on multiple grounds: the system had worked for centuries (confirmed by custom and usage);[126] Europeans could not be judged by Islamic law; Ottoman courts were unjust, corrupt, and not staffed by people trained in law; and furthermore, Europeans asserted, extraterritoriality was beneficial for their society by providing models of properly functioning judicial systems to help them improve their own legal system.[127] Extraterritoriality was not extinguished in Turkey until 1923.

Western powers exported extraterritoriality from the Ottoman Empire to locations around the world in the nineteenth century, including Zanzibar, Morocco, Tonga, Madagascar, Samoa, Japan, Congo, Iran, Thailand, Korea, and China.[128] All were independent nations at the time, not colonies. After Japan became an imperial power, it was freed from extraterritoriality, and in turn imposed it on China and Korea, the only non-Western power to engage

---

[124] Esin Orucu, "The Impact of European Law on the Ottoman Empire and Turkey," in Wolfgang Mommsen and J.A. de Moore, eds., *European Expansion and Law: The Encounter of European and Indigenous Law in 19th Century and 20th Century Africa and Asia* (Oxford: Berg 1992) 46–51.

[125] *Id.* at 49.

[126] Pears, *supra* note 106, at 421–25.

[127] Thayer, *supra* note 106, at 231–33; Todd, *supra* note 107, at 117–21.

[128] Kayaoglu, *supra* note 111, at 5.

in extraterritoriality. Familiar abuses in the Ottoman Empire arose elsewhere as well—particularly selling protected status and extending coverage to many thousands of people, foreigners and natives, through the protégé system.[129] Extraterritoriality generated bitterness from locals everywhere as an abusive imposition by external countries through raw power.[130] At its peak, there were 120 foreign courts functioning in China, where extraterritoriality continued until 1943.[131] At home European and American powers proclaimed the supreme, unified law state (as Chapter Three discusses with respect to indigenous native peoples in settler countries)—though they trampled this notion abroad when it served their interests.

Manifold Legal Pluralism in the Ottoman Empire

In the course of the nineteenth century (in shifting arrangements over time), five court systems applied different bodies of law in the Ottoman Empire. Islamic *kadi* courts had jurisdiction over Muslims in civil, commercial, and criminal cases, applying Sharia, state law, and local customary law, subject to final decisions by religious authorities (who were also state officials). (Sharia itself is pluralistic: differing across locations because it is intermingled with and influenced by local traditions; and Sunni has four schools of jurisprudence (*fiqh*)). The communal courts of non-Muslim *millets* heard civil, commercial, and criminal cases involving members of that group, applying religious law, subject to final decisions by the highest authority of the religious community. Extraterritorial consular courts had jurisdiction over foreigners and native Ottoman subjects with protégé status to civil, commercial, and criminal matters, applying the law of the foreign nation, subject to final decisions by the embassies or high courts established by foreign powers. Mixed courts comprised of natives and foreigners heard cases between Ottoman and foreign subjects in commercial cases, applying local and foreign sources of law, subject to final decisions by the Ministry of Commerce. Secular courts of the Ottoman state had jurisdiction over Muslims (and others) in certain types of civil, commercial, and criminal cases, applying

---

[129] See Francis Bowes Sayer, "The Passing of Extraterritoriality in Siam," 22 American Journal of International Law 70 (1928);

[130] See Ching-Chun Wang, "China Still Waits the End of Extraterritoriality," 15 Foreign Affairs 745 (1937).

[131] Kayaoglu, *supra* note 111, at 151.

state statutes and codes (modeled on French law), subject to final decisions by the Ministry of Justice.

These various courts and bodies of law were not organized in a comprehensive hierarchy. Exterritorial courts were outside the Ottoman state legal system. Mixed commercial courts were state courts but with institutional separation. Islamic *kadi* courts, initially located in religious houses, moved to government offices in the nineteenth century following legal reforms, yet functioned apart from secular courts.[132] Ottoman secular courts did not have final review over Islamic courts or over *millet* courts, and people unhappy with a decision in secular courts could thereafter apply to an Islamic court for a different outcome.[133] An appellate system for state courts was created in 1873, but there was no resolution of final authority between state and Islamic courts until Turkish reforms in the 1920s.

Under Mustafa Kemal Ataturk, a new unified secular legal system was created based on European Codes (primarily Swiss and German), adapted to Turkish elements, while sweeping away the preceding pluralistic system, including abolishing Sharia courts.[134] These legal reforms, along with concomitant social and economic reforms, were driven by Turkish elites who wanted to modernize and Westernize Turkey. Following this radical legal transformation, it took decades for social relations to align with the Westernized legal code, and it did not completely alter social behavior, particular over family law matters.

Unofficial Muslim law is still followed by a significant percentage of the population, including on matters explicitly illegal under the state legal system. Recent studies have found, for example, that in rural Southeastern and Eastern Turkey roughly 10 percent of people entered religious marriages without civil marriages (which is illegal), as much as 15 percent of women were married under the legally required age of 17 (including forced and arranged marriages), and 10 percent were in polygamous marriages prohibited by the state.[135] Women in illegal or unofficial marriages have brought cases in state courts seeking compensation from ex-husbands, to collect insurance for deceased husbands, protection from violent husbands, and benefits for second wives. State courts have a mixed record, some recognizing the de

---

[132] *Id.* at 117–18.

[133] *Id.* at 116.

[134] Orucu, *supra* note 124, at 51–54.

[135] See Ihsan Ilmaz, "Semi-official Turkish Muslim Legal Pluralism: Encounters Between Secular Official Law and Unofficial Shari'a," in A. Possamai, ed., *The Sociology of Shari'a: Case Studies from Around the World* (Basel: Springer 2015).

facto marriage and others denying claims on grounds of invalidity under state law. Legal pluralism through unofficial community law continues to exist in Turkey, interacting in complex ways with state law, notwithstanding an officially unified system of state law.

The British East India Company Law State

European overseas colonization in its initial stages was substantially carried out by private commercial actors. Two early leading actors were the British East India Company (EIC) and the Dutch East India Company (Vereenigde Oostindische Compagnie, VOC), joint stock companies owned by private investors.[136] Other private companies engaged in similar activities, including the Levant, Virginia, Africa, Russia, Hudson's Bay, and more.[137] Corporate entities—tracing back to medieval cities, guilds, universities, and other associations—governed themselves internally, exercising legal rights and powers within their organization and membership.[138] EIC extended its authority over an enormous expanse of land and people across Asia and elsewhere in the pursuit of corporate profits, giving rise to a fantastic jumble of pluralistic legal arrangements.

Created in 1600 by a royal charter that granted EIC the power to govern its employees and trading centers, in the course of the seventeenth and early eighteenth centuries EIC established a "network of plantations" in Asia and the Atlantic, exercising power to "erect and administer law; collect taxes; provide protection; inflict punishment; perform stateliness; regulate economic, religious, and civic life; conduct diplomacy and wage war; make claims to jurisdiction over land and sea; cultivate authority over and obedience from those people subject to its command."[139] Legal activities of the Company initially focused on advancing its own activities and maintaining order in its settlements. Out of a desire to save money and trouble, EIC had

---

[136] *See generally* H.J. Leue, "Legal Expansion in the Age of the Companies: Aspects of the Administration of Justice in the English and Dutch Settlements of Maritime Asia, 1600–1750," in Mommsen and Moor, *supra* note 124, at 129–58.

[137] Philip J. Stern, "'Bundles of Hyphens:' Corporations as Legal Communities in the Early Modern British Empire," in Lauren Benton and Richard J. Ross, eds. (New York: NYU Press 2013) 28.

[138] *Id.* at 22.

[139] Philip J. Stern, *The Company-State: Corporate Sovereignty and the Early Modern Foundations of the British Empire in India* (Oxford: Oxford University Press 2011) 6–7.

"an unmistakable tendency to keep clear of the natives' disputes and to leave them, as far as might be, to their own devices."[140]

Following a series of wars in the second half of the eighteenth into the nineteenth centuries, EIC expanded from governing its own employees and trading centers to governing much of the Indian subcontinent. The EIC took over administration and tax collection from the weakened Mughal Empire in the 1760s, thereafter deriving massive profits from tax collection as well as monopolistic trade between England and India. "It is very strange, very strange," parliamentarian Thomas Babington Macaulay remarked in 1833, "that a joint stock society of traders . . . should be intrusted with the sovereignty of a larger population, the disposal of a larger clear revenue, the command of a larger army, than under the direct management of the Executive Government of the United Kingdom."[141] The British Parliament enacted several statutes during this period to exert greater control over EIC, though the Company would continue to govern and administer courts in India until 1858. EIC blatantly contradicted juristic theories (then and today) that sovereignty necessarily inheres in states, that only states exercise legal powers, and that law is inherently public (not private).

"Very strange" is an understatement. EIC had a royal charter from England granting it public powers over its own employees, trading centers and plantations, including the rights to issue law, administer justice, and strike coins—but this gave it no power to rule India. Within India, their authority was derived from a fictional grant from the Mughal emperor.[142] The regular tributes EIC supplied for decades "signified that the Company's officials were theoretically vassals of the Mughal emperor," and EIC struck coins in the name of the emperor, who remained in a purely symbolic role.[143] "From the point of view of the Mughals, the Company was governing the empire on their behalf."[144] This façade was stripped off when, in response to the Revolt of 1857, the government tried the emperor (Bahadur Shah) for treason and exiled him. The following year the British government officially assumed rule of India from EIC, continuing the governmental and legal institutions the Company had already put in place.

---

[140] Leue, *supra* note 136, at 144.

[141] *Id.* at 3.

[142] Amar Farooqui, "Governance, Corporate Interest and Colonialism: The Case of the East India Company," 35 Social Scientist 44, 47 (2007).

[143] *Id.* at 48.

[144] *Id.* at 49.

Leading up to and following its de facto take over from Mughal rule, EIC established a dual system of law, one for its major trading cities and the second for elsewhere, while outside of this system pre-existing Mughal, aristocratic, village, and local courts continued to function. In Bombay, Madras, and Calcutta, designated as English Presidencies, EIC set up Mayor's Courts (accorded official King's Courts status) with English judges applying English civil and criminal law to Englishmen and other foreigners (early on also applying pre-existing Portuguese law for Portuguese parties in Bombay[145]), as well as to Company employees (including native Indians), later expanded to Indians generally when both parties agreed to jurisdiction. Court decisions could be appealed to a subsequently created Supreme Court in India, and ultimately to the Privy Council in London, intertwining EIC courts with the British legal system. Many Indian plaintiffs, "who quickly learned legal strategies that pitted one court against the other," resorted to British courts in matters over which Mughal courts also had jurisdiction.[146] Local elites protested this exercise of jurisdiction, which took cases away from them, diminishing their authority and income.[147] Large numbers of Indians brought cases to EIC Mayor's Courts seeking a better outcome than they expected to receive in a traditional forum, along with greater certainty that decisions would be enforced.[148]

In interior areas (*mofussil*), EIC established courts "administered Hindu and Muslim personal law, Islamic criminal law, and Company regulations."[149] Native Mughal officials (*kadis*) continued to administer criminal courts applying Muslim law, and in civil courts Muslim and Hindu experts become advisors on their respective forms of law as salaried Company employees.[150] Local aristocratic landowners (*zamindars*), although not officially recognized, continued to exercise jurisdiction over minor disputes as they had under Mughal rule. While Europeans could sue Indians in *mofussil* courts, Europeans had immunity from these courts in civil and criminal matters. Owing to cost and travel hurdles, "Indians in the interior were generally unable to bring their cases to Calcutta and were therefore extremely vulnerable to European violence and exploitation in both civil and criminal matters."[151]

---

[145] Stern, *supra* note 139, at 26–27.

[146] Benton, *supra* note 92, at 137.

[147] Leue, *supra* note 136, at 148.

[148] *Id.* at 149.

[149] Elizabeth Kolsky, "Codification and the Rule of Colonial Difference: Criminal Procedure in British India," 23 Law and History Review 631, 641 (2005).

[150] Benton, *supra* note 92, at 134.

[151] Kolsky, *supra* note 149, at 641.

Incidents between Europeans also went unaddressed. The immunity of Europeans from local courts outside the main cities created increasing distress as their numbers grew and disputes over land agreements, assaults, theft, and breaches of peace produced "a total denial of justice."[152]

A substantial proportion of dispute resolution at the village level between native Indians was outside the purview of the dual court system set up by EIC and pre-existing Mughal courts, held in caste or village tribunals (*panchayats*) comprised of important village elders applying local caste and customary law.[153] Community law in many locations was primarily local customary law and only secondarily Muslim or Hindu law.[154] Since these tribunals were outside the official system, there was no appeal from panchayat decisions to state courts—though cases could be brought directly to the latter—and panchayat decisions were not enforced by state courts. This weakened the authority of panchayats, though they continued to deal with many cases, imposing sanctions including fines, beating, shaming, and expulsion.[155]

Concerns in England in the mid-nineteenth century about injustices in India under EIC rule prompted a series of proposals for reform and the drafting of codes aimed at producing a uniform system of law that applied to everyone. Fierce opposition to these proposals was voiced in England as well as by expatriates in India. A British Judge on the Calcutta Supreme Court argued against equality that the European community, "a small but highly civilized community long accustomed to good laws and to a good administration of them," could not be put on the same level as "vast masses but lately emancipated from barbarism, and inspired with no traditional reverence for equal laws or incorruptible justice."[156] Indian judges—including those educated in England—could not preside over Englishmen, it was argued, because they could not judge fairly; and besides, it would invert the power structure to have a member of the subservient populace sit in judgment of an expatriate from the dominant polity.[157]

The Code of Criminal Procedure for India enacted by the British government in 1861 "secured the legal superiority of 'European-born British subjects' by reserving to them special privileges such as the right to a jury trial

---

[152] *Id.* at 648.
[153] Kolff, "The Indian and the British Law Machines: Some Remarks on Law and Society in British India," in Mommsen and Moor, *supra* note 124, at 205, 227.
[154] *Id.* at 229–33.
[155] *Id.* at 205.
[156] Statement of Arthur Buller, quoted in Kolsky, *supra* note 149, at 668.
[157] *Id.* at 669.

with a majority of European jurors, amenability only to British judges and magistrates, and limited punishments."[158] To justify their privileged position, a right to personal law was invoked. Prominent English jurist Fitzjames Stephen declared, "The Muhammadan has his personal law. The Hindu has his personal law . . . are English people to be told that, whilst it is their duty to respect all these laws scrupulously, they are to claim nothing for themselves?"[159] This is a dubious argument since the law at issue was a uniform criminal procedure code drafted by English applicable to English and everyone else—the sole objection was to Indian judges sitting in judgment over British. An 1872 amendment to the Code "formally introduced the principle of racial disability into the interior courts by barring Indian judges and magistrates from trying European British-born subjects in the mofussil."[160] In response to protests from Indians about this unequal application of law, an 1884 amendment finally allowed Indian judges to try Englishmen in the mofussil, albeit reserving to Europeans a right to a jury trial with at least half of the jury composed of Europeans or Americans.[161] This was, in effect, a carve-out form of tribunal extraterritoriality within territory governed by the British.

Official recognition of Muslim and Hindu law created many complicated issues and consequences. The EIC translator of Islamic legal treatises, Charles Hamilton, presented this as enlightened rule: "The permanency of any foreign domination requires that strict attention be paid to the advantage of the governed and to this great end, nothing can so effectively contribute except preserving their ancient established practices—civil and religious— and protecting them in the exercise of their own institutions[.]"[162] EIC also claimed this policy merely continued the existing legal arrangement under Mughal rulers, themselves initially external invaders, a Muslim minority ruling a Hindu majority. The Mughals established a comprehensive criminal code but refrained from a comprehensive family code. As described earlier, Muslim regimes generally allowed other religious communities to live in accordance with their own community law and institutions. Muslim courts were not mandatory for non-Muslims under Mughal rule; yet significant numbers of non-Muslim subjects during Mughal rule brought cases

---

[158] *Id.* at 658.

[159] Statement of Fitzjames Stephen, quoted in *id.* at 679.

[160] Kolsky, *supra* note 149, at 679.

[161] *Id.* at 682.

[162] Statement of Charles Hamilton, quoted in Partha S. Ghosh, "Politics of Personal Law in India: The Hindu-Muslim Dichotomy," 29 South Asia Research 1, 4 (2009).

to Muslim courts (just as Indians would later resort to EIC courts), often to register a legal transaction in official records or to obtain a better outcome than they would have received from their community-based tribunals.[163] In general however, "the spread of Mughal justice was no doubt thin on the ground, and the majority of disputes resolved at the village level by *panchayats* (councils, literally of five people) of various compositions and levels of formality."[164]

The incorporation of Muslim and Hindu law by English judges transformed the law in unintentional ways.[165] The translation and formulation of Muslim law and Hindu law into written compilations altered how they previously functioned as oral traditions involving normative judgments. English judges, furthermore, thought Muslim *kadi* decision-making, aimed at just outcomes, was insufficiently oriented to the application of clear legal rules. English judges applied the law in a common law fashion creating a body of precedent, while also rejecting local laws they found repugnant. "The result was reification, and rampant misinterpretation, of Hindu and Muslim law, and over time the effect was to allow English law and the common law practice of referring to precedents to alter indigenous law to make it more English."[166] Further Anglicizing Indian law, uniform law codes enacted at the time (which did not exist in Britain) restricted and fixed Muslim and Hindu law.[167] Transformed Indian law was thus absorbed within the transplanted English legal tradition producing a hybrid offspring.

Muslim and Hindu personal law still exists in India today outside the official legal system as well as recognized within the system, resilient in the face of repeated calls for greater legal uniformity. Outside the legal system, in rural villages mixtures of customary and religious law continue within the community. People are familiar with and arrange their affairs through this law, which is locally available and "is cheap and accessible."[168] Within the official state legal system, "the Indian legal system today recognizes and administers a complex system of personal (status) laws, whereby cases of

---

[163] Nandini Chatterjee, "Reflections on Religious Difference and Permissive Inclusion in Mughal Law," 29 Journal of Law and Religion 396, 408–410 (2014). For example, under Muslim law a daughter with brothers would inherit a share of the father's property, but under Hindu law she would receive nothing. *Id.* at 410.

[164] *Id.* at 414.

[165] Benton, *supra* note 92, at 139.

[166] *Id.* at 139.

[167] *Id.* at 151.

[168] Partha S. Ghosh, "Politics of Personal Law in India: The Hindu-Muslim Dichotomy," 29 South Asia Research 1, 12 (2009).

family, property, and religious institutions are decided on the basis of Hindu, Muslim, Parsi, and Christian personal law—depending on the religio-legal identity of the litigants in question."[169]

Progressive reformists, particularly on behalf of women's rights, have advocated abolishing regressive elements of religious law treatment of women, replacing them with a uniform secular law. Conservative and orthodox religious opponents claim that respect for their law is vital to their religion and protected by the religious freedom guaranteed in the Constitution.[170] Women's rights advocates invoke international women's rights and human rights declarations along with state law provisions in their efforts to reform religious law treatment of women, while in defense of their position religious leaders invoke international declarations protecting freedom of religion and the rights of indigenous peoples as well as state law protections for religion. A plurality of legal sources is enlisted on each side against the other, drawing from local community law, state law, and international law and human rights.

These debates take place against a backdrop of Hindu-Muslim political tension, always simmering and occasionally erupting into sectarian violence. There has been movement toward greater legal uniformity, but customary and religious community law remains within and outside of state law.

Uses and Abuses of the Monist Law State Image

The supreme, comprehensive, unified, monist theory of the sovereign territorial law state, first articulated by theorists in the sixteenth and seventeenth centuries, became the predominant view of European jurists by the nineteenth century. Significant progress had been made in bringing previously decentralized legal institutions under the ambit of state law, although exceptions remained, including imperial courts and ecclesiastical courts in England exercising jurisdiction well into the nineteenth century. Yet during this very period Europeans routinely acted toward other nations in ways contrary to the monist law state, exemplified in their insistence on extraterritoriality in the Ottoman Empire and across the world as well as the exercise of substantial legal powers by private companies pursuing European interests abroad.

---

[169] Nandini Chatterjee, "Reflections on Religious Difference and Permissive Inclusion in Mughal Law," 29 Journal of Law and Religion 396, 396–97 (2014).
[170] Ghosh, *supra* note 162, at 6–10.

More was involved than just hypocrisy. The monist theory of the law state was invoked by jurists to justify seizing political and legal powers over other lands. A historian of European imperialism, Andrew Fitzmaurice, articulates their rationalization:

> Territorial sovereignty, they argued, was only to be found in modern states. Such states were to be placed higher in the progress of history and therefore possessed superior rights, just as seventeenth-century Europeans had argued that agricultural society possessed superior rights to people living in a state of nature. Having thus extended the progressive theory of history, these jurists argued that it would be possible to occupy the territorial sovereignty of lands where such sovereignty had not already been 'taken,' including over the 'personal' sovereignties of Africa and Asia.[171]

Countries that did not meet the standards of the monist law state, in this view, were deficient, calling for takeover, as I show in the next two chapters. European colonization under the mantle of spreading civilized state legal systems resulted in widespread, intransigent legal pluralism inconsistent with the monist image.

Several points taken from this chapter bear emphasis in closing. Above all else, the monist law state image enhances and serves the power of state law— made explicit in the claim of comprehensive (monopolistic) supremacy. Yet forms of law have coexisted and intertwined in a remarkable, unruly, variegated, ever changing kaleidoscope of arrangements. As this chapter shows, the idea of the monist law state arose under specific social-political circumstances in Europe in response to conditions at the time to support the consolidation of power within states.

When regime law spans heterogeneous areas, sub-communities use their own laws in everyday social intercourse. People prefer to live by laws they are familiar with that serve their needs, through which their interaction is organized, using accessible fora and norms they understand to resolve disputes. At the same time, they will resort to alternative legal institutions when available, enlisting state law, customary and religious law, and cross-polity law (imperial, international conventions, human rights, etc.) when they perceive an advantage is to be gained thereby. Authorities that staff coexisting

---

[171] Andrew Fitzmaurice, Sovereignty, Property and Empire, 1500–2000 (Cambridge: Cambridge University Press 2014) 6–7.

courts and tribunals (state judges, imperial tribunals, religious authorities, traditional chiefs, village elders, etc.) maintain order and respond to disputes while enhancing their authority, prestige, and wealth by attracting litigants to their services. When the interests of coexisting tribunals coincide they cooperate, but they also compete. Situations of legal pluralism commonly involve alternative legal regimes with different norms, forum shopping by people, and coexisting legal authorities seeking to enhance their own respective bodies of law and positions.

Two
Postcolonial Legal Pluralism

Legal pluralism was initially raised in the early 1960s in a few pieces by anthropologists discussing law in postcolonial Africa and Asia. One of the earliest mentions of legal pluralism came in a 1962 article by anthropologist Lloyd Fallers about customary law in Uganda, the year it became independent from the United Kingdom:

> Among the long list of intractable problems faced by the new independent states of Africa, by no means the least severe is that of creating national legal systems out of the welter of indigenous and introduced bodies of law with which they come to independence. Bodies of customary law have survived, and in some cases have even been strengthened, during the period of colonial administration; European and, in some instances, Near Eastern and Asian elements have been added to the potpourri. . . . This legal pluralism is, of course, merely the legal aspect of the general cultural fragmentation which is so characteristic of the new African states. Consisting of congeries of traditional polities—some tiny clusters of a few villages, others great kingdoms numbering their subjects in the millions—thrown together by European diplomacy in the nineteenth century, the new states have little common culture to unite them.[1]

With a population comprised of different African tribal groups, Muslims, European settlers, and foreign laborers brought by Britain (many from India), "At least a dozen distinct customary legal systems exist there, along with elements of British, Indian, and Islamic law."[2] Another 1962 article about law in Africa, by jurist Denis Cowen, discussed the goal of African states to diminish existing legal pluralism in the belief that "a uniform national legal system may aid the development of national unity and sentiment,

---

[1] Lloyd Fallers, "Customary Law in the New African States," 27 Law and Contemporary Problems 605, 605 (1962).

[2] *Id.* at 616.

Legal Pluralism Explained. Brian Z. Tamanaha, Oxford University Press (2021). © Brian Z. Tamanaha.
DOI: 10.1093/oso/9780190861551.003.0003

and, if conceived on modern lines, may at the same time contribute toward the 'modernization' of a country previously regarded as 'backward.' "[3] A 1965 article about law in Indonesia by anthropologist Mervyn Jaspan described a similar situation, with introduced Dutch law coexisting alongside "regional and tribal customary law [adat], often combined with Islamic Law, and the legal usages of 'foreign oriental' minorities, mainly Chinese and Indian."[4] He discussed "the problem of plurality or unification of law";[5] and he remarked that the desire of elites and jurists to develop a modern uniform system of law showed few signs of coming to fruition.[6]

This chapter elaborates on postcolonial legal pluralism: how it came about, its consequences, and the situation of legal pluralism today. The primary focus of postcolonial pluralism has been on Africa, Asia, and the Pacific Islands. The areas involved are too vast and varied to detail, and the mountainous legal and anthropological literature on legal pluralism is too large to summit. Thus I focus on common patterns or findings in connection with legal pluralism, occasionally zooming in to specific situations to supply context and depth.

Colonization conventionally refers to European political, economic, and legal domination of large parts of the world from the sixteenth through the mid-twentieth centuries. Colonial powers were empires in the sense used in the previous chapter: a metropole exerting power over and exploiting subject peripheries for its own benefit. British control of India is a prime example. Earlier empires were largely land based, while European colonization involved ocean-based empires at great distances from the imperial center. European political domination involved various degrees of control over a peripheral territory as a colony, protectorate, or some other relationship; economic domination involved utilizing the land, labor, natural resources, and trade of a peripheral territory for the economic benefit of the metropole and its settler population; legal domination involved instrumental use of law by the colonial state to enforce its rule and achieve its exploitative economic objectives.

---

[3] Denis V. Cowen, "African Legal Studies—A Survey of the Field and the Role of the United States," 27 Law and Contemporary Problems 545, 552 (1962).

[4] Mervyn A. Jaspan, "In Quest of New Law: The Perplexity of Legal Syncretism in Indonesia," 7 Comparative Studies in Society and History 252, 252 (1965).

[5] *Id.* at 252.

[6] Another earlier piece on legal pluralism in Indonesia is Daniel S. Lev, "The Supreme Court and Adat Inheritance Law in Indonesia," 11 American Journal of Comparative Law 205 (1962).

Latin America, the Caribbean, North America, Australia, and New Zealand also involved colonization and all gave rise to legal pluralism. Much less has been written about these situations (until recently) because their legal pluralism has been compartmentalized. In these societies, large numbers of colonial settlers and laborers from elsewhere (brought as slaves or through indentured servitude) overwhelmed indigenous populations, which were further decimated by disease, forced labor, and killing. Unified legal systems were constructed, at least on the surface, relegating indigenous people to the margins, as I describe in the next chapter. Legal pluralism in postcolonial areas of Africa, Asia, and the Pacific, in contrast, is a pervasively standout feature of these societies.

European colonization evolved over time. For the first three centuries, roughly 1500–1800, European initiatives, aside from proselytizing by Christian missionaries in Spanish America, mainly focused on securing material resources and products for trade, creating markets for their goods, and establishing trading routes and towns. These early efforts were carried out mainly by trading companies, not by states themselves, and for the most part did not involve extensive control over territory. European states in this period were still in the process of consolidation themselves. England was internally riven by civil wars and revolution in the seventeenth century and the Dutch were embroiled in a decades-long war of independence from Spain. The late eighteenth century brought revolutions in the United States and France, and within a few decades thereafter most of Latin America secured independence from Spain. The Napoleonic Wars convulsed Europe in the early nineteenth century, followed by revolutions of 1848 in multiple countries. European polities throughout this period were occupied with pressing challenges to their rule at home.

European law initially applied to their own personnel, forts, and trading establishments at African and Asian outposts. Unless they impinged on colonial interests, matters between natives were seen by Europeans as best handled by natives. "Up to the late eighteenth century there was no serious European endeavor to develop jurisdiction over an autonomous population according to their own law. Nor were there attempts on a large scale to extend European law to the subject population."[7] Not only were native matters

---

[7] Jorg Fisch, "Law as a Means and as an End: Some Remarks on the Function of European and Non-European Law in the Process of European Expansion," in Wolfgang J. Mommsen and J.A. de Moor, eds., *European Expansion and Law: The Encounter of European and Indigenous Law in 19th and 20th Century Africa and Asia* (Oxford: Berg 1992) 23.

largely outside their economic concerns and beyond their capacity to address, it would have been costly and socially disruptive for Europeans to get involved in local law and disputes.

The colonial assertion of full political control over periphery territories did not widely occur until the second half of the nineteenth century.[8] EIC's penetration of India occurred a century earlier, but the British state did not take over from the Company until 1858. Although differences in attitude and approach existed among European colonizers, in practice they applied similar strategies. "Due to circumstances and scarce resources the European powers were forced to make use of the techniques of indirect rule, wherever possible, although in different degrees, depending on local circumstances."[9]

Colonial Indirect Rule

A conference of European powers was convened in Berlin in November 1884, involving England, Portugal, France, Belgium, the Netherlands, and Germany, to divide Africa amongst themselves. No African leaders participated. The territorial borders drawn by Europeans at the time remain largely the same today. Their assertion of rule over Africa was authorized under international law, jurists argued, because African countries lacked state sovereignty (*territorium nullius*), and therefore were not independent nations deserving of respect.[10] This argument conveniently overlooked that until recently India had been run by a British trading company, not a sovereign state; and at the Conference itself the Congo was allocated to a private company owned by King Leopold of Belgium (separate from the Belgian state)[11]— whose horrific exploitation of the territory resulted in the deaths of millions of Congolese.

Europeans justified seizing authority over the continent to end slavery, to bring civilized administration and law to Africans, and to better utilize its abundant natural resources. Frederick Lugard, the former Governor of

---

[8] See Heather Streets-Salter and Trevor R. Getz, *Empires and Colonies in the Modern World: A Global Perspective* (New York: Oxford University Press 2016) Part Four.

[9] Mommsen and Moor, "Introduction," *supra* note 7, at 7.

[10] Andrew Fitzmaurice, *Sovereignty, Property and Empire, 1500–2000* (Cambridge: Cambridge University Press 2014) Chapter 9.

[11] On the patent weaknesses in this position, see Casper Sylvest, "Our Passion for Legality: International Law and Imperialism in Late Nineteenth Century Britain," 34 Review of International Studies 403 (2008).

Nigeria (and previously of Hong Kong), explained: "Europe benefited by the wonderful increase in the amenities of life for the mass of her people which followed the opening up of Africa at the end of the nineteenth century. Africa benefitted by the influx of manufactured goods, and the substitution of law and order for the methods of barbarism."[12]

European colonizers copied administrative approaches from one another and applied methods from one context to the next as colonial administrators shared strategies and moved to new settings. Variations aside, they used a basic template: erect a colonial state, collect taxes from natives and customs fees and royalties, create courts, transplant law, accept local law on personal matters, and rely on local intermediaries. Administering substantial populations in faraway lands with vastly different ways of life required actions along these lines. Even France, which officially applied a universal code, recognized religious and customary law and tribunals in its African and Asian colonies.[13]

Lugard presents a vivid firsthand account of indirect rule utilized by the British in Africa and elsewhere in *The Dual Mandate in British Tropical Africa* (1922). "The essential feature of the system," he wrote, "is that the native chiefs are constituted as an integral part of the machinery of the administration."[14] The paramount chief was a regional ruler (advised by a British District Officer), supported by subordinate chiefs at lower levels of administration. The British Governor approved and could depose a paramount chief for abuse of power, but in general the colonial state supported and magnified the power of chiefs. "The native ruler derives his power from the Suzerain, and is responsible that it is not misused. . . . To intrigue against him is an offence punishable, if necessary, in a [British] Provincial Court. Thus both British and native courts are invoked to uphold his authority."[15] Only the British Colonial State had the power to impose taxation and to legislate. Only British courts had jurisdiction over non-natives and natives who lived in the townships. As for natives outside the township, "A native ruler, and the native courts, are empowered to enforce native law and custom, provided it is not repugnant to humanity, or in opposition to any ordinance."[16] State backing

---

[12] Frederick Lugard, *The Dual Mandate in British Tropical Africa* (London: Blackwood and Sons 1922) 615.

[13] Lugard's discussion of the French system in Africa shows its substantial resemblance to the British system; Lugard, *supra* note 12, at 568–69.

[14] *Id.* at 203.

[15] *Id.* at 203.

[16] *Id.* at 206.

for traditional leaders, who at the higher levels received payments from the state, enhanced their financial position and bolstered their authority within the community. This legal arrangement was widely replicated across colonial settings with differing degrees of penetration, albeit with differences in treatment between large indigenous populations with highly centralized chiefdoms and smaller dispersed populations.

British colonies were subject to the common law and equity, to laws passed in England for the colonies, and to laws declared by the colonial government. A hierarchy of courts was created: a British staffed "Supreme Court" in the colonial capital and commercial centers heard trials and appeals on matters within the city (with appeal therefrom to the Privy Council in London); "Provincial Courts" with British judges for large districts outside the major colonial cities; and "Native Courts" in each district staffed by chiefs (advised by British "Residents"). All three levels were created and funded by the colonial government. Courts staffed by British judges (informed by local assessors) as well as Native Courts would apply native religious law and customary law in cases involving natives, "especially in matters relating to property, marriage, and inheritance."[17] As one observer characterized the system: "the law of the colonizing power serves as the white man's own tribal law—a tribal law, however, of special status; for whereas Africans are compulsorily subject to certain branches of the colonizer's law, whites are not subject to any branch of African customary law to which they have not expressly or impliedly submitted themselves."[18]

Provincial Courts had exclusive jurisdiction in disputes involving non-natives as well as over natives in serious crimes like murder, applying British and colonial law, and concurrent jurisdiction with native courts in cases involving natives. Native Courts exercised jurisdiction only over natives, mainly involving "marital disputes, petty debts, trespass, assaults, and inheritance."[19] Muslim *kadi* courts heard the same kinds of matters subject to review by the chief native judge.[20] Although staffed by natives, Native Courts were not indigenous institutions but creations of and funded by colonial administrations. They were informal, citing little official law and barring the participation of lawyers.[21] Operating within the legal system subject

---

[17] *Id.* at 536.

[18] Denis V. Cowen, "African Legal Studies—A Survey of the Field and the Role of the United States," 27 Law and Contemporary Problems 545, 555 (1962).

[19] Lugard, *supra* note 12, at 550.

[20] *Id.* at 556.

[21] Martin Chanock, "The Law Market: The Legal Encounter in British East and Central Africa," in Mommsen and de Moor, *supra* note 7, at 302–33.

to higher review, with chiefs undergoing judicial training sessions, Native Courts developed hybrid forms of law that interwove elements of customary law and state law.[22]

At the lowest level were existing tribunals in villages, left to function as they did, remaining outside the official legal system, though de facto relied upon by the colonial state to manage a significant proportion of local disputes. "The headmen and the village chief will continue to exist, and their customary right to sit in arbitration for the settlement of small local disputes will not be interfered with,"[23] Lugard wrote.

Colonial state governments were economically self-sustaining, obtaining revenues by taxing natives along with customs fees on trading and royalties on mining. Head taxes or hut taxes superseded the former native systems of tributes. Local headmen collected regular taxes on behalf of the paramount chief. Although the tax rate was fixed by the British Governor, Lugard emphasized that "the actual assessment is in the hands of the native ruler and his representatives—the district and village heads—guided and assisted by the British staff. It therefore appears to the taxpayer as a tax imposed by his own, native ruler, though he knows that the vigilant eye of the District Officer will see that no unauthorized exactions are made, and that any injustice will be remedied."[24] Natives without income could provide labor to the government in lieu of tax payments, due on top of regular demands by colonial authorities for unpaid native labor on public projects.

Head or hut taxes, which could amount to the equivalent of a month's labor, also served the policy of compelling natives to work in the money economy for European plantations and mining enterprises, which were subsidized through "a rebate of half the amount if the occupier could prove that he had worked for a European for wages for a month."[25] Non-native settlers, almost all of whom were employed by the colonial government or European enterprises, many earning a "considerable" income, "are free from any form of local income tax in Africa."[26] The justification for exempting them from taxes paid by natives is that a tax on foreigners would be passed on to the

---

[22] See Roger Gocking, "British Justice and the Native Tribunals of the Southern Gold Coast Colony," 34 Journal of African History 93 (1993). Sue Farran, "Navigating Between Traditional Land Tenure and Introduced Land Laws in Pacific Island States," 64 Journal of Legal Pluralism 65 (2011).

[23] Lugard, *supra* note 12, at 553.

[24] *Id.* at 207.

[25] *Id.* at 256.

[26] *Id.* at 261.

companies that employ them through increased wages. Thus colonial tax policy was designed to support European economic enterprises.

Colonial law, as this recitation of Lugard's account shows, was geared to advancing the economic and political interests of the colonial power and its expatriate settlers, while also claiming to protect the native population and resources from gross exploitation by expatriates or their own native leaders.[27] "Colonial rule created new 'crimes,' many of which were offences against the imposed structure of colonial management."[28] Colonial criminal law unabashedly secured state power; for instance, it was a criminal offense to disobey any "reasonable order," defined as "any order which the circumstances may make necessary but which is not actually provided for in this or some other law."[29] Court enforcement of colonial tax and employment laws far exceeded cases for assault and larceny.[30] Detailed regulations were promulgated on methods of cultivation, sales of products, use of forests, movement, and much more, which were published only in English, although many natives did not speak the language. "The picture is one of a population subject to extensive regulation imposed by laws, the content of which they did not know, and randomly administered by officials, both white and African, who combined administrative and judicial roles."[31] This was British law and order, extolled by Lugard for replacing native barbarism.

The main economic activities were trade, plantations (coco, rubber, coffee, sisal, flax, cotton, etc.), harvesting timber, and mining diamonds and precious metals, run by European expatriates. Trade to and from colonies was protected by government granted monopolies up through the nineteenth century, until the rise of free trade views led to their reduction. Plantations and mining operations required securing land and a disciplined labor force. While native land tenure in many colonial contexts was held communally, the land utilized by European plantations (leased from the state, which had taken it, or purchased or leased privately from native chiefs) was based on transplanted British property regimes conferring fee simple ownership or long-term leases.[32] Land deemed unproductive was seized by colonial

---

[27] For an account of the various ways in which colonial states supported European exploitation, see Ann Seidman and Robert B. Seidman, "The Political Economy of Customary Law in the Former British Territories of Africa," 28 Journal of African Law 44 (1984).

[28] David Killingray, "The Maintenance of Law and Order in British Colonial Africa," 85 African Affairs 411, 413 (1986).

[29] M Chanock, *supra* note 21, at 283.

[30] *Id.* at 284.

[31] *Id.* at 284–85.

[32] Lugard, *supra* note 12, at 295–96.

authorities and used for public works or plantations. "In areas of European settlement," historian Christopher Bayly found, "these new definitions of property rights could become blunt instruments to bludgeon the weak. They made it possible for white settlers, and sometimes indigenous elites, to expropriate the common lands and labor of the original inhabitants."[33] Natives who lived on land claimed by European settlers were forced to enter tenancy agreements that required them to supply regular labor, enforced by criminal sanctions.[34] For mining, it was common across British and other colonies that "the ownership of all minerals is unreservedly vested in the Crown,"[35] which leased the right to mine to European run companies in return for royalties.

Procuring sufficient labor for European plantations and mines was a challenge because natives—who were portrayed as indolent and undisciplined—understandably were reluctant to engage in the back-breaking work.[36] The Dutch in Java and Germans in Samoa forcibly compelled natives to work under threat of criminal punishment.[37] The British preferred to avoid forced labor given their claimed justification to end slavery. In many colonial locations European enterprises brought large number of workers from outside, particularly Indians and Chinese, many on indentured servitude contracts.[38] To meet the need for laborers for mining and cash crops like sugar, cotton, coffee and rubber, "imperial officials supervised a system of indentured labor that resulted in the migration of nearly 1.5 million Indians, Africans, Chinese, and Pacific Islanders to other tropical colonies between 1834 and 1920."[39] Twenty million Chinese emigrated abroad via Chinese migration networks, 90 percent of whom went to Southeast Asia, many to work on plantations.[40] Employment contracts with native and immigrant labor were enforced by criminal penalties for "desertion,"[41] as well as "neglect of duties, negligence, and refusal to work."[42] "The criminal punishing of

---

[33] C.A. Bayly, *The Birth of the Modern World, 1780–1914* (Oxford: Blackwell 2004) 112, 134.

[34] Chanock, *supra* note 21, at 294.

[35] Lugard, *supra* note 12, at 347.

[36] *Id.* at 390–405.

[37] *Id.* at 417–18.

[38] *Id.* at 415–19. See Streets-Salter and Getz, *supra* note 8, at 157–60, 364–69.

[39] *Id.* at 366.

[40] *Id.* at 367. On a personal note, my grandparents emigrated from Okinawa to Hawaii in the 1920s via indentured servitude to work on a plantation.

[41] See Peter Fitzpatrick, "Law and Labor in Colonial Papua New Guinea," in Yash Ghai, Robin Luckham, and Francis Snyder, eds., *The Political Economy of Law: A Third World Reader* (Delhi: Oxford University Press 1987) 13–43.

[42] Chanock, *supra* note 21, at 294.

defaulting workers was one of the major occupations of the colonial courts."[43] The influx of immigrants, in turn, resulted in the recognition of community laws for immigrant communities, thereby multiplying legal plurality.

Colonial law thus consisted of transplanted law from the metropole oriented to maintaining the power of colonial governments and advancing the interests of their expatriate settlers, applied in British staffed courts; local customary and religious law applied by British judges as well as native judges in provincial and native courts to actions involving natives; British judges applying the laws of immigrant communities to their affairs; and unofficial village tribunals handling the bulk of disputes at the local level through customary and religious law. This basic framework structured legal pluralism within the colonial state, combining territorial regime law and local personal community law in the system, while leaving functioning local legal institutions to carry on outside the official system.

A wave of legal pluralism was created around the world in the wake of European colonization through the transplantation of legal norms and institutions and the movement of people and ideas. This occurred in five basic ways. First, colonizers implanted Western-derived laws and legal institutions in colonized areas to maintain colonial rule, further colonial economic enterprises, govern expatriate settlers, and maintain order in colonial towns and outposts, while local forms of customary and religious law continued to function for the bulk of indigenous people. Second, European leaders drew state boundaries over colonized lands in ways that disregarded pre-existing political-cultural-religious polities and communities, bringing within a single territorial state groups with different cultural and religious laws, while conversely groups with the same laws were divided across separate states.[44] Third, colonial economic enterprises like mines and plantations imported immigrant laborers in significant numbers (via slavery, indentured servitude, or voluntarily), who re-created communities with their own cultural or religious laws, especially on family law and inheritance matters. Fourth, powerful non-Western states that were not colonized (particularly Russia and China) created their own versions of the first and second approaches mentioned: some created states that spanned areas with different languages, ethnicities, and customary and religious laws; some

---

[43] *Id.* at 293.

[44] The continuing deleterious consequences of the arbitrary drawing of state boundaries in Africa and the Middle East are discussed in Tim Marshall, *Prisoners of Geography: Ten Maps that Explain Everything About the World* (New York: Scribner 2016) Chapters 5 and 6.

adopted Western laws and institutions in efforts to modernize, introducing transplanted forms of official state law alongside existing local law. Fifth, people from colonized countries emigrated to imperial centers, settling in immigrant communities, bringing their customary and religious laws with them, particularly on family law and inheritance, creating pockets of legal pluralism in the metropole. These five occurrences—which have commonly occurred in the history of multinational empires[45]—created legal pluralism along two axes: communities living side by side following different bodies of law and state law coexisting with contrasting bodies of community law, and in many locations both.

Legal Pluralism: An Introduction to Colonial and Neo-Colonial Law (1975),[46] by M.B. Hooker, is a monumental survey of legal pluralism produced in the course of colonization, focusing on the first four modes mentioned above. He covers the interaction of British colonial laws with Hindu law, Buddhist law, Islamic law, African customary law, Chinese customary law, and Adat law; French colonial civil law with indigenous forms of law in Africa and Indochina; Dutch colonial law with indigenous forms of law in Indonesia; Anglo-American common law with indigenous law in the United States, New Zealand, Australia, and South Africa; voluntarily adopted Western law in Turkey, Thailand, and Ethiopia; and finally, Marxist law in the USSR and China alongside customary and religious forms of law.

Colonial law in location after location accorded official recognition to customary or religious law in various ways and extents, sometimes through codification, more often by allowing courts to apply indigenous law, creating or supporting informal village or traditional courts, or simply leaving existing indigenous tribunals alone. Recognition of native law was not altruism on the part of colonizing powers. As the previous chapter shows, this is standard practice for empires throughout history. European colonizers "recognized" customary law because that was the most expedient way to maintain rule over subject populaces with the least expenditure and social disruption. It was a face-saving declaration by the colonial legal system claiming to "authorize" indigenous law that had long existed, which the colonial state did not have the power to replace.

---

[45] See generally Lauren Benton and Richard Ross, *Legal Pluralism and Empires, 1500–1850* (New York: NYU Press 2013).

[46] M.B. Hooker, *Legal Pluralism: An Introduction to Colonial and Neo-Colonial Laws* (Oxford: Clarendon Press 1975).

John Griffiths dismissed what Hooker discussed as not genuine legal pluralism because recognition by the colonial state amounts to another version of legal centralism. But this assertion takes state law's claim of recognition at face value. What it fails to appreciate is that native bodies of law did not owe their existence to state recognition (on paper), but rather to ongoing collective recognition within the community. The legal pluralism Hooker highlighted is undeniably genuine, with profound continuing significance for these societies. This was the legal pluralism in Yap, described in the Introduction, and across the Global South.

Hooker's encyclopedic study focuses primarily on legal materials like legislation and court decisions. Anthropological studies brought attention to the complex social and legal dynamics revolving around postcolonial legal pluralism. Now let us briefly examine the main issues discussed in the literature.

The Transformation-Invention of Customary Law

Colonial legal systems made overt efforts to alter and control customary law and religious law through statutory prohibitions and judicial rulings based on equity or the repugnancy clause that restricted slavery, child brides, polygamy, infanticide, witchcraft, ordeals, and other native practices opposed by colonial officials. More subtle changes were made to customary law and religious law through recognition and incorporation within the colonial legal system, a process that involved transformation and invention.

A fundamental aspect of this transformation is that native legal notions were translated for the purposes of recognition into Western categories that appeared to be roughly functionally similar (for example, divisions in property rights), though inevitably they did not match, resulting in significant changes. Another factor in the transformation of customary law is that the orientation of European legal systems differs substantially from indigenous justice systems. European law centers on the application of written legal rules to rights-bearing individuals involved in a given matter; indigenous systems are oriented to arriving at an equitable resolution of a dispute that takes into consideration applicable norms as well as broader social relations within the community.[47] The norms take contrasting forms—written

---

[47] See, e.g., Tess Newton Cain, "Convergence or Clash? The Recognition of Customary Law and Practice in Sentencing Decisions of the Courts of the Pacific Island Regions," 2 Melbourne Journal

versus unwritten—and those who preside have contrasting decision-making orientations—applying rules to determine outcomes versus striving to achieve outcomes satisfactory to the community.

The ascertainment of customary law for application in colonial courts proved to be elusive.[48] Customary laws norms "have been found to be in a state of flux with different versions; there are conflicting or contradictory norms; norms are described in a 'vague or elusive' manner; norms have multiple contingencies or exceptions; stated norms often do not match actual behavior; it is not always clear how to move from the abstract norm to application in a given case; and sometimes a number of normative orders coexist."[49] Contributing to these difficulties, norms are not applicable in the abstract, but rather are linked to the specific social relationships involved in given disputes. "This multiplicity not only makes it difficult to state the norms precisely, but sometimes may make it impossible, since the assortment of contingencies can vary so much from one case to another."[50] The flexibility of customary law matched the orientation of customary tribunals:

> An adequate account of a dispute therefore requires a description of its total social context—its genesis, successive efforts to manage it, and the subsequent history of the relationship between the parties. . . .
> . . . [I]ndigenous rules are not seen a priori as 'laws' that have the capacity to determine the outcome of disputes in a straightforward fashion. It is recognized, rather, that the rules may themselves be the object of negotiation and may sometimes be a resource to be managed advantageously.[51]

Evaluated from the standpoint of Western legal systems, this sounds defective. However, it is sensible in light of the objective of many customary tribunals to arrive at outcomes that restore peace within small communities

of International Law 48, 51 (2001); Guy Powles, "Common Law at Bay?" The Scope and state of Customary Law Regimes in the Pacific," 21 Journal of Pacific Studies 61, 64 (1997).

[48] Problems with the ascertainment of customary law are detailed in Kwamena Bentsi-Enchill, "The Colonial Heritage of Legal Pluralism," 1 Zambian Law Journal 1 (1969).

[49] Brian Z. Tamanaha, "A Proposal for the Development of a System of Indigenous Jurisprudence in The Federated States of Micronesia," 13 Hastings International & Comparative Law Review 71, 103–104 (1989) (citing multiple studies of customary law).

[50] Sally Falk Moore, "Descent and Legal Position," in Laura Nader, ed., *Law and Culture in Society* (1969) 374, 376.

[51] John Comaroff and Simon Roberts, *Rules and Processes: The Cultural Logic of Dispute in an African Context* (Chicago: University of Chicago Press 1981) 13–14.

that must live together. Strict rule application results in winners and losers, whereas dialogue and negotiation encourages acceptance.

Codifications of customary law suffered three difficulties.[52] First:

> What seems to be most misleading about these attempted codifications of customary law is not that the formulated rules would, in themselves, be necessarily wrong, but that they are fatally incomplete. For every 'rule' assumed, there are hundreds overlooked—'rules' which would qualify those stated, balance them, enlarge them or narrow them down. An enormous proliferation of rules will be needed if one insists on proceeding that way and no outsider will ever be able to do it. For those on the other hand who share the values of the community, the feeling of a balance will be something spontaneous and self-evident.[53]

Second, customary law varies by region, ethnic group, and religion; Namibia, for example, has forty-nine recognized traditional communities, most with their own customary laws.[54] Either one must write many customary law codes or a territorial or regional code that picks one set of customs over others, both unpalatable options, which is why relatively few customary law codifications were actually written.[55]

The third problem is that, whether taken from a code or informed by native law experts, European judges who apply customary law in the same manner they apply their own law distort its operation. "The essence of these customary systems may be said to have lain in their processes, but these were displaced, and the flexible principles which had guided them were now fed into a rule-honing and -using machine operating in new political circumstances."[56] Consequently, "the norms cannot retain their original

---

[52] For a balanced view of the challenges, see Anthony N. Allott, "What Is to Be Done with African Customary Law? The Experience of Problems and Reforms in Anglophone Africa from 1950," 28 Journal of African Law 56, 66 (1984).

[53] Alexander Nekam, Aspects of African Customary Law, 62 Northwestern Law Review 45, 48 (1967).

[54] Oliver C. Ruppel and Katharina Ryppel-Schlichting, "Legal and Judicial Pluralism in Namibia and Beyond: A Modern Approach to African Legal Architecture?" 64 Journal of Legal Pluralism 33, 40 (2011).

[55] R.E.S. Tanner, "The Codification of Customary Law in Tanzania," 2 East Africa Law Journal 105, 114 (1966).

[56] Martin Chanock, *Law, Custom, and Social Order: The Colonial Experience in Malawi and Zambi* (Cambridge: Cambridge University Press: 1985) 62.

content as components of a different system."[57] "The village elders, once having given evidence as witnesses in court, . . . find their opinions are then divorced from the particular context in which they were given and that an impersonal authority is bestowed on them."[58] Setting forth customary law in a code or judicial precedent further transforms customary law by rendering it fixed, while unwritten customary law changes in relation to changing circumstances.[59]

Owing to these differences, the codification and judicial application of customary law by European judges inevitably transformed their content and operation (as also occurred with Hindu and Muslim law in India, described earlier). Transformations of customary law also occurred in Native Courts staffed by natives. Native judges were not necessarily familiar with local customary law in the areas they presided over and lacked full awareness of the social relations and ramifications of the matters in dispute. The training they received in law and legal practices, and higher-level review of their decisions by British judges, carried legalistic imperatives that native magistrates imitated consciously and subconsciously. "It orients their minds toward the rule aspects of their task and thus it loosens their emotional comprehension of customary law and weakens their capacity to satisfy the balancing requirements of community."[60]

A number of anthropologists have argued that customary law was not truly customary at all, but rather was an invention that advanced the interests of colonial authorities as well as indigenous elites in situations undergoing massive changes in social, political, and economic relations.[61] What won the stamp of recognition in court was not customary law in the sense of lived social relations within the community, but involved selective formulations or interpretations of existing customs in new economic circumstances.[62] Once customary law was recognized by courts in the context of legal institutions and practices, it became "juridical customary law,"[63] the creation of legal

<hr>

[57] Gordon Woodman, "Customary Law, State Courts, and the Notion of the Institutionalization of Norms in Ghana and Nigeria," in Anthony Allott and Gordon R. Woodman, eds., *People's Law and State Law: The Bellagio Papers* (1985) 157.

[58] D.H.A. Kolff, "The Indian and the British Law Machines: Some Remarks on Law and Society in British India," in Mommsen and Moor, *supra* note 7, at 230–31.

[59] Kwamena Bentsi-Enchill, "The Colonial Heritage of Legal Pluralism," 1 Zambian Law Journal 1, 23, 27 (1969).

[60] Nekam, *supra* note 53.

[61] Frederick Snyder, "Colonialism and Legal Form: The Creation of 'Customary Law' in Senegal," 19 Journal of Legal Pluralism 49 (1981)

[62] Frederick Snyder, "Customary Law and the Economy," 24 Journal of African Law 34 (1984).

[63] Allott, *supra* note 52.

actors (British and native)—much like the common law in England, which was not the customs followed by people (notwithstanding claims about customs from time immemorial), but rather was an ongoing product of jurists.[64]

Socially Embedded Informal Village Tribunals

The official colonial legal arrangement, as we have seen, involves three layers: (1) colonial courts staffed by judges from the metropole presiding in major cities applied colonial law and transplanted civil codes or common law doctrines to expatriates and to state-related matters and commercial activities in the modern economic sector, and criminal law to everyone in the cities; (2) district or regional courts staffed by judges from the metropole applied colonial law, codes or common law, and when natives were involved customary law and religious law with assistance from native experts who served as assessors or gave evidence of the custom; and (3) Native or Village Courts staffed by natives, often chiefs or Big Men, applying customary law or religious law typically in an informal fashion with limited references to state law. When colonization ended this basic arrangement remained in place. Natives with professional legal training gradually assumed judicial positions in the first two layers and status distinctions between natives and Europeans were removed.

A significant bulk of legal activities in many of these societies during and after colonization, however, was not located within the official legal system just described, particularly in rural areas, but instead took place at the village level in informal tribunals. Some were officially acknowledged as carrying out judicial functions, but many were not, and the state legal system had little involvement in their operations.[65]

In many locations it was, and still is, a routinely followed customary practice expected within the community to take disputes to unofficial local tribunals first, rather than to state courts.[66] These tribunals are staffed by

---

[64] This transformation occurs in state courts that recognize customary law, in contrast to unofficial village courts. See Franz von Benda-Beckmann, "Law Out of Context: A Comment on the Creation of Traditional Law Discussion," 28 Journal of African Law 28 (1984).

[65] An example is Namibia's recognition of certain traditional authorities, which function much the say way as traditional authorities in other parts of Namibia that did not receive official recognition. See Oliver C. Ruppel and Katharina Ryppel-Schlichting, "Legal and Judicial Pluralism in Namibia and Beyond: A Modern Approach to African Legal Architecture?," 64 Journal of Legal Pluralism 33, 44–45 (2011).

[66] Lloyed Fallers, "Customary Law in the New African States," 27 Law and Contemporary Problems 605, 608, 613 (1962).

village chiefs, or elders, or respected members of the community applying local customary law, called together for the occasion, usually in open discussion with others present. They preside over disputes involving property, inheritance, divorce, adultery, custody of children, debt, theft, accidental injuries or damage to property, accusations of witchcraft, rape, and assaults short of homicide.[67] They do not mark a distinction between criminal and civil wrongs, and aim at restitution and reconciliation, though punishment is also involved. Decisions usually are not enforced by state legal officials, relying instead on social pressure from the community to abide by the outcome.

These tribunals are socially embedded in the sense that those who preside in the tribunal and those involved in the dispute are familiar with one another, have multiple ongoing connections, and share a past and future together within the community. "Judges and litigants, and the litigants among themselves, interact in relationships whose significance ranges beyond the transitoriness of the court or a particular dispute."[68] Since they are from the same community, furthermore, people are familiar with the situation and applicable norms. The hearing aims at achieving reconciliation, repairing the rupture among the kin groups and community, to enable people to continue live together—coming to an outcome seen as fair, or at least acceptable, all things considered. "To do this, they have to broaden their inquiries to cover the total history of the relations between the parties, and not only the narrow legal issue raised by one of them."[69] A decision is arrived at through a combination of open debate and discussion over the relevant facts and the appropriate norms and outcome, as well as negotiation, and social pressure to settle. A remedy is determined, often involving payment of goods or services and/or an apology, though it can also include corporal punishment or expulsion. A traditional feast or reconciliation ceremony involving the parties and the community closes the proceedings.[70]

Although they lacked official status, colonial legal systems implicitly relied on village tribunals to handle a substantial amount of dispute resolution.

---

[67] A dated yet informative account of these courts is J.H.M. Beattie, "Informal Judicial Activity in Bunyoro," 9 Journal of African Administration 188 (1957).

[68] J. van Velsen, "Procedural Informality, Reconciliation, and False Comparisons," in Max Gluckman, ed., *Ideas and Procedures in African Customary Law* (Oxford: Oxford University Press 1969) 138.

[69] *Id.* at 138.

[70] See William A. Shack, "Guilt and Innocence: Problem and Method in the Gurage Judicial System," in Gluckman, *supra* note 68, at 158.

Following decolonization, a number of newly independent states considered it important to assert the monopoly of state law, going so far as to abolish unofficial village tribunals. However, "in each of these enactments the holding of arbitration under customary law is either expressly or implicitly exempted so that arbitration under customary law continues to exist."[71] The state legal monopoly was maintained, in other words, by attaching the label "arbitration" to traditional tribunals, although they continued to function as before.

Unofficial tribunals have proven to be highly resilient. After Indonesia became independent from the Netherlands, lawyers advocating a uniform legal system led to the explicit abolishment of village *adat* courts (which had been recognized by the Dutch).[72] Yet little changed. State courts were too costly, with lengthy delays, and people avoided them whenever possible. Even after they were officially abolished, "because of the general desire to maintain local cohesion and solidarity, adat law continues to be operative in most cases. The village and *marga* [parish] heads no longer judge cases but are said to arbitrate or mediate."[73]

A recent comparative study of the relationship between non-state informal tribunals and state legal systems in postcolonial contexts across Africa, Asia, South America, and the Pacific found a range of treatments by the state: from active repression of the non-state tribunal (rare); to no formal recognition of the non-state tribunal but tacit acceptance and encouragement by the state (the vast majority); to formal recognition by the state of the non-state tribunal, granting it exclusive or non-exclusive jurisdiction over selected locations or matters, and in certain instances also providing state enforcement of its decisions (less common).[74] (To be clear, this survey excludes official Native or Village Courts created by colonial and postcolonial state, which are state courts; this is about informal tribunals not created or funded by the state.) Whatever the particular relationship with the state, non-state tribunals still play a significant role dealing with basic legal issues in rural communities of postcolonial societies. This point is borne out also in the one

---

[71] N.A. Ollennu, "The Structure of African Judicial Authority and Problems of Evidence and Proof in Traditional Courts," in Gluckman, *supra* note 68, at112.

[72] Mervyn A. Jaspan, "In the Quest of New Law: The Perplexity of Legal Syncretism in Indonesia," 7 Comparative Studies in Society and History 252, 260–61 (1965)

[73] *Id.* at 262.

[74] See Miranda Forsyth, "A Typology of Relationship Between State and Non-State Justice Systems," 56 Journal of Legal Pluralism and Unofficial Law 67 (2007). My description compresses Forsyth's seven model typology. The author's study examined Australia, New Zealand, Samoa, Kiribati, East Timor, Vanuatu, Fiji, Papua New Guinea, Solomon Islands, Tuvalu, Tokelau, South Africa, Malawi, Nigeria, Zambia, Mozambique, Lesotho, Botswana, Bangladesh, Philippines, Peru, and Columbia.

instance of state repression identified by the author. In an effort to create a unified state legal system with state courts applying customary law, Botswana made it illegal for people to preside over cases as a customary tribunal, but "in reality," it turns out, "not formally recognized chiefly courts are tolerated, or even supported, by the official police forces."[75] This example illustrates, once again, the allure of the image of the monistic law state in the minds of legal officials, but also the resilience of community law for ongoing social intercourse. Informal tribunals provide dispute resolution functions for the community that state legal systems lack the institutional capacity, orientation, and local knowledge to accomplish, and they do so in ways that matches the needs and comports with the understanding of the community.

The lines between non-state tribunals and state tribunals have become blurred and intertwined, often through *unofficial* arrangements and connections. State officials may refer cases to non-state tribunals to handle, relying on them to help manage social disputes, and may recognize their decisions (for example, deferring to land decisions); customary tribunals may refer cases to state courts when beyond their capacity to resolve or enforce. Some government officials also happen to sit on customary tribunals as respected members of the community.[76] While state and non-state tribunals have different norms and processes, and give rise to forum shopping, they can operate in a mutually supportive fashion, producing a de facto division of labor in the delivery of legal functions.

Enhancing Power of Traditional Elites

Indirect rule bolstered the power of traditional leaders in several ways. Chiefly authority had customarily been over tribes, but in the territorially based court system created by the colonial state, chiefs presided over native people living within their territory who were outside their tribes, a significant expansion of their authority, while still retaining personal authority over tribal members outside the territory.[77] Since the colonial state had limited reach in rural areas, chiefs and headmen bore much of the responsibility

---

[75] *Id.* at 73.

[76] See Noah Coburn and John Dempsey, "Informal Dispute Resolution in Afghanistan," United States Institute of Peace Special Report 247 (2010).

[77] Jarle Simensen, "Jurisdiction as Politics: The Gold Coast During the Colonial Period," in Mommsen and Moor *supra* note 7, at 263.

for criminal law, investigating and detaining wrongdoers, and serving as witnesses in criminal trials in state court.[78] They also presided over cases themselves. "Not only were African tribunals transformed in this way by being incorporated into the colonial system and by being made responsible for the administration of coercive colonial regulations, they also had at their command the unwritten customary criminal law, which could be used to punish conduct which they disliked which was not against any written law."[79] Chiefs have also been accused of utilizing their judicial powers for corrupt purposes, not just soliciting bribes, but also bringing cases against people in order to impose financial penalties.[80] Judicial fees and fines are significant sources of income to chiefs hearing disputes.[81]

A highly consequential increase in their power relates to authority over land. Under customary land tenure, land typically was not bought and sold in fee simple terms. Communal land tenure was common, providing people rights to control and use the fruits of the land, though not an unfettered right to dispose of it. Community and family social relations, including spiritual elements and connections with ancestors, were wrapped together with land in relations that extend back generations and carry future obligations. Drawing on familiar notions of feudal land tenure, British administrators presumed that paramount chiefs held the land in trust, with sub-chiefs arrayed below, each level exercising the power to allocate possession and use of the land. To prevent abuse by chiefs, it was common for colonial law to restrict land sales, particularly to foreigners, though land could be leased out, and final say was given to traditional leaders. In addition, colonial states designated traditional or tribal areas under state control as well as public lands (crown or state), which tribal leaders were given a say in administering.

Control over the allocation of land made people subject to chiefs in ways that did not previously exist, affecting rules of kinship and marriage, all of which were tied together.[82] Certain chiefs monetized their control over the land by imposing yearly rents on people living on the land, claimed as a form of customary tribute.[83] Chiefs also sold or leased the right to possess the land

---

[78] Chanock, *supra* note 21, at 284.

[79] *Id.* at 284.

[80] Simenen, *supra* note 77, at 271–72.

[81] Ulrike Schmid, "Legal Pluralism as a Source of Conflict in Multi-Ethnic Societies: The Case of Ghana," 46 Journal of Legal Pluralism 1, 33–34 (2001).

[82] Chanock, *supra* note 21, at 288.

[83] Simensen, *supra* note 77, at 264–65.

to large agricultural enterprises and granted mining concessions.[84] In one area, owing to "overlapping leases and double granting" by various chiefs, the area formally leased "exceeded the total area of the state."[85] Not only did this create disputes between paramount and lesser chiefs over the authority to grant leases, it also raised questions about how the proceeds were to be distributed, with hefty shares retained by the chiefs. One study concluded that traditional elites "were able to use their political platform to influence legislation governing local jurisdiction in their own favor and exploit the system of customary law to secure their material interests."[86] A World Bank report observed that "many forms of traditional law are seen to discriminate against marginalized groups and perpetuate entrenched discriminatory power structures within the local community."[87]

Traditional leaders exercise significant powers in many places across the Global South today, albeit with many variations. They have administrative authority in allocating land and benefits, legislative authority in declaring customary law and advising the legislature on the impact of proposed laws, and judicial authority in resolving local civil and criminal disputes. Their authority remains substantial in rural areas. In urban areas where multiethnic groups have settled, their power has been diluted, particularly in conflicts among young men from different ethnic groups who are less tied to traditional sources of authority.[88] "In the absence of strong common bonds, disputants have less incentive to accept an unfavorable outcome or to consider a ruling as binding."[89]

State officials are wary of traditional leaders as rival sources of power, but they also rely on traditional leaders to manage a range of political and legal functions at the local level. Traditional leaders defend their power and prerogatives against encroachments by the state, drawing on their support in the local community and ideological legitimation grounded in custom and tradition. Sometimes traditional leaders operate as a check on state officials,

[84] Pauline E. Peters, "Inequality and Social Conflict Over Land in Africa," 4 Journal of Agrarian Change 269, 290–300 (2004).

[85] Simensen, *supra* note 77, at 267.

[86] *Id.* at 257.

[87] Leila Chirayath, Caroline Sage, and Michael Woolcock, Customary Law and Policy Reform: Engaging with the Plurality of Justice Systems (Washington, D.C.: World Bank Legal Department Paper 2005) 4.

[88] See Jurg Helbling, Walter Kalin, and Prosper Nobirabo, "Access to Justice, Impunity and Legal Pluralism in Kenya," Journal of Legal Pluralism 8–13 (2015).

[89] Thomas Barfield, Neamat Nojumi, and J. Alexander Thier, "The Clash of Two Goods: State and Nonstate Dispute Resolution in Afghanistan," in Deborah Isser, ed., *Customary Justice and the Rule of Law in War-Torn Societies* (Washington, D.C.: United States Institute for Peace 2011) 17.

and vice versa. Sometimes both government officials and traditional leaders utilize their positions to obtain titles to or control over communal land for their own benefit.[90]

After decolonization traditional leaders in many countries suffered a backlash for collaborating with colonial authorities. Socialist governments, educated professionals, and other progressive sectors within society favored abolishing or diminishing the political and legal power of traditional leaders, seeing them as reactionary holdovers that stood in the way of creating a modern unified state legal system. Traditional chiefs have also been sharply criticized as local rent-seekers.

While abuses exist, however, traditional leaders are subject to social and political forms of accountability (as well as state legal restrictions), and many embrace their responsibility for the community and cultural tradition. Large portions of native populations today continue to support them. A study of nineteen African countries involving 26,000 face-to-face interviews found that "Large majorities believe that [traditional authorities] should still play a significant and increasing role in local governance; traditional authorities appear to enjoy a widespread popular legitimacy that undergirds the institution's resilience."[91] Contrary to what one might assume, the study found that popular support for traditional authorities holds not only among the rural population, but also among educated people, women, young people, and urban dwellers.[92] Their popularity appears to be based on appreciation for the important role they provide in resolving local disputes, underpinned by cultural views of respect for the chieftaincy that predated and survived the distortions introduced by colonization.

Uncertainty and Conflict Over Land

Among the many issues raised by legal pluralism those surrounding land are perhaps the most complex, fraught with conflict, and consequential. The conflicts involve overlapping claims to ownership or occupation rights, boundary disputes, enclosures, use of land for grazing, inheritance shares, government seizures of land, and the distribution of rents, royalties, and

---

[90] Peters, *supra* note 84, at 297.

[91] Carolyn Logan, "The Roots of Resilience: Exploring Popular Support for African Traditional Authorities," 112 African Affairs 355 (2013).

[92] *Id.* at 368–71.

income from land concessions. Although the circumstances vary greatly across countries, a broad generalization (most applicable in Africa) is that in urban areas state land law and registration is used—with the major exception of untitled peri-urban squatter settlements—while in rural areas customary land tenure is used within the community.

A continuous source of conflict from colonization through the present has been small-scale subsistence farming on family worked plots struggling to stave off large-scale consolidation of land for productive uses—with land often taken by state authorities or claimed by chiefs or Big Men then leased or sold to private enterprises. Frequent land conflicts arise today because population growth and migration of people to cities (seeking work or fleeing conflicts or famine) have made land scarcer and more expensive; land is increasingly becoming commoditized owing to extensive commercial ranching (cattle, pigs, etc.) and agriculture (plantations), and the construction of factories, offices, and apartments, leading to rising property values around urban areas.[93]

Land conflict takes place on a legal terrain with contrasting conceptualizations of property and land tenure rights (state versus customary), as well as coexisting systems of legal authority (formal state courts versus informal local tribunals), as well as different modes of land utilization (economic maximization versus subsistence farming). At the most general level, attitudes toward land involve a contrast between two very different world views and forms of social and economic organization.

In advanced capitalist societies land is an economic asset individuals utilize for various purposes: a place to live or to obtain rents from, an investment that appreciates in value, an asset to use as collateral for loans or to sell, a container of wealth to pass on to loved ones upon death. Land is *univocal*—an economic asset with multiple uses. Land in much of the Global South, particularly in rural areas, is far more complex and a central component of their life-world. Land involves wealth, a source of political power and social status, a place to live and source of subsistence, a basis of social security, a part of cultural and ethnic identity, an aspect of kinship and community relations, a locus of spirituality, and an ongoing link to ancestors that they hold in trust for future generations.[94] As just mentioned, moreover, land is a basis of the political, social,

---

[93] See Peters, *supra* note 84. My account is informed by an excellent overview of land conflicts, Klaus Deininger, *Monitoring and Evaluation of Land Policies and Land Reform* (World Bank Publications 2009).

[94] A sense of the integral role of land is conveyed in Zaid Abubakari, Christine Richter, and Jaap Zevenbergen, "Plural Inheritance Laws, Practices and Emergent Types of Property—Implications for Updating the Land Register," 11 Sustainability 1 (2019). An account of the clashes between these

economic, and legal powers of traditional leaders, who frequently have the authority to allocate land and receive rents therefrom for personal use and community distribution, as well as preside in customary tribunals that make determinations in land disputes. Land is *multivocal*—with multiple meanings, uses, and implications for manifold aspects of social existence.

Land issues are enmeshed in legal pluralism in several ways. One way is that customary land tenure is carved into different layers and slices inconsistent with state land law. State property regimes and registration systems typically are constructed in categories that treat real property as an economic asset held by individuals (including entities), with variations: fee simple, joint tenancy or tenancy in common, servitudes on the land, life estates and remainders, and contractually based lease rights and trusts. Customary land tenure often revolves around communal property that accords different rights and responsibilities to people within the family, kin group, lineage, or community to occupy or possess; to be consulted about; to seek permission from; to use for planting, hunting, or grazing; to reap present or future benefits from; to allow others to use; to pass on after death; and to dispose of. Customary land tenure combines individual and communal rights and responsibilities: "Research showed the vast majority of farms in Africa being worked by individual and small familial units who have separate claims, rights and responsibilities, even though land in its most general sense is usually vested in collectivities such as chiefdoms or clans."[95] Ownership titles and land registration recognized by state law do not capture the full gamut of customary land tenure rights and responsibilities, giving rise to conflicts between the two respective regimes, the former followed by the state and the latter by the community.[96] When titles are granted and land is registered, customary land tenure rights may be officially extinguished, and the official records may not reflect actual possession and understandings within the community. Because people with customary tenure can be illiterate and lack required documents or evidence, moreover, titling programs have resulted in many people being dispossessed.

two ideological understandings of law in Asia is Yuka Kaneko, "Origin of Land Disputes: Reviving Colonial Apparatus in Asian Land Law Reforms," in Yuka Kaneko, Narufumi Kadomatsu, and Brian Z. Tamanaha, eds., *Land Law and Disputes in Asia* (London: Routledge forthcoming 2021).

[95] Peters, *supra* note 84, at 269, 274. An overview of the debate over individual versus collective ownership is Tania Murray Li, "Indigeneity, Capitalism, and the Management of Dispossession," 51 Current Anthropology 385 (2010).

[96] Abubakari, Richter, and Zevenbergen, *supra* note 94, at 13.

In many of these countries a significant percentage of land acquired through customary transfer is not officially titled or recorded, including peri-urban property surrounding expanding cities; in Africa, only about 10 percent of land is formally recognized, and in major parts of Africa and Asia as much as 50 percent or more of the population in peri-urban areas live under informal arrangements.[97] Even when titling does occur and is registered under the formal system, parties who receive property through transfers or inheritance do not always register, so progress made through titling efforts may subsequently regress.

Uncertainty and conflicts arise from the coexistence of these systems. When land is sold, the outcome of an ownership dispute depends on whether the transaction was legally recorded or was conducted orally, as well as whether the dispute is taken to a customary tribunal or to a state court—or to both. When title is registered in state property records, a state court may order the sale valid, whereas a customary tribunal might decide otherwise on customary grounds. A study in Kenya found that 89 percent of land disputes filed in the local magistrate's court had previously been submitted to the customary council of elders.[98] This involved a sample of twenty-seven cases in one district, and it does not indicate how many cases were resolved satisfactorily by the council of elders, but the high percentage shows that people are willing to go to customary tribunals *and* to go to state courts when pursuing a desired outcome. A separate study of conflict over land in West Africa found evidence that levels of violence are higher where existing legal arrangements (de facto and de jure) allow cases to be brought to both state court and traditional courts, compared to unified systems in which people have only a single forum to adjudicate land claims—although the causes of this higher level of violence are unclear.[99]

Inheritance is a second land-related context in which legal pluralism regularly occurs. State laws on intestate succession (which specify how property passes when people die without wills), customary laws, and religious laws may all differ on the disposition of real property of a deceased.

---

[97] Emmanuel Frimpong Boamah and Margath Walker, "Legal Pluralism, Land Tenure and the Production of Nomotropic Urban Spaces in Post-Colonial Accra, Ghana," 36 Geography Research Forum 86, 97 (2016) (for example, 60 percent of peri-urban land in Accra is not registered). See Deininger, *supra* note 93.

[98] See Helbling, Kalin, and Norbirabo, *supra* note 88.

[99] See Kristine Eck, "The Law of the Land: Communal Conflict and Legal Authority," 51 Journal of Peace Research 441 (2014). The author recognizes that the existence of multiple jurisdictions might not causally enhance violence, but is itself a reflection of underlying factors that produce greater violence. *Id.* at 450.

A single country may include customary systems with patrilineal inherit-ance that sends property to sons or brothers if there is no son (daughters re-ceive nothing and widows have use rights); as well as matrilineal inheritance in which property passes through females and their children;[100] and also Islamic inheritance that provides shares for various family members, with wives entitled to one-eighth of the husband's estate (divided among all the wives), while sons receive twice the share of daughters.[101] People frequently do not record land transferred through inheritance, so official records of property ownership do not match ownership recognized within the family and community.

The coexistence of multiple inheritance regimes has particular signifi-cance for women, who head a significant number of households and are often land insecure. A study of fifteen sub-Saharan African countries in rural and urban settings found that, owing to customary inheritance rules, a majority of widows received *no* assets from their husband's estates upon death (going instead to his family and children).[102] Widows often stand to receive higher shares of the estate under state law than under customary law and religious law. During colonization women "learned quickly to seek relief in colonial courts" for better legal treatment under state family and inheritance laws.[103] Postcolonial state courts today similarly offer women better protections for their interests in divorce and inheritance cases, though they must overcome substantial hurdles to obtain these benefits. Access to state courts requires that they know about the law, have marriage certificates and property deeds, possess the financial wherewithal to retain legal assistance or enlist the support of a local woman's rights nongovern-mental organizations (NGOs), and be willing to suffer social condemna-tion within the community—"going to court to settle a marital dispute is regarded as an unforgivable offense."[104]

Among four possible combinations of land transactions, three produce uncertainty and the most secure fourth combination is the least common.[105] When transfers satisfy customary land tenure requirements, but titles are

---

[100] Abubakari, Richter, and Zevenbergen, *supra* note 94, at 6–9.

[101] Ruth Evans, "Working with Legal Pluralism: Widowhood, Property Inheritance, and Poverty Alleviation in Urban Senegal," 23 Gender & Development 77, 80 (2015).

[102] Amber Peterman, "Widowhood and Asset Inheritance in Sub-Saharan Africa: Empirical Evidence from 15 Countries," 30 Development Policy Review 543 (2012).

[103] Chanock, *supra* note 21, at 297.

[104] Evans, *supra* note 101, at 87.

[105] See Boamah and Walker, *supra* note 97, at 95–100.

lacking and/or are not recorded in the state land registry, ownership is not secure and banks are less likely to accept the property as collateral for loans. Titles may not be issued or registered because the cost may be high owing to the necessity to pay officials bribes, the titling or registration process can take years, those who inherit land fail to register, or other reasons. When property titles are registered with the state, but customary land tenure requirements are not satisfied, ownership is tenuous because it is subject to challenge on customary grounds.[106] The least secure combination is when the land is neither acquired under customary law nor reflected in titles registered with the state—the condition in many squatter settlements in major cities in Africa and Asia. The most secure combination is when customary law is satisfied *and* title is registered with the state, but this is the most expensive option and takes the most time and effort to accomplish.

As many as a billion people around the globe, according to one estimate, claim property rights and conduct property arrangements on terms inconsistent with official state law, ranging from urban squatter settlements (like favelas) where families have lived without official titles for generations (though still exchanging and passing on property) to rural areas where people follow customary land tenure; yet people *want* secure property rights under state law and hold up whatever documentation they might have to support their legal claim (old grants or deeds, tax payments, family records, sales agreements or leases, etc.) even if not legally valid for title.[107] People in possession of land without state legal recognition are perpetually vulnerable to eviction by the state or by those with official legal titles, who can invoke the coercive force of the state on their behalf.

Adding to the complexities, layered on top of the contrasts between state property law and customary and religious law on property is a pluralism of sequentially implemented contrasting official property regimes. In the span of several decades, parts of Africa and Southeast Asia went from colonially implemented property law, to socialistic property law, to liberal property law promoted by Western development organizations for economic development. These very different property approaches and their consequences have not been fully reconciled.

---

[106] *Id.* at 97.

[107] Daniel Fitzpatrick, "Fragmented Property Systems," 38 University of Pennsylvania Journal of International Law 137 (2016). An illuminating exploration of these issues is Christian Lund, *Nine-Tenths of the Law: Enduring Dispossession in Indonesia* (New Haven, CT: Yale University Press 2020).

Customary and Religious Law Clash with Human Rights

Constitutions and legislation in postcolonial societies commonly include provisions recognizing customary and religious law, as well as provisions recognizing international law and human rights. Many of these countries agreed to the Universal Declaration of Human Rights and the UN Convention on the Elimination of all Forms of Discrimination against Woman (CEDAW), among other international rights declarations. A latent tension is contained in these adoptions because certain customary law practices are said to violate human rights.[108] This tension reflects yet another layer of legal pluralism—state law, customary law, religious law, international law, and human rights—that has come to the fore in past several decades.[109] In these situations regime law, community law, and cross-polity law manifest various alignments, supportive and/or clashing, with parties invoking whatever advances their desired position.

International law stands on both sides of this tension. The UN Declaration of the Rights of Indigenous Peoples (2007) recognizes the right "to maintain and strengthen their distinct political, legal, economic, social and cultural institutions."[110] The Indigenous and Tribal Peoples Convention (1989) recognizes the right of indigenous people to live in accordance with "their own social, economic, cultural, and political institutions."[111] "In applying national laws and regulations to the peoples concerned, due regard shall be had to their customs or customary law."[112] On the other side, CEDAW, ratified by nearly every nation in the United Nations, recognizes the equality of women in "political, social, economic, and cultural fields," the same rights as men to enter and dissolve marriages, the same rights to ownership of property and to obtain employment, and other provisions that customary and religious law potentially run afoul of.

Objections to customary and religious tribunals come in three main themes: (1) discriminatory treatment of women, (2) harsh criminal

---

[108] A sobering account of the clash in Afghanistan is Per Sevastik, "Rule of Law, Human Rights and Impunity: The Case of Afghanistan," 12 Hague Journal on the Rule of Law 93 (2020).

[109] See Sue Farran, "Is Legal Pluralism an Obstacle to Human Rights?," 52 Journal of Legal Pluralism 77 (2006).

[110] UN Declaration of the Rights of Indigenous Peoples, Article 5 (2007). The four votes against the declaration were by settler societies: Australia, Canada, New Zealand, and the United States.

[111] Indigenous and Tribal Peoples Convention, c169, Article 1 (b), International Labor Organization (1989).

[112] Indigenous and Tribal Peoples Convention, c169, Article 8.1, International Labor Organization (1989).

sanctions, and (2) inadequate trial procedures. Women typically are not eligible to become traditional chiefs and do not sit on councils of elders, so they are excluded as decision-makers. Women often do not hold or receive land under customary and religious laws of possession, divorce, inheritance, or the death of a spouse. Customary law or religious law (or a blend) in some areas permit child brides; force a rape victim to marry the rapist; give girls to a victim's family as compensation for injuries or wrongs; condone honor killings; restrict women's work outside the home; and divorce, adultery, and inheritance laws are more favorable to men than women.[113] A recent report on customary tribunals by a prominent development agency—International Development Law Organization—summarizes:

> In many customary justice systems, women are routinely discriminated against with respect to their roles as guardians, their inheritance rights, and their right to freedom from sexual and domestic violence. Further, sanctions may be exploitative and/or abrogate women's basic human rights; such sanctions include the practice of wife inheritance (where a widow is forced to marry a male relative of her deceased husband), ritual cleansing (where a widow is forced to have sexual intercourse with a male in-law or stranger), forced marriage, and the exchange of women or young girls as a resolution for a crime or as compensation.[114]

Abhorrent to outsiders, it helps to view these practices in social context. The marriage of a widow to a relative of the husband is a means for her to obtain land to live on and obtain sustenance from; rape victims may suffer ostracism and discrimination, so marrying the rapist is a way to regain social respectability.[115] That said, these practices are difficult for outsiders to accept, and activists in these societies (often supported by international NGOs) have been working to reduce or reform them, invoking human rights, international declarations, and state law.

In connection with criminal sanctions, human rights concerns prompted by customary and religious law include torture, harsh physical punishment (spearing, beating, stoning), ordeals, and punishment for witchcraft.

---

[113] For details on customary and religious practices harmful to women, see Amnesty International, Afghanistan: Re-Establishing the Rule of Law (2003) 7, https://www.amnesty.org/download/Documents/104000/asa110212003en.pdf

[114] Erica Harper, Customary Justice: From Program Design to Impact Evaluation (Rome: IDLO 2011) 23.

[115] *Id.* at 25.

"Possibly the most salient criticism leveled at customary legal processes," the report states, "is that they fail to uphold international human rights and criminal justice standards. The sanctions imposed can include corporal punishment, humiliation, banishment, retaliatory murder, the betrothal of children and forced marriage. Such punishments violate, inter alia, the rights to life, protection against cruel, inhumane or degrading treatment, and protection from discriminatory treatment, as enshrined in international law."[116] Yet many people in these societies consider these punishments appropriate (while they may view Western incarceration as cruel and harmful to the family that depends on the prisoner). Objections to legal procedures include the following: "they can lack procedural safeguards that protect the rights of disputants, such as the presumption of innocence or the rights to a defense and due process"; "the methodology for ascertaining facts or assessing evidence may be arbitrary or violate human rights"; "unsound evidentiary practices not based on modern scientific rationalism often lead to equally unsound resolutions."[117]

Proposals to make indigenous customary and religious law conform to human rights norms are regularly put forth at the international level. The right to a fair trial guaranteed in UN Convention on Political and Civil Rights explicitly applies to "when a State, in its legal order, recognizes courts based on customary law, or religious courts, to carry out or entrusts them with judicial tasks." "It must be ensured that such courts cannot hand down binding judgments recognized by the State, unless the following requirements are met: proceedings before such courts are limited to minor civil and criminal matters, meet basic requirements of fair trial and other relevant guarantees of the Covenant[.]"[118] The core right in the Covenant is: "The right to a fair and public hearing by a competent, independent and impartial tribunal established by law is guaranteed,"[119] which "is an absolute right that is not subject to any exception."[120] This requirement is derived from Western trial conceptions, including an independent judiciary protected from dismissal and unbiased judges who do not "harbour any preconceptions about the particular case before them."[121]

---

[116] *Id.* at 24.

[117] *Id.* at 23.

[118] UN Human Right Committee, General Comment 32, Article 14, Right to Equality Before Courts and Tribunals and to a Fair Trial, 23 August 2007.

[119] *Id.* at Section III, 15, p 4.

[120] *Id.* at Section III, 19, p. 5.

[121] *Id.* at Section III, 20, 21, p. 6.

This cluster of proposals might sound appealing in the abstract but make little sense in these contexts. Keep in mind that customary tribunals involve gatherings where the adjudicators "generally know not only the disputants, but also the history to the dispute and other matters that may be regarded as important to its resolution, such as a transgressor's capacity to pay damages."[122] The strengths of socially embedded, informal customary tribunals seeking to restore community harmony in a timely fashion are among the very features that make them inconsistent with due process requirements in formal courts. (Recall the example of Yap in the Introduction.) To impose the due process requirements of formal state court systems on customary tribunals not only would distort how they function, but is not actually achievable. The chiefs or elders who preside in disputes are members of the community, connected through extended networks with others, and the community (including the people and families involved) often participates directly in the proceedings. This does not fit the model of an independent judge applying the law. Though it is not a perfect analogy for multiple reasons (particularly with respect to criminal sanctions), customary tribunals are more aptly compared to mediation or equity aimed at achieving outcomes acceptable to those involved and the broader community.

An unrealistic proposal was urged by Amnesty International in its report on establishing the rule of law in Afghanistan. The report details profound dysfunctionalities, corruption, and human rights violations of the state legal system; then it turns to address informal customary and religious law tribunals, *jirgas* and *shuras*, which are widely utilized for disputes in Afghanistan. The report recommends:

> Regulate the informal justice system: The competence of informal justice systems must be clearly set out in the law in order to remove any ambiguity regarding the role of Afghan informal justice mechanisms. The relationship between informal systems and the formal judicial system must be set out by law. In order to fulfil its obligation to exercise due diligence in protecting human rights, the [government] must ensure that *jirgas* and *shuras*, if they are allowed to continue to function, fully conform to international human rights law. If this cannot be ensured then these informal justice mechanisms must be abolished. All cases in which there are indications that a *jirga* or

---

[122] Harper, *supra* note 114, at 27.

shura has perpetrated human rights abuses must be thoroughly investigated and all those participating in them must be brought to justice.[123]

This recommendation is odd as well as hubristic.[124] The oddity is that, after expending many pages exposing the abject failures of the state legal system, the solution it proposes to human rights violations by customary tribunals is to place them under close supervision by the (dysfunctional) state legal system. The hubris is the suggestion that these tribunals "must be abolished" if they cannot be made to respect human rights. (What will take their place?) This presupposes that the government has the power to abolish these deeply rooted tribunals, many operating in rural areas where state institutions are absent. As a detailed overview of these systems observed, "Customary justice systems exhibit remarkable resilience, outlasting changes in government, conflict, natural disaster and state-based attempts to abolish them."[125] *Shuras* and *jirgas* have operated for centuries and currently handle the majority of civil and criminal disputes in Afghanistan; they are quick, accessible, and familiar to people in the community, who comply with the results.[126]

Jurists and development practitioners must drop their assumption that the only legitimate form of law is the formal Western state law model. Reducing human rights violations in connection with women and criminal justice is a long-term project that extends beyond the customary tribunals themselves. Their source lies in cultural notions embodied in customary law and religious law. When these ideas change to become less problematic, the human rights clash will diminish. Women's rights advocates who support customary tribunals—which are often popular among indigenous women despite their flaws—recommend education and consciousness raising among men and women, as well as organizing among indigenous women to press for reforms.[127] Customary and religious law and tribunals are not traditional institutions fixed in the past, it must be remembered, but continuously

[123] Amnesty International, *supra* note 113, at 47–48.

[124] An incisive critique of this recommendation and of Comment 32 is Haider Ala Hamoudi, "Decolonizing the Centralist Mind: Legal Pluralism and the Rule of Law," in David Marshall, ed., *The International Rule of Law Movement: A Crisis of Legitimacy and the Way Forward* (Cambridge, MA: Harvard Human Rights Program 2014).

[125] Harper, *supra* note 114, at 37.

[126] See J. Dempsey and N. Coburn, "Traditional Dispute Resolution and Stability in Afghanistan," United States Institute for Peace (2010) 2.

[127] See Rachel Sieder and Anna Barrera, "Women and Legal Pluralism: Lessons from Indigenous Governance Systems in the Andes," 49 Journal of Latin American Studies 633 (2017).

evolving *contemporary* creations at that reflect cultural attitudes and religious views within the community.

Recent Turn to Non-State Law by Development Agencies

Upon achieving independence, which occurred around the world following the end of World War II, it was seen by many as necessary to leave behind the badges of colonization, including legal pluralism. Educated indigenous elites and professionals, especially lawyers, many of whom had been educated in the West, promoted the enactment of a unified state legal system (the monist law state) as essential for economic development and joining the modern world. A backlash also occurred against traditional chiefs who were seen in many locations as collaborators with the colonial state and strategic actors who utilized their powers to advance their own interests and the groups they favored.

In the 1960s and 1970s, what came to be known as the law and development movement brought a wave of transplantation of Western laws and legal institutions across the Global South through voluntary borrowing, promoted by Western development agencies, welcomed by recipient governments in pursuit of economic and political modernization. In the 1990s and 2000s, following the collapse of communism, the "Washington Consensus" entailed the implementation of neo-liberal property, contract, foreign investment, and banking legal regimes, free market reforms (eliminating subsidies and government controls), known as structural adjustment programs, to facilitate entry to global capitalism. A host of legal reforms were required as conditions for foreign investment and development loans and grants from the World Bank and International Monetary Fund. "Rule of law" development—a concerted effort to improve state legal systems—became the mantra of the World Bank, USAID, and other development organizations. Despite these manifold efforts, however, state legal systems showed limited functional improvement and customary and religious law continued to thrive alongside state law.

A recent study found that the constitutions of sixty-one countries across the Global South "explicitly recognize forms of traditional governance and customary law" alongside state political and legal institutions.[128] Explicit

---

[128] Katharina Holzinger, Florian G. Kern, and Daniela Kromrey, "The Dualism of Contemporary Traditional Governance and the State: Institutional Setups and Political Consequences," 69 Political Research Quarterly 469, 469 (2016).

constitutional recognition of customary law and traditional authorities is highest in sub-Saharan Africa (about 50 percent of countries recognized both), South and East Asia and the Pacific (48 percent recognized customary law, 34 percent traditional authorities), followed by the Americas (20 percent recognized both).[129] An estimated 57 percent of the global population live in states with both customary law and state law.[130] Studies have found that very high percentages of people take their disputes to customary tribunals for resolution, for instance, between 80–90 percent in Afghanistan,[131] 80 and 90 percent in Malawi, 60 to 70 percent in Bangladesh, and 80 percent in Burundi.[132] "In many developing countries, customary systems operating outside of the state regime are often the dominant form of regulation and dispute resolution, covering up to 90 percent of the population in parts of Africa."[133] A survey of 2,300 households across Liberia found that 3 percent of civil cases went to state court, 38 went to customary tribunals, and 59 percent did not go to any forum, with similar percentages in criminal cases.[134] "It has become clear that in most of Africa, traditional authorities are here to stay, at least for the foreseeable future."[135]

People in these societies do not take their disputes to state courts for resolution for various reasons.[136] The state legal system may function poorly, with a dearth of trained lawyers and judges, poor funding, and inadequate staff and technological equipment. With a population of 7.5 million, for example, Rwanda in the early 2000s was served by about fifty lawyers, twenty prosecutors, and fifty newly recruited judges; Malawi had three hundred lawyers for nine million people.[137] Other common reasons are that state courts may be distant; lawyers and court fees are too costly for most people; the procedures and legal rules courts use are unfamiliar to people; the language used by the court differs from the local vernacular in societies with

[129] See Katharina Holzinger, Roos Haer, Axel Bayer, Daniela M. Behr, and Clara Neupert-Wentz, "The Constitutionalization of Indigenous Group Rights, Traditional Political Institutions, and Customary Law," 52 Comparative Political Studies 1775, 1794 (2019). These numbers are based exclusively on Constitutions, and do not include states that statutorily recognize customary law and tribal authorities.

[130] Holzinger, Kern, and Kromrey, *supra* note 128, at 469.

[131] Barfield, Nojumi, and Thier, *supra* note 89, at 161, at 17.

[132] Ewa Wojkowska, Doing Justice: How Informal Justice Systems Can Contribute (Oslo: UN Development Program 2006) 12.

[133] Chirayath, Sage, Woolcock, *supra* note 87, at 3.

[134] Harper, *supra* note 114, at 26–27.

[135] Logan, *supra* note 91, at 353.

[136] Harper, *supra* note 114, at 26–30.

[137] Laure-Helene Piron, "Time to Learn, Time to Act in Africa," in Thomas Carothers, ed., *Promoting the Rule of Law Abroad* (Washington, D.C.: Carnegie Endowment 2006) 275, 291.

multiple ethnicities; state court judges do not understand the social context or norms of the community; the state legal system may be seen as oppressive and/or corrupt; court cases take a long time to process; court outcomes, which have winners and losers, might not resolve the social rupture; and there may be social pressure to resolve the dispute within the community.[138] Local tribunals, in contrast, are easy to access, inexpensive, understandable, and transparent; they use familiar procedures and norms, produce immediate results, and effectively resolve the matter.

There is a deeper reason why people go to customary tribunals. State legal systems are doubly removed from the community. First, the legal institutions, norms, and processes have been derived from Western societies in which they evolved, and then grafted onto societies with entirely different social, cultural, economic, and political milieus—alien implants that have not lost this misfit even after generations. Second, state legal institutions entail highly technical languages, techniques, and processes that operate within bureaucratic legal organizations (legislatures, courts, prosecutors, police). Highly technical legal systems everywhere are dis-embedded from community relations. Informal tribunals, in contrast, involve people within the community directly participating in and carrying out their own law without the intervention and removal by legal specialists taking over with their own inscrutable terminology, processes, and actions. Traditional tribunals and customary and religious laws are what people know and identify with. As one commentator put it, "The customary legal framework is not seen as law at all, but as a way of life, how people live—State law on the other hand is something imposed and foreign."[139]

After several decades of efforts and billions of dollars spent on building the capacities of state legal systems in the Global South with limited positive results,[140] international development agencies lately have begun to advocate greater attention to and support for customary tribunals.[141] The United Nations Development Program (UNDP),[142] World Bank,[143] International Development Law Organization (IDLO),[144] and United States Institute for

---

[138] Wojkowska, *supra* note 132, at 13.

[139] Harper, *supra* note 114, at 28.

[140] See Brian Z. Tamanaha, "The Primacy of Society and Failures of Law and Development," 44 Cornell International Law Journal 209 (2011).

[141] An informative overview is Ronald Janse, "A Turn to Legal Pluralism in Rule of Law Promotion?," 6 Erasmus Law Review 181 (2013).

[142] Ewa Wojkowska, Doing Justice: How Informal Justice Systems can Contribute (Oslo: United Nations Development Programme 2006).

[143] Chirayath, Sage, and Woolcock, *supra* note 87.

[144] Harper, *supra* note 114.

Peace (USIP),[145] among others, issued reports on the significance of customary justice systems. The IDLO report states: "The question of customary justice and its role in promoting the rule of law has emerged as the most promising—and thorny—development in the field of justice reform."[146]

The World Justice Project (WJP) Rule of Law Index acknowledges that in many former colonized countries with weak state legal systems informal justice can be "timely and effective." Informal tribunals have not been factored into the country rankings, however, because "the complexities of these systems and the difficulties of systematically measuring their fairness and effectiveness make cross-country assessments extraordinarily challenging."[147] WJP's Index is yet another product of the image of the monist law state. Because WJP cannot measure the effects of informal justice tribunals, they are treated as if they do not exist. This gaping omission undermines the reliability of their Index given the high percentages of people using these systems in many countries.

The acknowledgment by Western development agencies of the functional utility of customary tribunals is by no means an enthusiastic embrace. Belatedly and almost begrudgingly, it is a pragmatic concession to reality. State legal systems in many of these countries are not working well, while non-state customary systems are serving local needs, and a majority of people in these societies prefer the latter. Continuing to ignore customary tribunals and law under these circumstances is senseless.

Indigenous rights activists in the Americas in the past three decades have also strongly advocated recognition of indigenous law, drawing on support from international recognition of indigenous rights. A number of Latin American countries enacted constitutional provisions in the 1990s with explicit acknowledgment of legal pluralism—Paraguay, Nicaragua, Mexico, Columbia, Peru, Bolivia, Ecuador, and Venezuela[148]—and Canada has recently made political commitments to support indigenous rights.[149]

---

[145] Isser, *supra* note 89.

[146] Forward by Deborah Isser, "Doing Justice," *supra* note 89, at 5.

[147] World Justice Project Rule of Law Index 2020 (Washington, D.C. 2020) 12.

[148] See Donna Lee Van Cott, "A Political Analysis of Legal Pluralism in Bolivia and Columbia," 32 Journal of Latin American Studies 207 (2000); Anna Barrera, "Turning Legal Pluralism into State-Sanctioned Law: Assessing the Implications of the New Constitutions and Laws in Bolivia and Ecuador," GIGA Working Papers (August 2011), https://www.giga-hamburg.de/de/system/files/publications/wp176_barrera.pdf

[149] See John Borrows, Larry Chartrand, Oonagh E. Fitzgerald, and Risa Schwartz, eds., *Braiding Legal Orders: Implementing the United Nations Declaration on the Rights of Indigenous Peoples* (Waterloo, Canada: Centre for International Governance Innovation 2019). Canadian jurists debate whether indigenous law exists. See Hadley Friedland, "Reflective Frameworks: Methods for Accessing, Understanding, and Applying Indigenous Laws," 11 Indigenous Law Journal 1 (2012).

Unlike postcolonial countries that underwent indirect rule, which all along acknowledged legal pluralism, this official recognition represents a significant shift. Unofficial customary law mechanisms have continued in existence without recognition in certain areas, whereas in other locations, where communities suffered greater disruptions through war, migration, or government suppression, current calls reflect a revival a of local justice. "One of the main reasons why indigenous peoples today ascribe legitimacy to their institutions of political-legal self-governance resides in their perception that these are constitutive elements of these groups' collective histories and identities."[150]

In addition to concerns about the treatment of women and human rights, and worries that these tribunals reinforce local power structures, two main objections have been lodged against greater recognition of customary tribunals. One objection is from state legal officials who are concerned that engaging with these tribunals diverts resources away from the development of state legal systems. "By working with informal mechanisms, they argue, the international community will promote and shift attention to nonstate institutions at a time when the state is in desperate need of support."[151] The response to this concern is that recognizing customary tribunals does not necessarily involve substantial funding—to the contrary, infusing money into them will warp existing incentives and affect how they function. More to the point, taking customary tribunals seriously does not entail abandoning efforts to build state legal systems. Rather, it involves constructing legal development efforts with a more holistic awareness of, attention to, and engagement with the full range of legal institutions operating in these societies.

Development practitioners who place their faith in building the monistic law state should also take a realistic look at how these systems function in their own societies. The high cost of legal services and lengthy court proceedings (which can take years) have resulted in large numbers of people in the United States and the United Kingdom with unmet legal needs. Purportedly well-functioning state legal systems are no panacea, therefore, even in far wealthier countries that expend vast sums on the legal system. Viewed in this

Australia has made limited accommodations of Aboriginal customary law. See James Crawford, "Legal Pluralism and the Indigenous Peoples of Australia," in O. Mendelson and U. Baxi, eds., *The Rights of Subordinated People* (Delhi: Oxford University Press 1994).

[150] Rachel Sieder and Anna Barrera, "Women and Legal Pluralism: Lessons from Indigenous Governance Systems in the Andes," 49 Journal of Latin American Studies 633, 643 (2017).

[151] Coburn and Dempsey, *supra* note 76, at 7.

light, the benefits of informal community tribunals that handle problems effectively should not be underestimated.

The other objection is that it creates opportunities for forum shopping and uncertainty: "strengthening the customary system can result in a competing and overlapping set of laws, which, while giving choice, can 'obstruct claim-holder's access to justice and impede effective handling of grievances. This may create confusion or promote instability."[152] Even when rules exist to clarify the respective jurisdiction of state courts and customary tribunals, legal pluralism inevitably creates opportunities for forum shopping, which the wealthy are better able to exploit than the poor. Undeniably this is problematic. Yet no perfect solution is available under the circumstances. And the presence of alternative tribunals can prompt improvements in the performance of each because their power and standing depends on attracting users and people will resort to accessible tribunals that function effectively over those that do not. The bottom line is that customary tribunals are popular and widely utilized and they serve people's needs.

Social, Cultural, Economic, Political, and Legal Pluralism

Postcolonial settings law are profoundly pluralistic today. Anthropologists John and Jean Comaroff, with decades of research on law in postcolonial societies, portray the current situation:

> Because of their historical predicaments, postcolonies tend *not* to be organized under a single, vertically integrated sovereignty sustained by a highly centralized state. Rather, they consist in a horizontally woven tapestry of partial sovereignties: sovereignties over terrains and their inhabitants, over aggregates of people conjoined in faith or culture, over transactional spheres, over networks of relations, regimes of property, domains of practice, and, quite often, over various combinations of these things; sovereignties longer or shorter lived, protected to a greater or lesser degree by the capacity to exercise compulsion, always incomplete.[153]

---

[152] Harper, *supra* note 114, at 34.

[153] John L. Comaroff and Jean Comaroff, "Law and Disorder in the Postcolony: An Introduction," in Jean Comaroff and John L. Comaroff, eds., *Law and Disorder in the Postcolony* (Chicago: Chicago University Press 2006).

To project the monist law image on these situations is fantastical. Law in postcolonial contexts is a complex bricolage within fragmented societies. The greater the degree of ethnic fractionalization there is in a society, the more likely the recognition of customary law and traditional authorities.[154]

To grasp the legal situation it helps to roughly distinguish three groups. These societies have modern governmental and commercial sectors (linked to global capitalism), based in urban centers, employing educated or semi-educated people, who purchase property, enter contracts, and so forth—the new middle classes who often desire modern rights-based legal systems.[155] State legal systems operate largely in connection with people and organizations (citizens as well as foreigners) in this modern sector. These societies also have rural regions where less-educated people live in villages clustered by ethnic groups or tribes, working for meager pay as laborers (crops, mining, forestry, fisheries, etc.), or outside the money economy engaging in subsistence farming, herding, fishing, hunting, trapping, gathering. Traditional leaders and customary tribunals continue to function effectively in these settings, while state courts are distant and infrequently utilized. Between these urban and rural settings are increasingly large multiethnic, peri-urban sectors in expanding cities, filled with migrants from rural areas seeking a better way of life, living as squatters and working in the informal economy. This third group lives at the margins of both the state legal system and customary tribunals: outside the state system because they work in the informal economy, they lack official property rights, and state law enforcement presence is limited in squatter areas (and mainly disciplinary); outside customary systems because the hold of customary tribunals is attenuated the further one goes from rural strongholds, particularly in multiethnic settings. These generalizations are porous and blurry at the edges, offered as illustrative.

These societies are highly pluralistic along multiple axes: cultural, ethnic, racial, caste, religious, insider/outsider, education, economic class, and political. The pluralism of law reflects these underlying divisions. Some people prefer secular state law while others are committed to the law of their own community or religion. People use the law with which they are most familiar—that comports with their expectations and normative views—and that is available to them. When they have access to more than one legal

---

[154] See Holzinger, Haer, Bayer, Behf, and Neupert-Wentz, *supra* note 129, at 1797–1801.
[155] See John L. Comaroff, "Reflections on the Colonial State in South Africa and Elsewhere: Factions, Fragments, Facts and Fictions," 4 Social Identities 321 (1998).

forum, they regularly seek out the one they consider most advantageous, and may approach more than one forum to obtain their objectives. This always occurs in situations of legal pluralism.

Another broad proposition is about the division of labor among governance institutions put into place during colonial rule. The colonial legal system focused on supporting the colonial state, maintaining order in major cities, and advancing expatriate-run commercial enterprises tied to trade; local governance and law and order was largely left to decentralized tribal authorities and religious authorities applying customary law and religious law. This institutional division of labor created path-dependent structures that became entrenched and self-reinforcing. Predatory, extractive, colonial states and legal regimes were taken over after colonization and all too often continued in their predatory mode of action under native management, with ethnic and religious conflict playing out through efforts to secure control of the state apparatus and its economic resources and coercive power. State legal authorities and their chiefly counterparts built and maintain institutional capacities to meet the tasks they have managed for generations, which provides them with prestige, power, and income. Many of these societies lack sufficient educational institutions and government revenues—lack social and economic capital—for state legal systems to efficiently function or to expand the reach of the state legal system to replace traditional authorities in rural area or at the village level. Nor is there a pressing need to undo the division of labor, particularly since state legal systems are struggling to handle their own tasks.

The respective state, traditional, and religious authorities may carry out conflicting legal norms, and they typically defend their turf from encroachment by the other, but in many locations they have established a working modus vivendi. Relations between coexisting legal systems can be thought of in three categories: cooperative, competitive, and combative.[156] Cooperative relations among these fora can be cohesive socially (though they may cooperate in ways that are jointly oppressive of certain disfavored groups). Competitive interaction can motivate coexisting fora to improve their functioning to meet the needs of people (though it can also result in pandering to attract users). Combative relations among coexisting legal forms exacerbates

---

[156] An insightful article of legal pluralism in post-conflict situations identifies four archetypes: combative, competitive, cooperative, and complementary. I drop complementary because cooperative relationships largely include those that are complementary. See Geoffrey Swenson, "Legal Pluralism in Theory and Practice," 20 International Studies Review 438 (2018).

legal uncertainty and may inflame social strife. One, two, or all three of these interrelations can exist in a single context of legal pluralism, shifting over time or arising on different matters.

Despite widespread expectations that postcolonial countries will eventually evolve toward unified legal systems, it is evident to most observers that legal pluralism is here for the foreseeable future. Recall the earlier discussion of empires that left community law in place—this is an inherited version of the same arrangement but on a national scale. From the standpoint of state law monism, legal pluralism appears hopelessly defective. Evaluated on its own terms, however, legal pluralism is a functional arrangement under circumstances marked by deep social and legal heterogeneity. The multi-sided pluralisms within these societies that legal pluralism reflects cannot be ignored or wished away.

The Rule of Law and Legal Pluralism

There are multiple accounts of what the rule of law means or requires.[157] A core idea common to most formulations is that *the rule of law exists when government officials and citizens are bound by and generally abide by the law.* This covers interaction between government and citizens (vertical) as well as the relations among citizens (horizontal). A major benefit of the rule of law is that people know in advance the legal consequences of their activities, providing them with security and predictability with respect to the government and other citizens. It is commonly assumed that legal pluralism in postcolonial countries is antithetical to the rule of law in so far as the very presence of coexisting legal systems creates uncertainty about legal matters. Eliminating legal uncertainty is one of the main justifications for developing a unified state legal system in the monist image.

A broader perspective, however, suggests that legal pluralism might actually help fulfill essential rule of law functions.[158] In many of these situations, as described, the state legal systems are transplants that do not match the norms and understandings of many people within the society, particularly in rural communities; and state legal systems function poorly for a variety

---

[157] See Brian Z. Tamanaha, *On the Rule of Law: History, Politics, Theory* (Cambridge: Cambridge University Press 2004).

[158] See Brian Z. Tamanaha, "The Rule of Law and Legal Pluralism in Development," 3 Hague Journal of the Rule of Law 1 (2011).

of reasons, including a lack of lawyers and judges, insufficient resources for legal institutions, and problematic social, economic, and political conditions. These conditions are fundamentally different from Western rule of law societies where law evolved over centuries interconnected with supportive social, cultural, economic, and political factors. The same model cannot be applied to both situations.

Customary and religious legal arrangements on property rights, marriage and responsibility for children, succession, debts and contracts, and personal injuries help manage the everyday lives and social intercourse within their communities. Customary and religious law utilized within the community are understood by people and comport with their normative expectations, and hence are generally predictable and provide a degree of certainty about their interaction and how disputes will be handled. Indeed, from the standpoint of people in the community it is state law that is unpredictable (not to mention practically unavailable to owing to excessive cost and distance). For these reasons, the existence of customary and religious law serve the horizontal rule of law function in which people are generally bound by and abide by the law in their social intercourse with others in the community. These bodies of law can also fulfill the vertical rule of law function in relation to the decisions and conduct of customary and religious leaders (though typically state government officials cannot be held accountable to informal customary and religious law tribunals, which must occur through the state legal system).

Another way to make this point is to imagine that all customary and religious law and tribunals are suddenly eliminated—through sustained repression—leaving the state law and legal system alone. When they wish to conduct a significant transaction (divorce, inheritance, etc.) or when trouble arises in their daily affairs (property dispute, redress for personal injury, etc.), people would have no familiar legal ground on which to stand and no accessible or understandable venue from which to seek resolution. This would entail a substantial reduction in legal certainty and the rule of law within the community. Understood in this way, legal pluralism in postcolonial societies serves the rule of law in relation to everyday social intercourse for people in many communities who otherwise would have no viable alternative.

Three
Legal Pluralism in the West

The belief that the state exercises a monopoly over law is widely held in the West. A closer look exposes large cracks in this idealized projection of the monistic law state. Romani (Gypsy) communities across Europe have lived in accordance with their own law for a thousand years. Indigenous law and tribunals exist in New Zealand, Canada, Australia, and the United States, in various relationships with state law. In a number of Western countries, Jewish law and Muslim law and institutions interact with state law as well as exist apart from state law. All of these examples involve the continuation of community legal orders (customary and religious) that long predate the modern state and have continued in different forms, adjusting to and surviving the extension and penetration of state law. In many of these contexts state law has tried to suppress, denigrate, or ignore these bodies of community law, denying their legal status, but despite this treatment they continue to exist and are considered law by adherents. This chapter (and the next) shows that the monist project to consolidate law in the state has not been fully accomplished even within highly developed Western legal systems, showing continuity with legal pluralism of the past owing to the survival of community law. As with previous chapters, this is not comprehensive coverage, but brief sketches of each form of community law and illustrative aspects their interaction with state law.

Romani Law

Several million Romani are scattered in communities across Europe, as well as the United States and Canada, in forty countries overall—a millennium old diaspora out of Northern India with a common culture, language, and law.[1] Romani communities historically have been nomadic or semi-nomadic,

---

[1] An informative collection on the Romani is Walter O. Weyrauch, ed., *Gypsy Law: Romani Legal Traditions and Culture* (Berkeley: University of California Press 2001).

Legal Pluralism Explained. Brian Z. Tamanaha, Oxford University Press (2021). © Brian Z. Tamanaha.
DOI: 10.1093/oso/9780190861551.003.0004

though many are now settled. For a thousand years they have lived by their own autonomous forms of community law, continuing to thrive even after the consolidation of law in the modern state, often subjected to persecution by the state and by the majority population. While maintaining tight-knit communities, Romani also participate in the societies in which they exist, often adhering to the locally dominant religion. Their legal practices vary by location, so a few generalizations will be offered that do not hold everywhere.

Romani law, an oral tradition carried out in community-based tribunals, is applied to a broad range of business arrangements (including contracts, debts, fraud, unfair competition), marriage and divorce, adultery, theft, offenses to honor, and other matters that give rise to disruptions within the community.[2] Disputes within the Romani community typically are resolved informally with the involvement of respected community figures. Only after this fails is an ad hoc court convened, known as *kris* (which means justice), although not all Romani communities hold a *kris*.[3] Actions can be brought by a plaintiff who suffered harm or by the community. Presiding at the *kris* are male judges selected for the occasion, often with each side picking a judge, balanced by a respected third judge.[4] The parties present their side, witnesses testify, and a discussion ensues among those attending until unanimity is reached on a fair result. Judges and participants cite "precedents, traditional practices, life stories, or folklore."[5] "Above all, the basic idea that determines the form and functioning of the Gypsy court is the concept of consensus. Every ruling of this court would have been adopted unanimously not only by its members, but by the entire community, including the defendants."[6]

Remedies mainly are money awards; in one community in Romania, the amounts ranged from 1,000 to 10,000 euros, rising as high as 100,000 euros in one instance.[7] The defendant's ability to pay is a factor in determining the size

---

[2] See Elena Marushiakova and Vesselin Popov, "The Gypsy Court in Eastern Europe," 17 Romani Studies 67, 92–97 (2007)

[3] *Id.* at 71–73.

[4] See Marushiakova and Popov, *supra* note 2; T.A. Acton, "A Three-Cornered Choice: Structural Consequences of Value-Priorities in Gypsy Law as a Model for More General Understanding of Variations of Justice," 51 American Journal of Comparative Law 639, 642–43 (2003).

[5] Marushiakova and Popov, *supra* note 2, at 87.

[6] *Id.* at 78.

[7] Claude Cahn, "Romani Law in the Timis County Ciambas Community," 19 Romani Studies 87, 93 (2009).

of the award.[8] A losing party can appeal by calling for another *kris*, at which the judges from the first *kris* appear to explain their decision. If the losing party does not pay the fine, the winner has the right to enforce the decision, including through force if necessary.[9] In rare instances a blood feud can result. The *kris* can also order banishment from the community, a sanction of last resort. Parties typically comply with decisions. In communities with *kris*, taking disputes among Romani to state courts is "absolutely unacceptable."[10]

State law and Romani law clash on various matters and Romani law and institutions are seldom recognized by state law, though Romani legal norms have been considered by certain state courts as a "cultural defense" for Romani charged with crimes.[11] (A cultural defense occurs when cultural views of a subcommunity are taken into consideration in state cases to negate criminal intent, to assess reasonableness of conduct, or to mitigate the seriousness of an offense.) In certain locations state legal officials decline to pursue criminal cases in actions between Romani out of deference to Romani legal processes.[12] State officials face difficulty also because Romani often do not cooperate with state inquiries and judicial processes. For these reasons, "host authorities often do not interfere with Gypsy society and in many respects are unequipped to deal with Romani culture when conflict occurs."[13]

From the standpoint of most Western legal systems, Romani law functioning within their societies do not exist as "legal orders." Despite this denial of their legal status, however, cohesive Romani communities live in accordance with, arrange their relations through, and resolve their disputes using their own community-based law—while also well aware of a rival legal system in state law. Romani see two legal systems, their own community law and state law, whereas the state legal system presents itself as the exclusive legal order, an image it maintains by applying blinders to any form of law other than its own.

---

[8] Marushiakova and Popov, *supra* note 2, at 87.

[9] Cahn, *supra* note 7, at 93.

[10] Marushiakova and Popov, *supra* note 2, at 83.

[11] See Ida Nafstad, "Legal Silencing of Minority Legal Culture: The Case of Roma in Swedish Criminal Courts," 28 Social & Legal Studies 839 (2018).

[12] Marushiakova and Popov, *supra* note 2, at 98.

[13] Walter O Weyrauch and Maureen Anne Bell, "Autonomous Lawmaking: The Case of the 'Gypsies,'" in Weyrauch, *supra* note 1, at 52.

Native Law in New Zealand, Canada, Australia, and the United States

New Zealand, Canada, Australia, and the United States are settler countries, which began as colonies much like those described in the preceding chapter, until indigenous populations were overwhelmed and marginalized through massive in-migration of settlers and aggressive military domination. Today these liberal democracies with capitalist economies project an image of highly developed unified, state legal systems. Yet significant manifestations of indigenous law exist in various relationships with (internal and external to) state law in ways that are not fully unified.

Treatment of native peoples by the colonial state and settlers went from wars, peace treaties acknowledging indigenous political and legal authorities, additional wars and massacres, seizure of native lands and resources for settlers, forced relocation and assimilation of indigenous people, to cultural, political, economic, and legal marginalization.[14] This history is marked by a pattern of state legal officials asserting the sovereign monistic law state image in a hostile and dominant posture toward native community law.

Signs have appeared in the last few decades of a degree of willingness in British Commonwealth settler countries (though not the United States) to re-examine the status of indigenous communities and their law, prompted by indigenous rights activists and by the UN Declaration of the Rights of Indigenous Peoples (UNDRIP) and other international support. Article 5 of UNDRIP states: "Indigenous peoples have the right to maintain and strengthen their distinct political, legal, economic, social and cultural institutions, while retaining their right to participate fully, if they so choose, in the political, economic, social and cultural life of the State." Adopted in 2007 by 144 states, with 11 abstentions, the only 4 states to vote against it, tellingly, were New Zealand, Canada, Australia, and the United States, although all four settler countries subsequently reversed their positions.

Studies of legal pluralism in setter countries have coincided with newfound attention to the plight of indigenous peoples. Discussions of indigenous law are part of larger cultural, political, and economic issues, including survival of indigenous languages and ways of life, self-determination within

---

[14] See Jane Burbank and Frederick Cooper, *Empires in World History: Power and Politics of Difference* (Princeton, NJ: Princeton University Press 2010).

the broader polity, ameliorating social and economic problems (poverty, poor health, poor education, lack of economic opportunities, domestic abuse, crime), and controlling or regaining tribal economic resources (forestry, fisheries, mining, hunting, casinos, etc.).

Indigenous rights advocates have asserted a range of positions: maintain or create informal or formal tribunals within indigenous communities; recognition of indigenous law in state law cases (particularly domestic relations, land tenure, and cultural defenses in criminal cases); transform official state law to better reflect indigenous values (i.e., resource management, respect for nature, restorative justice); and, most ambitiously, complete political and legal sovereignty of native peoples. A common stance across these varied positions is that indigenous legal traditions pre-existed the settler state for millennia, weathered repeated efforts at repression by the state, and have survived in one form another (at least within the community) to the present.[15] Even when state law recognizes indigenous law, in this view, indigenous law has existed all along independent of said recognition. Another common position is that indigenous law is values-based rather than strictly rules-based, and encompasses relations between people within a community (including ancestors and future generations), relations with the environment, and spiritual aspects of nature and existence. And like all legal traditions, indigenous law is not frozen in the past but consists of continuously evolving bodies of legal norms, values, principles, and practices suitable for contemporary circumstances.

Among settler countries, New Zealand has the most proportionally sizable indigenous population, with Maori about 15 percent of the populace. The foundational document for relations between the British Crown and the Maori is the Treaty of Waitangi (1840). At its making there were roughly 125,000 Maori and only a few thousand settlers, though rapidly increasing in number through immigration; there were regular skirmishes and bouts of violence between Maori and settlers (and their Maori allies), often involving abusive land purchases by settlers.[16] The Treaty has been the subject of controversy from the outset owing to a difference between the English and the Maori translation of Article One. In the English version the Chiefs gave the Queen "all the rights and powers of sovereignty," while the

---

[15] See Valmaine Toki, "TIkanga Maori—A Constitutional Right? A Case Study," 40 Commonwealth Law Bulletin 32, 34 (2014).

[16] See Maori Customary Law, Library of Congress, New Zealand, https://www.loc.gov/law/help/customary-law/maori.php

Maori translation used a word for governance or government, which lacks connotations of absolute supremacy that attached to the English conception of sovereignty.[17] This linguistic-conceptual divergence generated legal pluralism in the meaning of a single document with great significance. Article Two confirmed that the existing powers of Chiefs over land, estates, forests, fisheries, and other properties would remain intact.

As with other British colonies, initially the colonial state did not replace indigenous tribunals and laws outside settler towns, which was impractical given the limited power of the colonial state.[18] The New Zealand Constitution Act of 1852 recognized Maori districts "be maintained for the government of themselves, in all their relations to and dealings with each other, and that particular districts should be set apart within which such laws, customs, or usages should be so observed."[19] "The situation meant that some, if not most Maori communities, remained subject to their traditional values, customary laws, usages, norms and institutions after the Treaty [of Waitangi]."[20] For serious crimes against settlers, chiefs would deliver the Maori wrongdoers to British magistrates. The system was bi-jural, "whereby the settlers would govern settlers and Maori would govern themselves according to their customary laws and institutions."[21] A number of state ordinances and court decisions recognized Maori customary law, particularly with respect to land rights and criminal punishment.[22] In cases brought within the state legal system in disputes involving only Maori (in settled areas), magistrate courts relied on Maori chiefs in advisory roles as native assessors.[23]

When settlers had become a substantial majority of the population by the final decades the nineteenth century (numbering a half million by 1880), attitudes toward Maori customary law changed and hardened from acceptance to extinguishment. Maori chiefdoms suffered a series of losses in land wars in the 1860s, losing significant tracts of land to the Crown. The demise of Maori law, at least from the standpoint of the official state legal

---

[17] See "Treaty of Waitangi," Encyclopedia of New Zealand, page 2, https://teara.govt.nz/en/treaty-of-waitangi/page-2

[18] The account is substantially indebted to a special report on Maori Law issued by Law Commission, Maori Custom and Values in New Zealand Law (2001), https://www.lawcom.govt.nz/sites/default/files/projectAvailableFormats/NZLC%20SP9.pdf

[19] Quoted in Robert Joseph, "Re-Creating Legal Space for the First Law of Aotearoa-New Zealand," 17 Waikato Law Review 74, 78 (2009).

[20] *Id.* at 75.

[21] *Id.* at 78–79.

[22] Law Commission, *supra* note 18, at 18–19.

[23] *Id.* at 20.

system, was proclaimed in an 1877 case, *Wi Parata v Bishop of Wellington*. Chief Justice Pendergast declared the Treaty of Waitangi a "simple nullity," "worthless," because it had been signed by "barbarians without any form of law or civil government" incapable of entering a treaty with a civilized nation.[24] Furthermore, he concluded, the Native Rights Act of 1865 and Native Land Act of 1873, which recognized Maori customary law property rights, were nullities because "no such body of law existed," and "a phrase in a statute cannot call what is non-existent in being."[25] Subsequent legislation abolished the use of native assessors, criminalized certain Maori practices, and replaced collectively held native land tenure with individual title under colonial law.[26] Maori law thereafter was marginalized within the state legal system.[27] Despite its official erasure, Maori legal values and practices survived informally within villages in tribal regions as late as World War II,[28] and continuously to the present in traditional gatherings (*Marae, hui*) and among the values within Maori communities.

Beginning in the 1970s, and steadily accelerating thereafter, political pressure to improve the position of the Maori and the sustained effort of Maori legal scholars and lawyers prompted a series of initiatives for greater recognition of Maori customary law norms and values, albeit in the face of substantial resistance from jurists and the public.[29] This effort has borne fruit of late.

Through various legislative acts and court decisions, including a revival of the Waitangi Treaty, native rights have been recognized in fishing, native land title, native relationships with ancestral lands and natural resources (water, soil, forests), native values of extended kin relationships in Family Court decisions on disposition of a child, customary relationships in criminal sentencing, community justice gatherings for juvenile offenders, and the protection of Maori cultural symbols.[30] A recent Supreme Court decision recognized, for the first time, that Maori customary law (*tikanga*) (a burial custom in this instance) should be considered within the common law,

[24] Wi Parata v. Bishop of Wellington (1877) 3 NZ Jur. (N.S.) S.C., language cited in John Tate, "The Three Precedents of Wi Parata," 10 Canterbury Law Review 273 (2004).

[25] Quoted in Joseph, *supra* note 19, at 80.

[26] Law Commission, *supra* note 18, at 22–25.

[27] See John Dawson, "The Resistance of the New Zealand Legal System to Recognition of Maori Customary Law," 12 Journal of South Pacific Law 56 (2008).

[28] Joseph, *supra* note 19, at 75; Joseph Williams, "Lex Aotearoa: An Heroic Attempt to Map the Maori Dimension in Modern New Zealand Law," 21 Waikato Law Review 1, 11 (2013).

[29] On the backlash against recognition of Maori law and rights, see David V. Williams, "Indigenous Customary Rights and the Constitution of Aotearoa New Zealand," 14 Waikato Law Review 120 (2006).

[30] See Williams, *supra* note 28.

though questions remain about the criteria for recognition of customary law and its impact in a given case.[31] If Maori law is to obtain increased recognition within the legal system, advocates urge, judges must be better trained to ascertain *tikanga* and its implications, particularly because Maori law is value based, with customary norms interpreted within overarching values emphasizing relationships, community, balance, reciprocity, spirituality, and others.[32] Even when this is done with sensitivity, however, Maori law advocates warn that common law doctrine will control and shape incorporation in ways that maintain the dominance of state law.[33]

A remarkable recent action was legislative recognition of the Whanganui River and its surrounds as "an indivisible and living whole" with legal personality.[34] This is a hybrid blend of Maori spiritual values toward nature combined with modern legal status, rights, duties, and liabilities, demonstrating how Maori legal principles and values can influence the state legal system more broadly in ways that are not limited to the Maori community. A few locations around the world have recently accorded legal personhood to natural objects for environmental purposes, but uniquely Maori aspects of this action are recognition that the river is living whole as well as inseparably interconnected with the attendant Maori community, not something that can be owned.[35]

Historical and contemporary treatment of indigenous law in New Zealand bears notable parallels to that in Canada and Australia, as I show next (the United States is different in certain respects). Contemporary advocates of indigenous law regularly refer to the work of fellow native scholars, creating a transnational network and body of work. Despite recent strides, however, like indigenous law in other settler societies, Maori law continues to have a limited place within New Zealand state law.

Law in Canada consists of three officially recognized streams: English common law, French civil law (in Quebec), and elements of native law (not to forget unofficial Romani law, and Jewish law and Sharia law, mentioned

---

[31] The case is *Takamore v. Clarke* [2012] NZSC 116, [2013] 2 NZLR 733, described in Williams, *supra* note 28, at 15–16.

[32] Carwyn Jones, "A Maori Constitutional Tradition," New Zealand Journal of Public and International Law 187 (2014).

[33] Ani Mikaere, "Tikanga as the First Law of Aotearoa," 10 Yearbook of New Zealand Jurisprudence 24 (2007).

[34] Te Awa Tupua (Whanganui River Claims Settlement) Act 2017, http://www.legislation.govt.nz/act/public/2017/0007/latest/whole.html

[35] Abigail Hutchison, "The Whanganui River as a Legal Person," 39 Alternative Law Journal 179 (2014).

shortly). For several centuries after initial contact native peoples maintained community-based legal systems that coexisted with English and French legal institutions.[36] Relations between native peoples and the Crown were initially arranged through treaties between sovereigns. Over time the state shifted to claim total sovereignty, treating native peoples as subjects rather than co-equal nations, engaging in repeated efforts at assimilating natives from the mid-nineteenth through the twentieth centuries.[37] As late as 1969, an official statement of government policy proposed the complete termination of Indian status, ultimately withdrawn in the face of sharp criticism from advocates of native rights.[38] Canadian courts up through the early 1980s indicated that the Parliament held the power to extinguish all native rights.[39] The Constitution Act of 1982 placed indigenous rights on a firmer footing with a clause that "existing aboriginal and treaty rights of the aboriginal peoples of Canada are hereby recognized and affirmed,"[40] although subsequent Court interpretations of this language again placed native law and rights in a subservient position.[41]

Native legal norms and practices presently exist in various contexts, recognized by state law as well as outside the state system, particularly on issues relating to family law, land rights, and disputes generally, as well as hunting, fishing, and cultivation, and ecological management.[42] State law treatment of indigenous law involves five main approaches: (1) giving legal effect to native arrangements like adoption and marriage; (2) taking native beliefs into consideration in evaluating the reasonableness of conduct in criminal and civil cases; (3) delegating power to recognized indigenous bands to make rules that are enforced in state court; (4) deferring to zones of autonomy and

[36] See James Sakej Youngblood Henderson, "'First Nations' Legal Inheritances in Canada; The Mikmaq Model," 23 Manitoba Law Journal 1 (1996).

[37] *Id.* at 27–28.

[38] John F. Leslie, "The Indian Act: An Historical Perspective," 25 Canadian Parliamentary Review 32 (2002).

[39] See John Borrows, "Tracking Trajectories: Aboriginal Governance as an Aboriginal Right," 38 University of British Columbia Law Review 285, 307–308 (2005).

[40] Canada Constitution Act 1982, Section 35 (1).

[41] See Brenda L. Gunn, "Beyond Van der Peet: Bringing Together International, Indigenous and Constitutional Law," in John Borrows, Larry Chartrand, Oonagh E. Fitzgerald, and Risa Schwartz, eds., *Braiding Legal Orders: Implementing the United Nations Declaration on the Rights of Indigenous Peoples* (Waterloo, Canada: Center for International Governance Innovation 2019) 135–44.

[42] See John Borrows, Indigenous Legal Traditions in Canada, Report for the Law Commission of Canada (2006), http://publications.gc.ca/collections/collection_2008/lcc-cdc/JL2-66-2006E.pdf 13–76.

self-determination for indigenous communities; and (5) incorporating customary law into state law.[43]

A variety of arrangements exist. The Metis people in Alberta have an official tribunal that hears disputes over land and usage rights.[44] The Carrier people have informal tribunals presided over by chiefs who render decisions in disputes involving marriage, succession, resource management, and other matters.[45] The Nisga'a nation entered a treaty with the government that incorporates their legal principles on family law, succession, resource usage, land, etc., in so far as they are consistent with provincial law.[46] The Nunavut Territory government recognizes an array of Inuit values, principles, and practices in legislation, regulations, and procedures.[47] Various native communities engage in traditional deliberation, apology, and reconciliation processes in response to disputes.[48] More generally, the First Nations Land Management Act (1999) allowed bands on Indian reserves to create their own land use codes.

Notwithstanding these examples, indigenous legal traditions have significantly eroded in native communities and have received limited recognition within the state legal system. Recent work pushes for the "recognition and revitalization"[49] or "recovery and renaissance of Indigenous laws."[50] A review of the literature on indigenous law in Canada observed that "the common starting point of the scholarship reviewed in this report is the legal fact that over the past 150 years the Canadian state, its legislation and its courts, have left little space for the recognition and application of Indigenous law."[51]

State court efforts to incorporate indigenous law have had limited success. The coexisting systems have incommensurable ideologies and different values, principles, and decision-making orientations. In crimes, for example, state law has a punitive orientation focused on applying legal rules to individual actions, while indigenous law has a restorative orientation focused on

---

[43] This list is taken from an informative essay on the dilemmas of recognition by Kirsten Anker, "Post-Colonial Jurisprudence and the Pluralist Turn: From Making Space to Being in Place," in Nicole Roughan and Andrew Halpin, eds., In Pursuit of Pluralist Jurisprudence (Cambridge: Cambridge University Press 2017) 272–74. For simplicity, I have deleted the labels Anker provided for each strategy: translation, accommodation, delegation, deference, and incorporation.

[44] Borrows, *supra* note 42, at 58–59.

[45] *Id.* at 59–65.

[46] *Id.* at 65–73.

[47] *Id.* at 74–77.

[48] See Michael Coyle, "Indigenous Legal Orders in Canada: A Literature Review," Western University Law Publications (2017)

[49] *Id.* at 9.

[50] Our Vision, Indigenous Law Research Unit, University of Victoria Law Center, https://www.uvic.ca/law/about/indigenous/indigenouslawresearchunit/index.php

[51] Coyle, *supra* note 48, at 4.

the community. State judges have a superficial understanding of indigenous law, moreover, and little guidance on how to reconcile the two. A recent landmark decision by the Supreme Court held that questions about Aboriginal land title claims must consider both the common law and native law;[52] although in practice courts treat indigenous law as questions of historical and evidentiary facts, rather than as law, thereby distorting, limiting their scope, and freezing them.[53]

These issues always arise when Western state legal systems are juxtaposed with and attempt to incorporate indigenous law, as preceding discussions have shown. Law is an integrated aspect within the social whole in which it develops. Extracting particular elements of law from one system and injecting it into another inevitably results in transformations—not only because it is detached from its original social-legal context of operation, but also because it is absorbed on the terms of a wholly different recipient legal system.

The UN Declaration on the Rights of Indigenous Peoples (UNDRIP) provided a major political boost for the cause of indigenous law and rights.[54] To meet its commitment to UNDRIP the Canadian government recently issued a plan for forthcoming legislation with greater acknowledgment of indigenous law and rights. The legislative Preamble states: "Indigenous peoples have repeatedly expressed that recognition legislation must be framed by an understanding that rights, including title, *are inherent and not premised on Crown understandings, standards or recognition.*"[55] If the legislation confirms this assertion, it would acknowledge that indigenous law and rights have their own independent basis, portraying Canadian law as pluralistic at its very foundation (deeper than the coexistence of civil law and common law within state law), a braiding of independently derived legal orders: state law and indigenous law.[56] Significantly, advocates insist that indigenous legal orders have independent standing without regard to recognition by state law, and retain this standing even if state law explicitly denies that they exist. The

---

[52] Tsilhqot'in Nation v British Columbia, 2014 SCC 44.

[53] See Fraser Harland, "Taking the Aboriginal Perspective Seriously," 16 Indigenous Law Journal 21 (2018); Don Coutuvier, "Judicial Reasoning Across Legal Orders: Lessons From Nunavut," 45 Queens Law Journal 319 (2020).

[54] See Borrows et al., *supra* note 41.

[55] Preamble and Purpose, Overview of a Recognition and Implementation of Indigenous Rights Framework, https://www.rcaanc-cirnac.gc.ca/eng/1536350959665/1539959903708

[56] It does not bode well for the legislation that a recent poll found 34 percent of Canadians favored greater independence and self-control for indigenous communities, while 66 percent felt they should have the same rules and systems as all Canadians. See Kerry Wilkins, "Strategizing UNDRIP Implementation: Some Fundamentals," in Borrows et al., *supra* note 41, at 179 n. 13.

status of indigenous legal orders is grounded in the communities that live by them, not in how the state chooses to treat them.

In broad outline Australia followed the same pattern as New Zealand and Canada. A major difference is that Aborigines were hunter-gatherers who lacked large political structures like chiefdoms that existed elsewhere. Consequently, British colonizers and settlers faced less formidable resistance to their incursions, and did not enter treaties with Aborigines to justify their takings. Invoking the monist law state image, they claimed that Australia was terra nullius and territorium nullius, respectively, unoccupied land with no semblance of civil society, sovereignty, or law.[57] Since Aborigines did not have law, jurists reasoned, there was no existing law to respect or accommodate—so British common law and colonial enactments were written on a blank legal slate. Jurists serving the state and settler interests used this reasoning to justify the seizure of lands occupied by Aborigines on the theory that they lacked property rights and accordingly did not own the land on which they had lived for thousands of years.

At the outset colonial policies were the same as those utilized elsewhere: English law was applied to dealings between settlers, and between settlers and Aborigines, while Aborigines were left to apply their own practices in disputes among Aborigines, particularly in remote areas. Over time, the Crown claimed the power to handle all matters, including between Aborigines, although in practice intervention by the state was limited.[58] Aborigines were not allowed to give testimony in cases because they were considered untrustworthy,[59] making it especially difficult to deal with legal matters involving natives, to their detriment. An official policy of non-recognition of Aborigine law, part of a broader policy of assimilation, held until well into the twentieth century. Clashes between these coexisting bodies of law occurred throughout this period—particularly when actions considered legal under customary law were illegal under state law. Aboriginal customary law allowed killing or spearing as punishment (payback), for example, but those who carried out these actions violated state law against murder and assault, and were prosecuted by the state.[60] The perceived unfairness of this situation for Aborigines acting in accordance with their own

---

[57] See Recognition of Aboriginal Customary Laws, Australian Law Commission Report 31 (1986) paragraphs 39, 60, available at https://www.alrc.gov.au/publication/recognition-of-aboriginal-customary-laws-alrc-report-31/

[58] *Id.* at paragraphs 39–45.

[59] *Id.* at paragraph 46.

[60] *Id.* at paragraphs 49–57.

community law led to legislation and court decisions that permitted consideration of customary law as mitigation—in the face of much opposition from jurists and the settler population. Beyond that accommodation there was scant official recognition of customary law.

In a 1971 case involving Aboriginal claims to land rights, the Court explicitly addressed whether Aborigines have law. The Solicitor General argued that Aboriginal customs are not law because law requires institutional enforcement. Justice Blackburn responded:

> Implicit in much of the Solicitor-General's argument . . . was . . . an Austinian definition of law as the command of a sovereign. At any rate, he contended, there must be the outward forms of machinery for enforcement before a rule can be described as law . . .
>
> None of these objections is in my opinion convincing. . . . The specialization of the functions performed by the officer of an advanced society is no proof that the same functions are not performed in primitive societies, though by less specially responsible officers. . . .
>
> I do not believe that there is utility in attempting to provide a definition of law which will be valid for all purposes and answer all questions. . . . I prefer a more pragmatic approach. . . . The evidence shows a subtle and elaborate system highly adapted to the country in which the people led their lives, which provide a stable order of society and was remarkably free from the vagaries of personal whim or influence. If ever a system could be called 'a government of laws, and not of men' it is that shown in the evidence before me.[61]

Blackburn's account of law apart from the monist law state is more sophisticated than the view expressed by many jurisprudents at the time as well as today. Two decades later, the High Court decided in the *Mabo* case that Aboriginal customary law conferred property rights entitled to legal recognition. "The facts as we know them today do not fit the 'absence of law' or 'barbarian' theory underpinning the colonial reception of the common law of England," the court held.[62] Legislation was enacted following this decision to provide for native title claims.

---

[61] Milirrpum and Others v. Nabalco Pty Ltd and the Commonwealth of Australia (1971) 17 FLR 141, at 266–68.

[62] Mabo v Queensland (No 2), ((1992) 175 CLR 1), paragraph 38.

Today, in addition to customary land tenure, pockets of Aboriginal law exist within and outside the state legal system. Informal tribunals still handle matters among Aborigines in tribal communities. State-created Aboriginal courts staffed by Aborigines have operated in Queensland and Western Australia for several decades.[63] State courts have taken Aborigine law into consideration in criminal cases on issues of reasonableness, duress, and punishment in criminal cases, compensable injuries in civil liability, as well as in family law (marriage, adoption) and inheritance matters.[64] There is also legislation protecting Aboriginal hunting and fishing rights and sacred spots.[65]

Opponents of more extensive recognition raise several objections: the customary "payback system" violates human rights against cruel punishment, and customary law permits child brides and treats women poorly.[66] A general objection based on state law monism is that consideration of Aboriginal customary law creates the unequal application of law among Australian citizens.[67] Proponents of greater recognition point out that support for and compliance with Aboriginal law remains high within the native community, that non-recognition undermines community cohesion as well as the traditional authority of elders, that it is unfair to apply laws alien to their way of life, and that indigenous people understand that their law evolves and must comport with contemporary conditions and human rights norms.[68] Although two substantial Law Commission reports in the past four decades have urged greater recognition of customary law, the "recommendations have, by and large, been ignored."[69]

The United States, like other settler countries, underwent several changes in policies toward and relations with Native Americans.[70] Across settler countries

[63] Recognition of Aboriginal Customary Laws, *supra* note 57, paragraph 83.

[64] *Id*. at paragraphs 70–82.

[65] Excellent sources on customary law are the 1986 Australian Law Commission Report, and Aboriginal Customary Law: The Interaction of Western Australian Law with Aboriginal Law and Culture, Final Report, Project 94, Law Reform Commission of Australia (2006), https://www.alrc. gov.au/publication/recognition-of-aboriginal-customary-laws-alrc-report-31/

[66] See Aboriginal Customary Law, *supra* note 65, at 69–71.

[67] See Recognition of Australian Customary Laws, *supra* note 57, at paragraph 38, 166–68.

[68] See *id*. at 103–12; Tom Calma, "The Integration of Customary Law into the Australian Legal System," Australian Human Rights Commission, https://humanrights.gov.au/about/news/speeches/ integration-customary-law-australian-legal-system-calma

[69] AJ Wood, "Why Australia Won't Recognize Indigenous Customary Law," The Conversation, June 9, 2016, https://theconversation.com/why-australia-wont-recognise-indigenous-customary-law-60370

[70] A concise overview is Matthew L.M. Fletcher, "A Short History of Indian Law in the Supreme Court," October 1, 2014, Human Rights Magazine, American Bar Association, https://www. americanbar.org/groups/crsj/publications/human_rights_magazine_home/2014_vol_40/vol--40--no--1--tribal-sovereignty/short_history_of_indian_law/

the pattern of treatment was a function of relative power: treated as equals when native tribal populations were formidable—then unilateral domination when settler populations increased substantially and state power became overwhelming. This is evident in the fact that the independent Kingdom of Hawaii was forcibly seized by the considerably more powerful United States in 1893, and consequently does not enjoy recognition of sovereignty today on a par with Native American tribes despite their similar native status.

Early on Native Americans were dealt with as sovereign nations entitled to respect. However, they were subjected to steadily growing pressure from settlers seeking land, backed by the US government, resulting in wars and the forcible relocation of many tribes onto reservations, as well as programs aimed at assimilation.[71] Early nineteenth-century decisions by the US Supreme Court established that tribes are "domestic dependent nations" with the right of self-governance free from regulation by the states.[72] By the close of the nineteenth century, the Supreme Court asserted that Congress has plenary power over Indian tribes, a reversal of previous acknowledgment of Indian sovereignty. A series of twentieth-century cases confirmed Indian self-governance on tribal lands—including the right to enact and enforce laws applicable to tribal members—but also the power of Congress to unilaterally abrogate treaties and alter the extent the Indian authority.[73] This assertion, first stated by the Supreme Court in 1886, was grounded on the theory of the sovereign monist law state. Although Indian tribes held certain attributes of sovereignty, the Court declared, "within the geographical limits of the United States" (on territories not recognized as states) "the right of exclusive sovereignty must exist in the national government."[74]

As the Supreme Court recently acknowledged, Congress and individual states repeatedly broke promises and treaties with Native American tribes.[75] One notorious example occurred when Congress promised the Creek Nation complete self-governance in 1833 as they were forcibly ejected from Georgia and Alabama to make way for settler plantations, and relocated to eastern Oklahoma. This was the infamous Trail of Tears, during which thousands of Creek and other Native Americans died en route. Violating

---

[71] Burbank and Cooper, *supra* note 14, at Chapter 9.

[72] These cases are known as the Marshall Trilogy: Johnson v. M'Intosh, 21 US 543 (1823); Cherokee Nation v. Georgia, 30 US 1 (1831); Worcester v. Georgia 31 US 515 (1832).

[73] See United States v. Kagama, 118 US 375 (1886); Lone Wolf v. Hitchcock, 187 US 553 (1903).

[74] United States v. Kagama, *supra* note 73, at 380.

[75] These events are described in McGirt v Oklahoma, Slip Opinion, 591 US ___ 2020.

its agreements, in 1901 Congress abolished Creek tribal courts (to pressure them for other concessions). Thereafter, for many decades state courts in Oklahoma as well as other states exercised criminal jurisdiction in cases between Indians on Indian land, although this was contrary to treaties with Indian tribes and federal law.

The Supreme Court has depicted the relationship in terms of overlapping sovereign powers, but with the United States absolutely superior. On the one hand, it recognized that Indian tribes have "inherent powers of a limited sovereignty which has never been extinguished."[76] On the other hand, incorporation in the United States entailed their subjection to national power, so the sovereignty of Indian tribes "exists only at the sufferance of Congress and is subject to complete defeasance."[77] The result of this combination is that "Indian tribes still possess those aspects of sovereignty not withdrawn by treaty or statute."[78] Reflecting their separate and denigrated treatment, Native American tribe members were not granted US citizenship until 1924. A significant number of federal statutes have been enacted specifying the respective powers of Indian tribes, the federal government, and states relating to various matters on tribal lands.[79]

There are 574 federally recognized tribes today, spread across the United States. A range of indigenous legal institutions exist within tribal societies, from small community associations to substantial tribal governments. "Traditional non-judicial dispute resolution mechanisms continue to function in some tribes along with Peacemaker courts, courts of specialized jurisdiction, such as administrative commissions, gaming, small claims courts, and courts of general jurisdiction."[80] Formal tribal courts apply customary and traditional law, often in consultation with elders, and they also apply tribal codes and constitutions, their own precedents as well as decisions from other tribal courts, and state and federal law, producing a thoroughly hybrid body of law.[81] Navajo Nation has a highly developed government, administering a population of 200,000, with territory extending across Utah, Arizona, and New Mexico, and a court system handling about 20,000 cases in a given

---

[76] United States v. Wheeler, 435 U.S. 313, 322–23 (1978).

[77] See Fletcher, *supra* note 70, at 23.

[78] *Id.*

[79] For a detailed list, see Public Law 280, Tribal Court Clearing House, http://www.tribal-institute.org/lists/pl280.htm

[80] Nell Jessup Newton, "Tribal Court Praxis: One Year in the Life of Twenty Indian Tribal Court," 22 American Indian Law Review 285, 292–93 (1998).

[81] *Id.* at 293, 304.

year (civil, criminal, traffic, family, etc.).[82] The Creek Nation has a legislature, executive, courts with criminal and civil jurisdiction, a police force, and an annual budget over $350 million. There are myriad arrangements and variations among the tribes, which range greatly in size, organization, and institution development. Outside of well-established court systems like the Navajo Nation, not a great deal is known about tribal law and native tribunals, including how many are operating (at least 188 tribunals were confirmed in a survey, but the actual number may be double that).[83]

Here I will address legal powers and jurisdictional rules, which exhibit a mix of personal and territorial jurisdiction.[84] Tribal governments have full legal powers over their own citizens on tribal lands, including the power to tax; the most extensively organized tribes have enacted a range of criminal and civils laws, with their own police, prosecutors, and courts.[85] Tribal governments have jurisdiction over criminal and civil cases between their tribal members for incidents that occur on tribal lands, though the federal government has jurisdiction over major crimes (murder, kidnapping, incest, etc.). But tribal governments have limited powers to regulate and adjudicate non-members on tribal lands. They have no jurisdiction over crimes between non-Indians on tribal land and almost none over crimes by non-Indians against Indians (with a recent exception for domestic abuse),[86] and they generally lack civil jurisdiction over non-members, albeit with unclear exceptions based on consent or significant harm to the tribe.[87] A federal law gave a few designated states concurrent jurisdiction with tribal authorities over criminal and civil matters. A number of tribes have objected to this as an encroachment on their authority, while the states have complained that they lack the funds to handle these cases, are uncertain about their jurisdictional authority, and are unfamiliar with tribal communities.[88]

[82] See Welcome to the Navajo Nation, Official Site of the Navajo Nation, https://www.navajo-nsn.gov/history.htm

[83] See Elizabeth A. Reese, "The Other American Law, 73 Stanford Law Review, forthcoming 2021, https://papers.ssrn.com/sol3/papers.cfm?abstract_id=3660166

[84] This discussion is indebted to Matthew L.M. Fletcher, *American Indian Tribal Law* (New York: Aspen 2011); Andrea Wilkins, *Fostering State-Tribal Collaboration* (Lanham, MD: Rowman & Littlefield 2016); Robert J. Miller, "American Indian Sovereignty Versus the United States," *Routledge Handbook of Critical Indigenous Studies* (forthcoming 2020), available at https://papers.ssrn.com/sol3/papers.cfm?abstract_id=3541054

[85] Miller, *supra* note 84, at 23.

[86] Oliphant v. Suquamish Indian Tribe, 435 U.S. 191 (1978).

[87] Montana v. United States, 450 U.S. 544 (1981); Strate v. A-1 Contractors, 520 US 438 (1997).

[88] Wilkins, *supra* note 84, at 51–54.

In general, then, tribal governments and courts exercise criminal and civil power over actions between tribal members on tribal lands, but not over actions involving non-Indians on tribal lands.[89] There are two sides to this arrangement. When it originated, the exercise of jurisdiction by Indians over Indians was considered fairer than subjecting them to the standards of civilized people. As the Supreme Court explained in 1883, if Indians who commit criminal acts on fellow Indians are brought before a state court, "it tries them not by their peers, not by the customs of their people, nor the law of their land, but by superiors of a different race, according to the law of a social state of which they have an imperfect conception and which is opposed to the traditions of their history, to the habits of their lives, to the strongest prejudices of their savage nature; one which measures the red man's revenge by the maxims of white man's morality."[90] The obverse of this reasoning, naturally, is that a white man cannot be held accountable to the laws and tribunals of Indians. While the stark differences between the coexisting systems of justice viewed through assumptions about the superiority of white civilization justified the arrangement at the time, that does not explain why this basic arrangement continues today.

The current combination of tribal authority based on territorial jurisdiction over tribal lands, but with personal jurisdictional exemptions for non-Indians, strongly resembles extraterritorial demands by Western countries across the globe in the nineteenth and early twentieth centuries that Westerners not be tried by less civilized legal systems. The continuing significance of personal status for community law and native rights is reflected in controversies surrounding who—which groups and which individuals (how much blood is enough)—qualifies for native or indigenous status.

More generally, this discussion of settler countries shows state (regime) law and indigenous (community) law in various combinations and modes of interaction. Not only have we seen that sovereignty and arrangements with coexisting forms of law are malleable and change over time—from mutual acknowledgment to suppression to limited recognition—but also that changes are driven by the economic interests at stake and attitudes of the dominant regime that strives to dictate the terms of the relationship. And in all four countries the image of the monistic law state, and theories of law based

---

[89] Although tribal authority is limited over non-members, which includes both non-Indians and Indians who are not tribal members, initially the exemption was declared in relation to non-Indians and the bulk of people it applies to are non-Indians.

[90] Ex Parte Crow Dog, 109 US 556, 571 (1883).

thereon, have been weaponized by jurists to derive conclusions that erase and suppress indigenous law. Juristic theories have genuine consequences by shaping concepts and providing arguments through which jurists construct law. The Austinian (Bodin, Hobbes) theory of law as exclusively the product of the sovereign has been invoked by jurists again and again on behalf of state law supremacy and exclusivity in this centuries-long contest. Yet denials by state legal officials of the existence of indigenous law and efforts to stamp it out did not succeed, as it continued to be manifested within the community in various forms.

Another point worth noting in closing is that discussions of legal pluralism usually center on state law treatment of indigenous law as one-directional incorporation of the latter by the former. However, formal state legal systems can learn from and integrate indigenous legal practices. In the 1990s a "restorative justice" movement arose in the context of criminal law, particularly for juveniles who commit crimes. The idea behind restorative justice is that the offender, victim, and immediate community meet face to face to help achieve reconciliation through dialogue and an apology. Community participation and informality are essential components of this process, which takes place outside ordinary state law treatment of criminal offenders. Proponents of restorative justice identify their roots in indigenous dispute resolution, citing examples from Native American groups, Hawaiians, Maori, and others. Both victims and perpetrators who participate in the process indicate higher levels of satisfaction compared to ordinary judicial processes,[91] and restorative justice programs have spread around the world in many different contexts in the past two decades.[92] Of more general application, as the costs of legal services increase beyond the means of ordinary people in many societies, a possible forum for resolution of disputes might be informal community based settings, at least in close-knit communities where people have multiple long-standing connections with one another. These tribunals work across the Global South and in native communities in the West, and have the potential to work more generally.

[91] See David B. Wilson, Ajima Olaghere, and Catherine S. Krimbrell, "Effectiveness of Restorative Justice: Principles in Juvenile Justice: A Meta-Analysis," June 2017, National Criminal Justice Reference Service, https://www.ncjrs.gov/pdffiles1/ojjdp/grants/250872.pdf; Jeff Latimer, Craig Dowden, and Danielle Muise, "The Effectiveness of Restorative Justice Practices: A Meta-Analysis," 85 The Prison Journal 127 (2005).

[92] For an overview, see Declan Roche, "Dimensions of Restorative Justice," 62 Journal of Social Issues 217–38 (2006). See John Braithwaite, Restorative Justice and Responsive Regulation (Oxford: Oxford University Press 2002).

Rabbinical Courts and Sharia Tribunals

Religious tribunals, as previous chapters have shown, have operated for many centuries in various arrangements prior and subsequent to the development of the state system: independent bodies of ecclesiastical law like medieval canon law; a part of state law in theocracies or official state churches; semi-autonomous systems like *millets*; unofficially in religious communities in societies hostile to the particular religion; and as arbitration bodies whose rulings are enforced by state courts. The relationship between religious law and state law within any given context is a product of historical and political circumstances. Across these different arrangements are several commonalities: the laws are observed within the community of believers; the religious laws are considered divinely mandated and thus binding on believers and *superior* to state law (and to laws of other religions); they cover marriage, divorce, responsibility for offspring, sexual relations, inheritance, transactions and debts, and sacred matters, though certain of these matters are removed by state law; and they make adjustments that enable them to continue to function in relation to ruling regime law. Throughout history regime legal orders have coexisted in one way or another with pockets of religious community law following different sets of rules.

Within the religious community, it is important to emphasize, these bodies of religious law have always been considered binding *law*—regardless of how state law officially characterizes it. Consider Jewish law (*halakhah*) in contemporary US society. A minority religious group regularly subjected to persecution by state regimes, for over two millennia Jews have maintained rabbinical courts (Beth Din) to resolve disputes within the community.[93] Jewish law holds that state law is binding on Jews ("the law of the regime is law"), at least if the regime is not unjust, but Jews are required to take their disputes to Beth Din rather than to state courts.[94] Jewish authorities have a long history of construing the operation of their community laws in ways that are able to function effectively within state law.

Beth Din of America (BDA), for instance, the most prominent rabbinical court in the United States, renders decisions in divorce, personal status, and commercial disputes. BDA presents itself as working together with state law, stating "The Beth Din of America adjudicates disputes in a manner

---

[93] See Moishele Fogel, "Synagogue and State: The Evolution of the Relationship Between the Jewish People, Halacha, and the State," February 11, 2019, Cardus Religious Freedom Institute.
[94] *Id.* at 8–12.

consistent with secular law requirements for binding arbitration so that the resolution will be enforceable in the civil courts of the United States of America and the various states therein."[95] Section 2a of BDA's official Rules and Procedures specifies "The parties shall be deemed to have made these Rules a part of their agreement to seek arbitration[.]"[96] While thus emphasizing enforceability within state law, BDA also makes clear that it is a Jewish tribunal bound by and applying Jewish law. Section 3c states "The Beth Din of America accepts that Jewish law as understood by the Beth Din will provide the rules of decision and rules of procedure that govern the Beth Din or any of its panels."[97] Section 3e provides that when the parties accept common commercial practices in their profession or trade, the Beth Din will apply these commercial practices in the decision "to the fullest extent provided by Jewish law."[98]

The two legal systems at play in these contexts construe the same situation quite differently. Courts in the United States do not enforce Jewish court decisions or law; instead, Beth Din decisions are enforced under ordinary contract law; and US courts, consistent with their general deference to arbitration decisions, "have never overturned a BDA-issued arbitration award."[99] On its own terms, in contrast, the Beth Din is a rabbinical court applying Jewish law within the context of a state legal system—a hybrid combination. BDA models its procedures on standard arbitration rules and its rabbinical judges are versed in both Jewish and state law.[100] "'*Beth dins*' ability to interweave religious and secular law is their key to success," observed Michael Broyde, an Emory law professor and rabbi judge for BDA.[101] As far as state law is concerned, only one legal system is operating, whereas BDA sees two legal systems. From the standpoint of Jewish law, furthermore, Jewish law is supreme over state legal systems—the former determines that the latter is binding on adherents—although it makes pragmatic accommodations to state law out of necessity.

[95] Rules and Procedures, Beth Din of America, Preface, https://bethdin.org/wp-content/uploads/2018/04/BDA118-RulesProcedures_Bro_BW_02.pdf

[96] *Id.* at 1.

[97] *Id.* at 5.

[98] *Id.* at 5.

[99] Michael J. Broyde, Ira Bedzow, and Shlomo C. Pill, "The Pillars of Successful Religious Arbitration: Models for American Islamic Arbitration Based on the Beth Din of America and Muslim Arbitration Tribunal Experience," 30 Harvard Journal of Racial & Ethnic Injustice 33, 36 (2014).

[100] Michael J. Broyde, *Sharia Tribunals, Rabbinical Courts, and Christian Panels* (New York: Oxford University Press 2017) Chapter 7.

[101] *Id.* at 15.

The claimed supremacy of Jewish law over state law is evident in Israel, where rabbinical courts have defied efforts by the Israeli Supreme Court to curtail their jurisdiction. "The Rabbinical courts judges met and formally declared that they were rejecting the decision [restricting their jurisdiction] and would not comply with it on the grounds 'that they consider themselves bound only by the religious law and not by the state law or by precedents set by the [Supreme Court].'"[102] This creates a direct clash between two legal systems, religious and state, each claiming supremacy over the other on the matter at issue. A willingness to defy state law for religious law reasons is not limited to rabbinical courts. A recent poll in Israel asked, "If a contradiction arose between religious law and a state court ruling, which would you follow?"—in response to which 97 percent of ultra-Orthodox Jews and 56 percent of Muslims said they would follow their religious law.[103]

Sharia tribunals exhibit many parallels to rabbinical courts, except that the former are far more controversial in the West. Sharia combines religious, moral, and legal obligations for the community of believers (*Ummah*) based on the Quran and the teachings of Muhammad (*Hadith*), supplemented by the writings of Islamic scholars and jurists. There is no single or unified body of Islamic law. In addition to the divide between Sunni and Shi'a Muslims, Sunni has four classical schools of Islamic jurisprudence (*fiqh*). Furthermore, Muslim law varies by country and region, and much of what is seen as Islamic law in a given location includes a mix of local customs and traditions (Arabic, Turkish, South Asian, etc.). Muslims in Western countries have also created hybrid versions of Islamic law through interaction with surrounding cultural views and restrictions imposed by state law.[104]

Islamic law and tribunals exist within Muslim communities in the United States,[105] though with a less visible presence owing to the rise of populist anti-Muslim public sentiment. Following the 9/11 attacks, ten US states passed laws banning state courts from applying Sharia (one of which has been declared invalid),[106] and a dozen have enacted facially neutral laws

---

[102] Rabea Benhalim, "Religious Courts in Secular Jurisdictions: How Jewish and Islamic Courts Adapt to Society and Legal Norms," 84 Brooklyn Law Review 745, 798 (2019).

[103] Tamar Hermann, Ella Heller, Chanan Cohen, Dana Bubil, and Fadi Omar, The Israeli Democracy Index 2016 (Jerusalem: The Democracy Institute 2016) 84–85, 176.

[104] See Prakash Shah and Werner Menski, Migration, Diasporas, and Legal Systems in Europe (London: Routledge 2006); Ihsan Yilmaz, Muslim Laws, Politics, and Society in Modern Nation States (Burlington: Ashgate 2005).

[105] An established instance is the Islamic Tribunal located in Dallas, Texas, at https://www. islamictribunal.org/

[106] See Erin Sisson, "The Future of Sharia Law in American Arbitration," 48 Vanderbilt Journal of Transnational Law 891, 899–908 (2015).

that ban all religious or foreign law.[107] (The effort to avoid the appearance of targeting Muslims poses a threat to rabbinical courts, which heretofore have generated little public controversy.) A recent poll found that half of Muslims had personally experienced anti-Muslim discrimination in the past twelve months.[108] Despite this overt hostility, a number of state laws provide accommodations for Islamic law requirements in the name of religious freedom, including the wearing of head scarfs and other religious restrictions.[109]

European countries have made greater accommodations to Islamic law.[110] Two factors contribute to this: between 5–10 percent of the population in Western European countries are Muslim (compared to only 1.1 percent in the United States), many of whom immigrated in the past few decades, so their ways of life cannot be ignored; and Article 9 of the European Convention on Human Rights recognizes the right of everyone "to manifest his religion or belief, in worship, teaching, practice and observance," along with the freedom of assembly and association of Article 11.[111] Belgian, Spanish, German, and French courts have on occasion directly applied Sharia law in family law issues (subject to limitations),[112] as well as other matters, including the ritual slaughter of animals by butchers, and the wearing of head scarfs at work; German social security treats polygamous marriages as legally valid for the purposes of awarding pension support for second (or more) wives.[113] A province in Greece has official Sharia courts that render decisions on family law and inheritance (a residual legacy of Ottoman times and Turkish-Greek

---

[107] Maurits S. Berger, "Understanding Sharia in the West," 6 Journal of Law, Religion and State 236, 262 (2018); Benhalim, *supra* note 102, at 775.

[108] "U.S. Muslims Concerned about Their Place in Society, but Continue to Believe in the American Dream," July 26, 2017, Pew Research Center, https://www.pewforum.org/2017/07/26/findings-from-pew-research-centers-2017-survey-of-us-muslims/

[109] See Eugene Volokh, "Religious Law (Especially Islamic Law) in American Courts," 66 Oklahoma Law Review 431 (2014).

[110] Polls show that views toward Muslims are much more negative in Eastern and Southern Europe (Hungary, Italy, Poland, Greece—two-thirds negative) than they are in Western Europe (Netherlands, Sweden, France, Germany, United Kingdom—one-third or below negative). See Michael Lipka, "Muslims and Islam: Key Findings in the US and Around the World," Aug. 9, 2017, Pew Research Center, https://www.pewresearch.org/fact-tank/2017/08/09/muslims-and-islam-key-findings-in-the-u-s-and-around-the-world/

[111] Article 9 (1), European Convention on Human Rights. For an analysis of various European laws supporting the recognition of Sharia law, see Dorota Anna Gozdecka, "Religious Pluralism as a Legal Principle," in Russell Sandberg ed., Religion and Legal Pluralism (Surrey: Ashgate 2015) Chapter 11.

[112] See Ludovica Decimo, "The Relationship Between Religious Law and Modern Legal Systems," 6 Calumet—Intercultural Law and Humanities Review 1, 8 (2018).

[113] See Mathias Rohe, "Application of Sharia Rules in Europe: Scope and Limits," 44 Die Welt des Islams 323 (2004).

separation treaties), as do Bulgaria and Macedonia.[114] A significant amount of Islamic legal practices and dispute resolution in Europe takes place in informal settings like local mosques, although information about their quantity is limited because few have been studied.[115]

Much of the recent attention to Sharia law in Europe has centered on the United Kingdom, which has a significant Muslim population. Archbishop Rowan Williams provoked a public uproar in 2008 when he advocated greater recognition of Islamic law within the British legal system.[116] Informal Islamic Sharia Councils (a network) had already been functioning since the 1980s within Muslim communities. They operated outside the arbitration framework, in a non-transparent fashion, and their decisions were not enforceable in state court—which Williams suggested should be remedied. In 2008, the British government officially recognized the Muslim Arbitration Tribunals (MAT), enabling their decisions to be enforced in court.[117] Most Sharia councils are less formalized and transparent than MAT, however, and their decisions do not qualify for enforcement by state courts. Indeed, some Sharia councils have expressed reluctance to obtain formal recognition under state law, which they consider to be "un-Islamic."[118]

Once again what has emerged are hybrid combinations of religious and state law. Procedure Rules of MAT specify that decisions are made "in accordance with Qur'anic Injunctions and Prophetic Practice as determined by the recognized Schools of Islamic Sacred Law"; and "In arriving at its decision, the Tribunal shall take into account the Laws of England and Wales and the Recognized Schools of Islamic Sacred Law."[119] Their rules specify procedures consistent with the Arbitration Act of 1996 (posted on their page), and provide for notice of hearings, right to be represented, an opportunity to be heard, and other standard arbitration requirements. Each tribunal must consist of a scholar of Islamic law as well as a qualified Solicitor or

---

[114] Konstantinos Tsitselikis, "The Legal Status of Islam in Greece," 44 Die Welt des Islams 402, 414–19 (2004).

[115] Berger, *supra* note 107, at 246–48.

[116] Rowan Williams, "Civil and Religious Law in England: A Religious Perspective," 10 Ecclesiastical Law Journal 262 (2008).

[117] Broyde, *supra* note 100, at 176.

[118] See Samia Bano, "In Pursuit of Religious and Legal Diversity: A Response to the Archbishop of Canterbury and the 'Sharia Debate' in Britain," 10 Ecclesiastical Law Journal 283, 299 (2008). A critical study of Sharia councils is Elham Manea, Women and Sharia'a Law: The Impact of Legal Pluralism in the UK (London: Taurus 2016).

[119] 1(1) and 8(2), Procedure Rules of Muslim Arbitration Tribunals, http://www.matribunal.com/rules.php

Barrister of England or Wales. These tribunals look to Islamic jurisprudence as well as "the juridical and practical realities of life in England."[120]

Public opposition to recognition of Sharia by Western state legal systems has been vociferous, along with less vehement opposition to recognition of Jewish law. Criticisms fall into two basic categories: both bodies of religious law are unfair or oppressive to women; and the monist argument that a uniform system of law should apply to everyone in society.[121] Both religions grant men the right to divorce but not women. Under Jewish law, the husband must grant a *get* for his wife to be divorced—and he can prevent his wife from remarrying by withholding the *get*. Under Islamic law, the husband ends a marriage by uttering a divorce formula called *talaq*.[122] Husbands thus have substantial leverage over their wives, controlling whether they can divorce and remarry as well as affecting the status of their ex-wife's future children. Moreover, Muslim wives who obtain a civil divorce but not a religious one, and remarry civilly, risk being prosecuted for criminal adultery if they travel to an Islamic country (when the estranged ex-husband lodges a complaint). These requirements, needless to say, are inconsistent with divorce and equal rights laws in liberal democratic societies as well as human rights norms on the equality of women. The situation is further complicated because over half of Muslim marriages in the United Kingdom are not registered as civil marriages.[123] A Muslim marriage (*nikah*) can take place at private homes or mosques. Unless they also undergo a civil marriage, however, under state law they are not legally married.

These are parlous situations for women. Jewish and Muslim women have the right to go to state courts to dissolve a civil marriage, but this would not dissolve their religious marriage. They are able to engage in forum shopping among religious courts because multiple tribunals exist and there is no unified hierarchy, and studies have found that parties select courts they believe will be favorable; they can even bring a case before a second tribunal if unsatisfied with the results at the first.[124] Judges in these tribunals, well aware

---

[120] John R. Bowen, "How Could English Courts Recognize Shariah?," 7 University of St. Thomas Law Journal 411, 422 (2010).

[121] An account of the objections is in Broyde, *supra* note 100, at Chapter 9.

[122] Bowen, *supra* note 120, at 414.

[123] See Gillian Douglas, Norman Doe, Sophie Gilliat-Ray, Russel Sandberg, and Asma Khan, "The Role of Religious Tribunals in Regulating Marriage and Divorce," 24 Child & Family Law Quarterly 139 (2012).

[124] See Russel Sandberg, Gillian Douglas, Norman Doe, Sophie Gilliat-Ray, Russell Sandberg, and Asma Khan, "Britain's Religious Tribunals: Joint Governance in Practice," 33 Oxford Journal of Legal Studies 263, 287 (2013).

of the tension with surrounding societal norms and state legal systems, have made efforts to help wives avoid untenable positions. The Orthodox Jewish community in the United Kingdom successfully sought a provision in the Divorce (Religious Marriages) Act 2002 that delayed the granting of the civil divorce until the husband granted the *get*.[125] The Rabbinical Council of America issued a Resolution in 2015, endorsed by Beth Din America, advocating the use of prenuptial agreements to contractually assure that "the *beit din* will have the proper authority to ensure that the get is not used as a bargaining chip."[126] Sharia Tribunals in the United Kingdom have granted divorces notwithstanding the husband's refusal to utter the *talaq* in cases where a civil divorce has already been obtained.[127] And Dutch courts have entertained torts claims by women against husbands who refuse to grant a divorce when they live separately.[128] Jewish and Muslim women in the West have led movements for equal treatment of women, advocating reforms through state law as well as within religious law.[129] These various actions involve multi-sided strategies to improve the position of wives; some pit the state legal system against religious tribunals while in other instances the two systems work together.

Muslim women express ambivalent attitudes toward Sharia councils.[130] Over 90 percent of the cases are brought to Sharia councils by women (men can divorce unilaterally through declaration of *talaq* so they do not need a decision).[131] Some of the women are committed to Islam and want to obtain a religious divorce, while others only have a religious marriage, without a corresponding civil marriage, so this is their only means of obtaining a divorce. Judges in Sharia councils are almost exclusively men who tend to urge reconciliation, including for women with physically abusive husbands. A study in the United Kingdom found, "Many women reported that they were expected to be reconciled with their husbands and were encouraged to be more understanding of their husband's limitations because women were presented as nurturers of the Muslim family and more open to compromise."[132] A woman

---

[125] Douglas et al., *supra* note 123, at 152.

[126] Benhalim, *supra* note 102, at 791.

[127] Douglas et al., *supra* note 123, at 153.

[128] Berger, *supra* note 107, at 271–72.

[129] For examples, see KARAMAH: Muslim Women Lawyers for Human Rights, https://karamah.org/; Women Living Under Muslim Laws, Channel Foundation: Supporting Women's Rights Around the Globe, https://www.channelfoundation.org/grants/wluml/; Benhalim, *supra* note 102, at 781–82.

[130] See Bano, *supra* note 118.

[131] See Executive Summary, Independent Review into the Application of Sharia Law in England and Wales (2018) 5.

[132] Bano, *supra* note 118, at 303.

who told the Imam she wanted a divorce because her husband was violent was asked, "Oh, how violent was that? Because in Islam a man is allowed to beat his wife!"[133] Not only do traditionalist views of the role of women predominate, but some husbands used the proceedings to negotiate on other matters like child custody and financial settlements, matters that state law requires be resolved by state courts.[134] Women's rights activists, furthermore, have expressed concerns that Sharia councils might condone child brides, forced marriage, marital rape, domestic abuse, polygamy, and other violations of women's rights.[135] A recent UK government report on Sharia councils vaguely asserted that "there is evidence that the rights and freedoms of some women are indeed infringed in some proceedings by some councils," though it provided no details.[136]

Two further points should be made in connection with the controversy over Sharia and women's rights. First, UK law already makes a number of exemptions from generally applicable laws for religious reasons not specific to Sharia, for example: not requiring doctors to participate in abortions if they have religious objections; allowing facilities to restrict men or women from a location or service on religious grounds; allowing sex discrimination in employment if a religion dictates that the position must be done by a particular gender; permitting different treatment on sexual orientation grounds when religiously motivated; and more.[137] Second, other legal accommodations to Sharia unrelated to women or gender have not raised objections. In particular, Sharia principles prohibit the charging or paying of interest on loans, so special regulations and laws have been issued for Islamic banks and insurance companies, and for banks issuing mortgages for Muslim home purchasers, to conduct transactions in ways that comply with Sharia strictures.[138] Islamic legal authorities and Islamic banks, on their end, have made efforts to construe transactions in ways that conform to Islamic and Western legal requirements on financial issues.[139]

---

[133] *Id.* at 303.

[134] *Id.* at 303.

[135] See Executive Summary, *supra* note 131, Annex C, Letter Received from Women's Rights Groups.

[136] *Id.* at 9.

[137] See Dominic McGoldrick, "Accommodating Muslims in Europe: From Adopting Sharia Law to Religiously Based Opt Outs from Generally Applicable Laws," 9 Human Rights Law Review 603, 631 (2009).

[138] *Id.* at 631.

[139] An informative description is Nima Mersadi Tabari, "Islamic Finance and the Modern World: The Legal Principles Governing Islamic Finance in International Trade," 31 Company Lawyer 249 (2010).

A European based group of Islamic jurists issued a *fatwa*—a legal opinion drawing on Islamic legal teachings—in 1999 that allows Muslims to enter into mortgages on the grounds that housing is a necessity and ownership is an important way to improve their lives and financial condition; they also recognized that many Muslims had already been obtaining mortgages out of necessity, and the ruling helped ease their qualms.[140] A poll of Muslims taken a few years thereafter found that 65 percent had paid interest on mortgages,[141] many of which undoubtedly predated the *fatwa*.

The second main objection to state recognition of Islamic law comes from people who believe that there should be one uniform system of law for everyone. This is monistic state law advocated under the mantle "One Law for All."[142] Archbishop Williams acknowledged the objection "that the law is the law; that everyone stand before the public tribunal on exactly equal terms, so that recognition of corporate identities or, more seriously, of supplementary jurisdictions is simply incoherent if we want to preserve the great political advances of Western legality."[143] He responded that the monist image of law fails to take account of the reality in multicultural societies that people have multiple affiliations, and religious communities provide foundational meaning in people's lives.[144] He also emphasized that state law establishes basic liberties that everyone in society is entitled to, although a person can choose to forgo this:

> [T]he criterion for recognizing and collaborating with communal religious discipline should be connected with whether a communal jurisdiction actively interferes with liberties guaranteed by the wider society in such a way as definitively to block access to the exercise of those liberties; clearly, the refusal of a religious believer to act upon the legal recognition of a right is not, given the plural character of society, a denial to anyone inside or outside the community of access to that right.[145]

---

[140] Alexandre Caeiro, "The Social Construction of Sharia: Bank Interest, Home Purchase, and Islamic Norms in the West," 44 Die Welt des Islams 351, 369–70 (2004).

[141] McGoldrick, *supra* note 137, at 619.

[142] See Dennis MacEoin, Sharia Law or "One Law for All? Civitas: Institute for the Study of Civil Society (Trowbridge: Cromwell Press 2009).

[143] Williams, *supra* note 116, at 270.

[144] *Id.* at 271–73.

[145] *Id.* at 273.

Williams also pointed out that British law already provides limited accommodations for Orthodox Jewish and Roman Catholic legal practices, so his argument merely extends the same treatment to Muslims.[146]

The debate over the treatment of Sharia in Western legal systems continues, with potential implications for Beth Din and other institutions of religious law. Efforts have been made on both sides at mutual accommodations. Ultimately, however, *both* state law and religious law assert that *their* law is *binding* and *superior*. The direct clash is evident in a *fatwa* on divorce issued by the Islamic Council of Europe:

> In conclusion, I would like to affirm that the divorce issued by the civil court in response to the wife's request *is neither a valid divorce nor legitimate marriage dissolution*. This means that such a wife remains a wife and is not free to marry another man. Marrying another man while the original marriage is still in place is *a violation of Islamic law and a crime*. What is more dangerous than this is the fact that all children she gives birth to before obtaining a proper marriage dissolution may be considered to be of the first husband from whom she assumed she had been divorced. Wives who face intolerable situations may seek marriage dissolution by a recognized body that is known and accepted in acting as a judiciary body for Muslims.[147]

This is not a unique stance. Analogous assertions are made by the Roman Catholic Church and Orthodox Judaism. State law asserts a parallel position on the opposite side. In February 2020, a British Court of Appeal ruled that a *nikah* marriage is a "non-marriage" under state law, so no legally cognizable marital rights attach to Islamic marriages.[148]

Thus Islamic law does not recognize the validity of state law marriages and divorces, while state law does not recognize the validity of Islamic law marriages and divorces. A person subject to both forms of law—a citizen of the state and a member of the *Ummah*—lives with and navigates legal pluralism. State legal officials might insist that the official state legal system

---

146 *Id.* at 279–80.

147 Shaykh Haitham Al-Haddad, "Fatwa: A Civil Divorce is Not a Valid Islamic Divorce," The Islamic Council of Europe, https://iceurope.org/fatwa-a-civil-divorce-is-not-a-valid-islamic-divorce/ (emphasis added).

148 Harriet Sherwood, "Islamic Faith Marriages not Valid in English Law, Appeal Court Rules," February 14, 2020, The Guardian, https://www.theguardian.com/world/2020/feb/14/islamic-faith-marriages-not-valid-in-english-law-appeal-court-rules

controls, so the views of adherents about their own law does not matter, but community-based adherence to Islamic law says otherwise.

Adherence to religious law is a complex matter involving individual, familial, community, and political factors. A 2007 poll of Muslims in the United Kingdom responded to the statement, "If I could choose, I would prefer to live in Britain under sharia law rather than British law." Responses varied by age: 75 percent of respondents over the age of 45 preferred British law, whereas about 50 percent of the respondents between 16 and 34 preferred British law.[149] The older generation, perhaps surprisingly, also proportionally expressed greater tolerance than the younger generation toward Muslim women marrying non-Muslims, marrying without consent of their guardian, and homosexuality. Thus younger people, those more likely to have grown up in Britain, tended to be more supportive of living under strict versions of Sharia than did older generations. Compare these results with an extensive poll conducted in 2013 in thirty-nine countries across Eastern Europe, Africa, and South Asia, nearly all with Muslim majorities.[150] Support for Sharia to be enforced as state law varies across countries from highs above 90 percent (Iran and Afghanistan) to lows of 12 percent and below (Albania, Turkey, Kazakhstan, Azerbaijan). In the few countries where support for Sharia as state enforced law varied by age—"older Muslims tend to favor enshrining sharia as the law of the land more than younger Muslims do."[151] Additionally, substantial majorities of Muslims in Southern and Eastern Europe (86 percent) and Central Asia (70 percent) believe women should have a right to initiate divorce, more than double the percentage in the Middle East, North Africa (33 percent), and Southeast Asia (32 percent).

A wide range of views, from progressive to traditionalist, evidently exists among Muslims about whether Sharia should be enforced as state law as well as the content of Sharia law. Attitudes toward Sharia and state law depend on the total mix of surrounding cultural, economic, religious, political, and legal circumstances. A significant proportion of Muslims in the West have developed cosmopolitan forms of Islam influenced by Western attitudes and conditions[152] (just as manifestations of Islamic law vary around the world

[149] Munira Mirza, Abi Senthilkumaran, and Zein Ja'far, Living Apart Together: British Muslims and the Paradox of Multiculturalism (London: Policy Exchange 2007) 46–47, https://policyexchange.org.uk/wp-content/uploads/2016/09/living-apart-together-jan-07.pdf

[150] See "The World's Muslims: Religion, Politics and Society," April 30, 2013, Pew Research Center, https://www.pewforum.org/2013/04/30/the-worlds-muslims-religion-politics-society-overview/

[151] Id.

[152] See Muslims for Progressive Values, https://www.mpvusa.org/

owing to surrounding influences); another segment of Muslims in the West prefer traditionalist interpretations of Islamic law.[153] Younger generations express attitudes that recognize both Islamic law and state law, making this pluralism a part of their identities.[154]

Community Law and Territorial State Law

The Western legal systems covered in this chapter have highly developed institutionalized systems that claim a monopoly over the territory. Yet as we have seen in this chapter significant forms of community law continue to thrive. A jurist might insist that these forms of law exist today only by leave of, and on the terms set by, the state legal system—evident in the state law enforcement of rabbinical court decisions not as "law" but as "arbitration." This position is convincing only if one assumes that state law dictates reality by virtue of its own fiat. Consider, on the other side, that all of the forms of community law discussed in this chapter have existed in one form or another for a thousand years or more prior to and alongside state law. They are likely to continue as long as these communities live in accordance with their own forms of law. If that is correct, the price to pay for achieving the monist ideal might be the extinguishment of or full conformity of all community law to regime law. What this suggests is that state law monism—the assertion of exclusive, uniform, supreme law in the state—has a potential affinity with totalitarianism.

[153] A 2017 poll of American Muslims found that 52 percent believe Islamic law should be reinterpreted consistent with modern conditions, compared to 38 percent who preferred traditional understandings. See "U.S. Muslims Concerned about Their Place in Society," *supra* note 108.
[154] See Mathias Rohe, "Sharia and the Muslim Diaspora," in Peri Bearman, ed., *The Ashgate Research Companion to Islamic Law* (Aldershot: Ashgate 2014) 261–76.

Four

National to Transnational Legal Pluralism

The latest wave of legal pluralist studies goes under the labels global or transnational legal pluralism (used interchangeably), written by comparative law, international law, and transnational law scholars.[1] This work focuses on legal-regulatory phenomena that extend beyond nation-states. A thickening profusion of international and transnational law and regulation (public, private, hybrid) exists to address cross-border matters like commerce in goods and services, migration, money flows and banking, pollution control and environmental regulation, shipping and air travel, telecommunications and the internet, terrorism, global health threats like pandemics, illicit drug trade, intellectual property protection, and more. There has also been a growth in transnational organizations with legal functions, including the United Nations, European Union, World Trade Organization, and many more. And internationally generated legal regimes, like human rights law or the UN Declaration of the Rights of Indigenous Peoples, have increasingly penetrated local settings. Global legal pluralist theorists assert that what they identify "closely resembles" the legal pluralism discussed decades ago by legal anthropologists.[2] These developments, as I show in this Chapter, are best understood in terms of the modern proliferation of law and regulation at every level.

The primary focus of this chapter is on official forms of law and regulation (shading into private regulation) at local, regional, national, transnational, and international levels. I start with pluralism internal to the US legal system, then move to constitutional pluralism in the European Union, and finally to global legal pluralism. As with previous chapters, the discussion reveals rich legal pluralism inconsistent with the image of the monist law state. To replace this image, I offer a descriptive account of official forms of law as innumerable distributed institutions exercising different functions with various connections and disconnections to other political and legal institutions,

---

[1] Paul Schiff Berman, "The New Legal Pluralism," 5 Annual Review of Law and Social Sciences 225 (2009).

[2] Ralf Michaels, "Global Legal Pluralism," 5 Annual Review of Law and Social Sciences 243, 244 (2009).

Legal Pluralism Explained. Brian Z. Tamanaha, Oxford University Press (2021). © Brian Z. Tamanaha.
DOI: 10.1093/oso/9780190861551.003.0005

which do not constitute a unified, hierarchically organized (monistic) whole. Unlike previous chapters, which have been largely descriptive, the latter part of this chapter, when discussing global legal pluralism, will be analytical and critical as well, the first encounter in this book with theories of legal pluralism.

Legal Pluralism in the United States Legal System

American jurists commonly assert that the United States is a system of dual sovereignty. Dual sovereignty (or "dual federalism") is "the concept that state and national governments enjoy exclusive and non-overlapping spheres of authority."[3] (Accounts of dual sovereignty typically omit mention of Native American tribes, reflecting their marginality in the minds of American jurists.) Prominent federal judge Jack Weinstein expressed this understanding: "The coexistence of state and federal systems accords each person the benefits of dual citizenship while subjecting all individuals to two sovereignties. This dichotomy becomes particularly striking when considering the state and federal courts, two independent systems whose interplay often perplexes the citizen as well as the theorist visualizing the law as an integrated whole."[4] "Visualizing the law as an integrated whole," as Weinstein put it, is the monist image jurists project on state law, a widely shared implicit faith that law in the United States comprises a unified, hierarchical arrangement.

A leading case on dual federalism by the Supreme Court declared that the Constitution "recognizes and preserves the autonomy and independence of the States, independence in their legislative and independence in their judicial departments. . . . Any interference with either, except as thus permitted [authorized or delegated to the national government by the Constitution], is an invasion of the authority of the State and, to that extent, a denial of its independence."[5] States manage health, safety, and welfare, which includes crimes, family and inheritance law, tort law, property law, contracts and commercial law, corporations, sanitation, safety regulations, education, and much more. The laws of the fifty states vary significantly from one another as well as from the federal government. Although the federal legal system looms large in the

---

[3] Robert A. Schapiro, "Toward a Theory of Interactive Federalism," 91 Iowa Law Review 243, 246 (2005).

[4] Jack B. Weinstein, "Coordination of State and Federal Judicial Systems," 57 St. John's Law Review 1, 1 (1982).

[5] Erie R.R. Co. v Tompkins, 304 U.S. 64, 78–79 (1938).

minds of many observers, in excess of 99 percent of cases are filed in state courts. The federal government manages activities with consequences across state lines, especially commerce, everything related to the functions of the federal government and its agencies, and international affairs. Legal doctrine builds on this basic division of authority, with a substantial and contested amount of overlap. "The federal governments and states have extensive areas of concurrent authority. In many realms, from narcotics trafficking to securities trading to education, federal and state laws regulate the very same conduct."[6]

An immense volume of law exists within the United States:

There are more than 89,000 separate governmental units operating in the United States. Beneath the national government and 50 state governments, 3,033 counties, 19,492 municipal governments, 16,519 town or township governments, 37,381 special district governments. . . . Within the national government itself, the division, separation, and distribution of power can be overwhelming. The legislative branch includes 2 houses, 435 congressional districts, and more than 200 committees and subcommittees. The judicial branch encompasses 94 separate federal judicial districts as well as a host of special courts. The executive bureaucracy reaches across 15 separate departments and more than 137 federal agencies and commissions that in 2006 alone printed almost 80,000 pages of proposed rules, regulations, and orders in the Federal Register.[7]

Law is thus produced and utilized at countless sites, from local to regional to national. The monist state law image projects that this coheres in a unified, hierarchical, "integrated whole."

As a descriptive account of US law, the monist law image is patently false. What exists is a vast array of legal institutions—creating, enforcing, and applying law—in innumerable settings tied to specific functions that are not all directly or indirectly connected to an overarching whole. These are widely distributed, decentralized institutions, each with its own legal purposes, powers, obligations, and hierarchies of authority, with its own material and financial resources, often with interests and concerns that conflict with other

---

[6] *Id.* at 246.

[7] William J. Novak, "The Myth of the 'Weak' American State," 113 American Historical Review 752, 765 (2008).

legal authorities, loosely connected, if at all, at certain points of intersection or coordination.

It functions in the aggregate, with each legal entity handling its designated tasks. But situations regularly arise that expose disjunctions. For example, police, judges, and prosecutors carry out legal activities that link together in the enforcement and application of law, but they also have different incentives and responsibilities that regularly set them at odds (sometimes checking, ignoring, or undermining actions of the others). A multitude of clashes occurred between government officials with legal powers at all levels during the COVID-19 pandemic, including clashes between governors and mayors over authority and legality of lockdowns and face mask ordinances; a number of sheriffs vocally refused to enforce masking ordinances (considering them unconstitutional infringements on liberty). City and state officials sharply opposed the deployment of federal law enforcement officers in cities by the Trump Administration in response to Black Lives Matter demonstrations. New York law enforcement officials continued to investigate President Donald Trump and his financial organizations for various criminal activities over the opposition of the US Department of Justice. These are just a few recent examples. The belief that law in the United States is a unified legal system requires a large leap of faith.

The pillar of this faith is the Supremacy Clause of the Constitution: "This Constitution, and the Laws of the United States which shall be made in Pursuance thereof; and all Treaties made, or which shall be made, under the Authority of the United States, shall be the supreme Law of the Land; and the Judges in every State shall be bound thereby, any Thing in the Constitution or Laws of any State to the Contrary notwithstanding."[8]

The Supremacy Clause in itself, however, does not create a unified system. A unified legal system requires a legally articulated arrangement that organizes respective realms of legal authority and a judicial system that operates across state and federal lines that ensures uniform and consistent results. Under monistic state law, unitary states, and federations and confederations with degrees of autonomy at lower levels, are organized in a coherent and consistent manner, at least in theory, with clear and consistent legal arrangements that tie everything together in a unified hierarchical arrangement. By that standard the United States does not have a unified legal system. An example that affects millions of people is that eleven states and

---

[8] Article VI, United States Constitution.

the District of Columbia (a federal enclave) have legalized the possession of marijuana, which is a crime under federal law punishable by a fine of $1,000 and up to a year in prison. A person can legally consume marijuana under state law but be sentenced to jail under federal law.

Two characteristic signs of legal pluralism, highlighted in previous chapters, are forum shopping by parties seeking favorable outcomes and competition among coexisting courts for business and authority. Forum shopping is common in the US legal system. Parties can choose from among different courts within a single state; they can choose which state (among fifty states) to bring a claim; they can choose whether to file their claim in a state or federal court; and they can choose which federal district court to file their claim in.[9] The appropriate forum for a case depends on subject matter (subject matter jurisdiction), contacts parties have with the location of a forum (personal jurisdiction), and considerations of convenience for parties and witnesses (venue). State courts generally can hear both state and federal claims, although federal courts have exclusive jurisdiction in bankruptcy, patent infringement, immigration, admiralty, and other matters; federal courts can hear state claims under diversity jurisdiction when parties are from different states and the amount in controversy exceeds 75,000 dollars.

Thus a significant overlap exists in the types of cases heard by state and federal courts. Since federal courts hearing state claims apply the law of the state in which they are sitting, the US District Court in St. Louis, Missouri, for example, may apply a different law to a case than the US District Court in East St. Louis, Illinois, across the Mississippi River a few miles away. These respective district courts are also in different federal appellate circuits, which can diverge on interpretations of federal law (discussed shortly). When an issue under state law has not been resolved by the state high court, the federal judge must determine how state courts are likely to rule, which on multiple instances state courts subsequently decided otherwise. State courts applying federal law, meanwhile, have asserted that they are not bound by interpretations of federal law by lower federal courts (beneath the US Supreme Court), thereby creating different interpretations of federal law between state and federal courts.[10] Savvy litigators consider these differences in laws and interpretations when deciding in which court to file a lawsuit.

<hr>

[9] See Debra Lyn Bassett, "The Forum Game," 84 North Carolina Law Review 333 (2006); Mary Garvey Algero, "In Defense of Forum Shopping: A Realistic Look at Selecting a Venue," 78 Nebraska Law Review 79 (1999).

[10] Amanda Frost, "Inferiority Complex: Should State Courts Follow Lower Federal Court Precedent on the Meaning of Federal Law," 68 Vanderbilt Law Review 53 (2015).

A major motivation behind forum shopping is the perception that certain states and certain federal districts are conservative or liberal along various lines: pro-defendant or pro-plaintiff, pro-government, pro-civil liberties, pro-business or pro-labor, and so forth. This perception is based on legislation, prevailing legal doctrines, court procedures, and on the perceived ideological attitudes of judges—which can affect the outcomes of cases.

States have created "a kind of competitive market for law," observes legal historian Lawrence Friedman.[11] This competition revolves around the substantive laws and regulations as well as the courts that apply them. "A core feature of U.S. corporate law is regulatory competition. Companies can choose which state's corporate law will govern their affairs and states vie—to some extent—to attract companies to incorporate."[12] By crafting business- and tax-friendly corporate laws, and creating a special chancery court to hear corporate actions staffed by judges who have created flexible standards, Delaware became favored by large companies, with roughly 60 percent of all public companies incorporated in that state, along with a disproportionate number of corporate cases.[13] Forum shopping in torts claims is also common. States courts in small districts in Illinois and Missouri in the 1990s and 2000s attracted a disproportionate number of mass torts and class actions cases owing to a perceived pro-plaintiff bent.[14] Congress passed a law directing large class actions to federal court,[15] and the Supreme Court has tightened the law on personal jurisdiction in mass torts cases,[16] though forum shopping in torts cases continues. The American Tort Reform Foundation—funded by major corporations—publishes an annual list of "judicial hellholes" that serve as "magnet jurisdictions" through plaintiff-friendly laws and judicial decisions attracting products liability and other torts suits against corporations.[17]

Even when the same federal law is applied in federal district courts, individual courts entice litigants through attractive procedures and rulings.

---

[11] Lawrence M. Friedman, *American Law in the 20th Century* (New Haven, CT: Yale University Press 2002) 596.

[12] See John Armour, Bernard Black, and Brian Cheffins, "Delaware's Balancing Act," 87 Indiana Law Journal 1345, 1345 (2012). The number of cases filed in Delaware has been dropping in recent years, while the number of incorporations remains high.

[13] *Id.* at 1348–50.

[14] *Id.* at 286–91.

[15] Class Action Fairness Act of 2005, Public Law No. 109-2, 119 Stat. 4 (2005).

[16] See Bristol-Myers Squibb Co. v. Superior Court of California, 137 S. Ct. 1773 (2017).

[17] See American Tort Reform Foundation, Judicial Hellholes 2019/2020, https://www.judicialhellholes.org/wp-content/uploads/2019/12/ATRA_JH19_layout_FINAL.pdf

Among ninety-four federal district courts, the Eastern District of Texas presided "over a quarter of all patent infringement suits in 2014 and almost one-half in the first part of 2015 . . . in spite of the fact that this district is home to no major cities or technology firms."[18] The District of Delaware also has a disproportionate share of patent cases, which comprise over half of the filings in that court. A study found that "forum shopping in patent law is driven, at least in part, by federal district courts competing for litigants," attracting cases through procedural and administrative norms and practices preferred by plaintiffs.[19] Another study concluded that "there is little doubt that forum shopping occurs in bankruptcy."[20] The choice of where to file a federal claim may also take into account whether the federal judicial circuit that hears the appeal is perceived as liberal or conservative.[21] The Center for Individual Rights brought its successful challenge of affirmative action in the Fifth Circuit, known to have a bevy of conservative judges.[22] Significant variations exist in the interpretation of federal law among federal appellate circuits, called circuit splits, which can remain unresolved for decades,[23] contributing to forum shopping as parties seek favorable doctrines and courts.[24]

Legal pluralism within the US legal system is structural—fifty state legal systems from which to choose, plus the federal legal system, plus Native American tribes. But a deeper source of this pluralism are background cultural, economic, and political differences across the country: blue state/red state, urban/rural, secular/religious (Evangelical, Catholic, Jewish, Islamic, etc.), and ethnic (White/Black/Latino/Asian/Native American). Legal pluralism, preceding chapters have shown, is the product of heterogeneity within society that gives rise to differences within the law.[25] The heterogeneity of US

<hr>

[18] Daniel Kerman and Greg Reilly, "Forum Selling," 89 Southern California Law Review 241, 246 (2016).

[19] J. Jonas Anderson, "Court Competition for Patent Cases," 163 University of Pennsylvania Law Review 631, 634–65 (2015).

[20] Todd J. Zywicki, "Is Forum Shopping Corrupting America's Bankruptcy Courts?," 94 Georgetown Law Journal 1141, 1160 (2006). Forum shopping in bankruptcy is demonstrated in Lynn M. LoPucki, *Courting Failure: How Competition for Big Cases Is Corrupting the Bankruptcy Courts* (Ann Arbor: University of Michigan Press 2005); Samir D. Parikh, "Modern Forum Shopping in Bankruptcy," 46 Connecticut Law Review 159 (2013).

[21] See Andreas Broscheid, "Comparing Circuity: Are Some U.S. Courts of Appeals More Liberal or Conservative Than Others?," 45 Law & Society Review 171 (2011).

[22] See Hopwood v. Texas, 78 F.3rd 932 (5th Cir. 1996), cert. denied, 518 US 1033 (1996).

[23] See Amanda Frost, "Overvaluing Uniformity," 94 Virginia Law Review 1567 (2008).

[24] Wayne A. Logan, "Constitutional Cacophony: Federal Circuit Splits and the Fourth Amendment," 65 Vanderbilt Law Review 1137, 1183–85 (2012).

[25] Margaret Davies emphasizes legal pluralism of legal doctrine within highly developed legal systems. Margaret Davies, "Pluralism and Legal Philosophy," 57 Northern Ireland Legal Quarterly 577 (2006).

society is manifested in multiple streams of legal doctrine, different legislation, and judges with different attitudes, which results in an internally pluralistic legal system.

Two additional factors render it practically impossible to wrap all the law in the United States together within a consistent, unifying umbrella of hierarchical legal arrangements under the Supremacy Clause. First, state legislatures and high courts have final say on all matters of state law that do not infringe on the US Constitution or federal laws. Consequently, by grounding their decision in an interpretation of state law, state courts can issue directly contrary decisions on the same point of law as federal courts. A recent instance with immense political significance involves gerrymandering—the practice of surgically crafting voting districts to maximize the votes of the party in power, taken to extreme lengths in recent decades, particularly by Republican legislators. (State legislatures draw voting districts for state and federal elections.) In the 2018 election in Wisconsin, for example, although Republicans received only 49 percent of the vote, they secured 63 of 99 seats in the State House legislature.[26] In a 2019 case challenging the legality of gerrymandering in North Carolina, the US Supreme Court denied federal courts the power to invalidate state voting districts on the grounds that there is no way to determine how much gerrymandering is too much.[27] (Republican drawn voting districts resulted in 10 of 13 State House seats going to Republicans although candidates for the two parties received almost equal votes.) On the very same issue, a few months later, a state court in North Carolina came to the opposite conclusion, invalidating the Republican drawn voting map on the grounds that excessive gerrymandering violates the state Constitution's equal protection and free speech clauses (language also in the US Constitution), and its free election clause.[28] The Supreme Court of Pennsylvania likewise struck gerrymandered voting districts in a similar ruling. Tribal courts, it bears adding, are not bound by federal court precedent when interpreting the Indian Civil Rights Act applicable to Indian tribes, although the language is similar to the Bill of Rights of the US

[26] Craig Gilbert, "New Election Data Highlights the Ongoing Impact of 2011 GOP Redistricting in Wisconsin," December 6, 2018, Milwaukee Journal Sentinel, https://www.jsonline.com/story/news/blogs/wisconsin-voter/2018/12/06/wisconsin-gerrymandering-data-shows-stark-impact-redistricting/2219092002/

[27] Rucho et al. v. Common Cause, 139 S. Ct. 2484 (2019).

[28] See Michael Li, Thomas Wolf, and Annie Lo, "The State of Redistricting Litigation," May 14, 2020, Brennan Center for Justice, https://www.brennancenter.org/our-work/research-reports/state-redistricting-litigation

Constitution. The power of state legislatures and courts and Native American tribal legislatures and courts to have final say on their own law renders legal pluralism irreducible.

The second more fundamental reason legal pluralism within the US legal system cannot be construed away through the Supremacy Clause is that an overarching unified system requires clear rules on the allocation of respective *powers* between the state and federal governments, as well as a clear specification of the respective *jurisdiction* of courts—neither of which exists. The main difficulty in the respective allocation of state and federal powers lies with the Commerce Clause in the US Constitution, which authorizes Congress to "regulate commerce with foreign nations, and among the several states, and with the Indian tribes."[29] Based on this Clause, Congress has enacted volumes of legislation on matters that fall squarely within state powers. The problem is that the meaning of the Commerce Clause has changed a great deal over time, and continues to change unpredictably in connection with the views of a majority of Justices at a given time on the issue at hand, rendering the extent of federal power unclear and subject to shifting lines. For example, the Supreme Court held Congress does not have the power to enact a law that prohibits guns in schools because that does not involve commerce between states;[30] a decade later, the Court held that Congress has the power to criminalize homegrown marijuana cultivation intended by the grower solely for personal medicinal consumption (legal in California) because it potentially implicates commerce between states;[31] a half dozen years thereafter, when evaluating the validity of the Affordable Care Act, the Court held that Congress does not have the power under the Commerce Clause to mandate people to buy health insurance, although health insurance is a national market.[32] If the scope of national power vis-à-vis states is unclear and perpetually subject to change, their respective legal authority cannot be coherently articulated within an overarching scheme.

A clear set of jurisdictional rules necessary to ensure that cases are funneled to courts in order to produce a coherent overarching legal arrangement is also lacking. Jurisdictional rules allocate authority to hear cases between state courts, between state and federal courts, among federal courts, and between courts and administrative agencies. For decades scholars have decried

---

[29] Article I, Section 8, Clause 3, US Constitution.
[30] United States v. Lopez, 514 U.S. 549 (1995).
[31] Gonzales v. Raich, 545 U.S. 1 (2005).
[32] NFIB v. Sebelius, 567 U.S. 519 (2012).

the confusing state of jurisdiction doctrines. A legal scholar observed in 1981, "In many cases . . . federal jurisdictional rules are extremely unclear. They are also extremely complex."[33] Three decades later another scholar declared: "jurisdictional doctrine is riddled with uncertainty and complexity."[34] A number of the central tests for jurisdiction (arising under federal law, finality of decision, standing, domicile, minimum contacts, etc.) involve vague standards or rules with multiple exceptions, and courts can exercise discretion to decline jurisdiction even when it does exist (abstention). Adding to the uncertainty and complexity, beyond legal technicalities, the policies behind the allocation of jurisdiction are several and not entirely clear or mutually consistent. These policies include respecting state legal authority and courts, protecting out-of-state parties from biased state courts, maintaining comity between state and federal authorities, maintaining uniform interpretations of federal law, not overburdening federal courts, preventing duplication of efforts, ensuring that the correct party brings a claim in a forum with a connection to the action. Cases arise in which these policies conflict—as when respect for state courts comes up against consistent interpretations of federal law—with no preestablished hierarchy or balance.[35] As a result of these factors, although court jurisdiction is straightforward in run-of-the-mill cases, cases regularly arise where it is unclear and uncertain. (Conflicts of law and choice of law issues add further layers of complexity and uncertainty, which cannot be addressed here.)

Another source of legal pluralism is that various legal officials assert their own power to interpret law. Jurists typically assume courts have final say, but that assumption is neither necessary nor assured. Various officials at local, state, and federal levels press their own views of the constitution and laws, which they may maintain in the face of contrary court interpretations, producing legal pluralism among different legal officials with significant consequences.[36]

The manifold pluralisms that run through law in the United States along multiple axes challenge the image of the monist law state. A defender of

---

[33] Martha Field, "The Uncertain Nature of Federal Jurisdiction," 22 William & Mary Law Review 683, 684 (1981).

[34] Scott Dodson, "The Complexity of Jurisdictional Clarity, 97 Virginia Law Review 1, 13 (2011)

[35] *Id.* at 24–26.

[36] See Daniel Halberstam, "Constitutional Heterarchy: The Centrality of Conflict in the European Union and the United States," in Jeffrey L. Dunhoff and Joel P. Trachtman, eds., *Ruling the World? Constitutionalism, International Law, and Global Governance* (New York: Cambridge University Press 2009) Chapter 11.

retaining this ideal might insist, in response, that it nonetheless serves as a regulative ideal to bring greater uniformity and consistency than would exist in its absence. Perhaps, the point remains that this is not a completely unified, internally consistent, hierarchical legal system. Remember that standard arguments raised on behalf of monism are the elimination of uncertainty, inconsistent law, and forum shopping—which are common in the United States.

Legal Pluralism in European Legal Systems

The legal system of the United Kingdom is also pluralistic, with legal variations in relation to England and Wales, Scotland, and Northern Ireland. For historical and political reasons, Scotland has maintained separate substantive law doctrines as well as court institutions. Heavily influenced by the civil law tradition, Scotland has distinctive private law on family law, succession, and property, as well as criminal law and procedure;[37] appeals on civil cases can be taken from Scottish courts to the recently created United Kingdom Supreme Court, but not criminal cases. Legal systems develop in patchwork ways shaped by history, culture, power, and politics, not drawn up in accordance with a tidy organized scheme.

"Many national constitutional systems are, in fact, full of legal pluralism," asserts comparative constitutional theorist Alec Stone Sweet,[38] providing examples from Germany, Spain, Italy, and France—the latter three considered unitary states. "The legal systems of each of these states can be characterized as pluralist: jurisdiction is fragmented rather than unified and final authority to determine outcomes is distributed among autonomous supreme courts that manage functionally-specialized legal domains."[39] A significant source of pluralism is that constitutional courts exist alongside ordinary courts, including high courts, generating questions about the extent to which decisions of constitutional courts are binding on other courts and legal and administrative officials, as well as about the power of ordinary courts to engage in constitutional interpretation. This involves degrees of cooperation as

[37] Neil Walker, Final Appellate Jurisdiction in the Scottish Legal System (Edinburgh: Scottish Government 2010) 18–19.

[38] Alec Stone Sweet, "Constitutionalism, Legal Pluralism, and International Regimes," 16 Indiana Journal of Global Legal Studies 621, 623 (2009).

[39] *Id.* at 634.

well as conflict and non-cooperation. The Constitutional Council in France "has no formal means of imposing its rights interpretations on the Supreme Court (Cassation) or Supreme Administrative Court."[40] Germany has experienced "resistance and a long struggle" and Italy has seen periodic eruptions of "wars of judges" between the constitutional court and other courts.[41]

Similar conflicts exist in Eastern European countries, detailed by Lech Garlicki, a former judge on the Polish Constitutional Tribunal and judge on the European Court of Human Rights. The Polish Supreme Court has taken the position that it is not bound by interpretations of the Constitutional Tribunal; the Czech Supreme Court has refused to be bound by Constitutional Court precedent; and similar conflicts have occurred in Hungary and Russia.[42] Tensions between constitutional and ordinary courts is "systemic," Garlicki asserts, owing to "the natural inclination of judges to expand the scope of their authority."[43] The very existence of coexisting courts allows people to resort to one or another, whichever they deem most favorable to their interests, pressing claims that potentially place these courts at odds.

On top of uncertainties and conflicts within coexisting national courts, the full picture of legal pluralism in European countries includes additional layers of laws and courts brought by membership in the European Union, with the Court of Justice of the European Union, and the adoption of the European Convention on Human Rights, enforced by the European Court of Human Rights.

Constitutional Pluralism of the European Union

Following the continent-wide devastation of World War II, European political leaders endeavored to tightly weave together their countries in mutually beneficial economic arrangements to reduce the likelihood of future wars. Beginning with six nations enacting the Treaty of Paris (1951) and Treaty of Rome (1957), intertwining further with the Treaty of Maastricht (1993) and

---

[40] Alec Stone Sweet, "The Structure of Constitutional Pluralism: Review of Nico Krisch, Beyond Constitutionalism: The Pluralist Structure of Post-National Law," 11 I-Con 491, 494–95 (2013).

[41] Sweet, *supra* note 38, at 634–35. A more detailed account of the conflicts in Germany and Italy is in Lech Garlicki, "Constitutional Courts versus Supreme Courts," 5 International Journal of Constitutional Law 44 (2007).

[42] Garlicki, *supra* note 41, at 57–63.

[43] *Id.* at 64.

Treaty of Lisbon (2009), today the European Union consists of twenty-seven states across Western and Eastern Europe, creating a common market of over 400 million people. It has a parliament, executive bodies (European Council, European Commission), a council of ministers, a Court of Justice, a central bank, an auditor; it has a common currency (with exceptions); it issues laws and regulations; it has external borders with internal free movement and a European Union passport, and enters treaties with other nations. These are standards markers of a sovereign state, though, as discussed shortly, everyone insists it is *not* a state.

The Court of Justice of the European Union (CJEU), the final interpreter of EU law, over time built a legal order on top of skeletal treaties, using structural features to derive a set of overarching legal principles: the supremacy of EU law over conflicting national law, direct effect of EU law, the duty of national courts to abide by and enforce EU law, the obligation of national high courts to refer unresolved questions involving EU law to the CJEU, and the ability of individuals to enforce EU rights against states as well as other individuals.[44] These legal principles, the Court held, are necessary for the functional efficacy of the EU and for uniformity in the interpretation of its law.

National courts generally acknowledge and abide by these principles, and EU law is highly effective. But there is a large caveat: "For the most part national courts have not accepted that EU law is the supreme law of the land. But nor have they simply assumed that national constitutional law is the supreme law of the land."[45] This applies not only to substantive law but also to which court has final say. Potential clashes arise in two main situations: when a national court determines that an EU law exceeds the powers delegated to the EU (ultra vires), and when national constitutional courts consider whether an EU law violates national constitutional provisions or rights. In these instances, national constitutional courts (led by the German Federal Constitutional Court) have asserted the power to make their own final determination. "[T]he acceptance of the supremacy of EU rules over national constitutional rules has not been unconditional, if not even, at times, resisted by national constitutional courts. This confers to EU a kind of contested or

---

[44] The key case was Case 106/77, Amministrazione delle Finanze dello Stato v. Simmenthal, [1978] ECR 629. For a concise description of these developments, see Julio Baquero Cruz, "Another Look at Constitutional Pluralism in the European Union," 22 European Law Journal 356, 359–60. (2016).

[45] Mathias Kumm, "How Does European Law Fit into the World of Public Law?," in Jurgen Neyer and Antje Wiener, eds., *Political Theory of the European Union* (Oxford: Oxford University Press 2011) 127.

negotiated normative authority."[46] National courts and the CJEU have made efforts to avoid direct confrontations over the issue of supremacy, though multiple clashes have occurred on significant issues.[47]

In a 2020 case, Germany's Federal Constitutional Court (GFCC) declared that it is not bound by a ruling of the Court of Justice of the European Union (CJEU) on the propriety of the European Central Bank's public sector asset-purchase program during the Great Recession.[48] EU treaty law gives CJEU exclusive power to adjudicate matters relating to the European Central Bank. Nevertheless, GFCC ruled that because the CJEU improperly applied the proportionality principle, the ruling was beyond the court's authority (ultra vires) and therefore is not binding. What makes this a direct power confrontation is that this was not a German court insisting on its authority to rule on matters of German constitutional law; rather GFCC ruled that it is not bound by a decision of the high court of the European Union on matters governed by European Union law in connection with a European institution. This reasoning traces back to the *Maastricht-Urteil* decision, issued in 1993 by the German Constitutional Court, holding that the EU has limited powers delegated by member states and does not have the competence to determine its own competence, so Germany is not bound by EU actions that extend beyond what the treaties provide for.[49] Courts in ten member states adopted some version of this position in the ensuing dozen years, subsequently joined by Hungarian and Czech judicial decisions refusing to follow particular provisions of EU law on the grounds that they are ultra vires and hence not binding.[50] European jurists have condemned the latter two decisions as bad faith acts of defiance, a departure from more typical efforts of national courts to comply with EU law absent a compelling clash with the national constitution.[51]

[46] Miguel Poiares Maduro, "Interpreting European Law: Judicial Adjudication in a Context of Constitutional Pluralism," 2 European Journal of Legal Studies 137, 137 (2007).

[47] For a list, see Neil Walker, "Constitutional Pluralism Revisited," 22 European Law Journal 333, 340 (2016).

[48] The case is described in Katharina Pistor, "Germany's Constitutional Court Goes Rogue," May 8, 2020, Project Syndicate, https://www.project-syndicate.org/commentary/german-constitutional-court-ecb-ruling-may-threaten-euro-by-katharina-pistor-2020-05

[49] See Julio Baquero Cruz, "Legacy of the Maastricht-Urteil and the Pluralist Movement," 14 European Law Journal 389, 391–94 (2008).

[50] See Julio Baquero Cruz, "Another Look at Constitutional Pluralism in the European Union," 22 European Law Journal 356, 366 n. 16 (2016).

[51] See Leonardo Pierdominici, "The Theory of EU Constitutional Pluralism: A Crisis in a Crisis?," 2 Perspectives on Federalism E-119 (2017).

An additional layer of legal pluralism within the EU is created by the European Convention on Human Rights (ECHR), enforced by the European Court of Human Rights (ECtHR), a body of the Council of Europe, which is separate from the EU. Individuals are entitled to bring claims in this court against their own nations for actions that violate the Convention. In its half century of operation, the ECtHR has issued over 22,500 decisions, 84 percent of which have found state violations of the Convention; over 40,000 new applications have been filed by individuals with the Court annually in recent years.[52] The forty-seven European states that have signed on to the Convention accord it a range of weight: from standing above domestic law, to special status, to significant but defeasible in the face of national constitutional considerations. The case law of the ECtHR is treated by national courts along a continuum, from binding to respectful consideration but non-binding dialogue.[53] Multiplying the pluralism, neither the Court of Justice of the European Union (in Luxembourg) nor the European Court of Human Rights (in Strasbourg), both of which enforce rights, albeit with differences, has accepted the superior authority of the other.[54] As a result, human rights in Europe involves a pluralism of legal doctrines and rights declarations (multiple domestic and European laws, treaties, and charters) as well as a pluralism of courts (domestic, CJEU, ECtHR).[55]

Stone Sweet summarizes the pluralistic situation:

Today one finds multiple sources of rights that are judicially enforceable against all conflicting infra-constitutional legal norms, including statutes: there are multiple high courts that enforce these rights; and often there

[52] See ECHR Overview: 1959–2019, European Court of Human Rights, Council of Europe, https://echr.coe.int/Documents/Overview_19592019_ENG.pdf; Analysis of Statistics 2019, European Court of Human Rights (January 2020), https://www.echr.coe.int/Documents/Stats_analysis_2019_ENG.pdf

[53] This is the position expressed by a Justice of the Supreme Court of the United Kingdom. See Brenda Hale, "*Argentoratum Locutum*: Is Strasbourg or the Supreme Court Supreme?," 12 Human Rights Journal 1 (2009). An informative study that compares national treatment of EU law and the ECHR, see Giuseppe Martinico, "IS the European Convention Going to be 'Supreme'? A Comparative-Constitutional Overview of ECHR and EU Law Before National Courts," 23 European Journal of International Law 401 (2012).

[54] See Tobias Lock, "The CJEU and ECtHR: The Future Relationship between the Two European Courts," 8 The Law and Practice of International Courts and Tribunals 375 (2009). An excellent study of the two courts is by Hanneke Ceciel Katrijn Senden, Interpretation of Fundamental Rights in a Multilevel System, 46 School of Human Rights Research Series (2011), https://openaccess.leidenuniv.nl/bitstream/handle/1887/18033/Manuscript%20H.%20Senden.pdf?sequence=2

[55] See Samantha Besson, "European Human Rights Pluralism: Notion and Justification," in Miguel Maduro, Kaarlo Tuori, and Suvi Sankari, eds., *Transnational Law: Rethinking European Law and Legal Thinking* (Cambridge: Cambridge University Press 2014) Chapter 7.

is no agreed upon conflict rule or procedure to settle conflicts of norms and authority. In most national legal systems, three such sources of rights—the national constitution, the EU treaties, and the ECHR—overlap. Individuals have a choice of which source to plead, and judges have a choice of which right to enforce.[56]

This is not just a matter of individuals resorting to EU law or the ECHR to force changes in domestic law, or national courts cooperating with or staving off inroads from European courts, but can also involve domestic courts leveraging this interaction in an internal national contest.

Ordinary judges may seek to limit the impact of the jurisprudence of the European courts; but they may also prefer to apply it rather than domestic constitutional case law in order to enhance their own authority and subvert that of constitutional courts. The German labor courts, for example, have partnered with the CJEU to raise German standards of rights protection in employment law, regaining the authority they had lost to German Federal Constitutional Court (GFCC), which has been steadily marginalized. Indeed, the German labor courts have invested heavily in the development of EU rights, as a means of cajoling the GFCC to change its (less-progressive) positions.[57]

Conflicts between coexisting domestic courts, enlisting EU law in support when possible, have long been a source of pluralistic interaction between European and national constitutional courts.

European scholars, in the past two decades, have discussed relations between the EU and member states in terms of "constitutional pluralism."[58] High courts of member states and the CJEU posit contrasting starting presuppositions: national courts insist that legal primacy remains with sovereign member states and the EU is a derivative order; the CJEU position is that the EU is an emergent autonomous legal order with legal supremacy in relation to the purposes of the Union. The former theory underlies the assertion of national courts that they have the power to determine whether an EU

---

[56] Alec Stone Sweet, "The Structure of Constitutional Pluralism: Review of Nico Krisch: The Pluralist Structure of Post-National Law," 11 I-Con 491, 495 (2013).

[57] *Id.*

[58] For a collection with key contributors to and critics of constitutional pluralism, see Matej Avbelj and Jan Komarek, *Constitutional Pluralism in the European Union and Beyond* (Oxford: Hart Publishing 2012).

law exceeds the powers states delegated to it, and must protect national rights and constitutional provisions from intrusion; the latter theory underlies the CJEU claim of primacy in the interpretation of EU law and the supremacy of EU law over national law. Both theories have a sound basis.

Each is superior in its own domain, legal theorist Neil MacCormick observed in a pair of articles in the 1990s. "It follows also that the interpretative power of the highest decision-making authorities of the different systems must be, as to each system, ultimate."[59] Expanding on MacCormick's analysis, a decade later Neil Walker argued that these are conflicting foundational positions in which the constitutional order of the EU coexists with the constitutional orders of nation-states, with no established legal hierarchy to reconcile conflicting assertions of legal supremacy or which court has final say.[60] Constitutional pluralism, Walker elaborates, recognizes that the European legal order originally built on treaties "developed beyond the traditional confines of inter-*national* law and now makes its own independent constitutional claims, and that these claims exist alongside the continuing claims of states. The relationship between the orders, that is to say, is now horizontal rather than vertical—heterarchical rather than hierarchical."[61] Theorists of constitutional pluralism press *descriptive* as well as *normative* claims: constitutional pluralism accurately describes the situation, and seeing it in these terms is beneficial in so far as it encourages all sides to act in a measured and flexible manner, a mutual dialogue between courts involving signaling and adjustments that help make the arrangement work.

Critics have raised multiple challenges to the descriptive and normative claims of constitutional pluralists: the EU is not an autonomous constitutional order in its own right (but rather is a treaty-based international organization with limited function-based powers); constitutional pluralism is oxymoronic because entailed within constitutionalism is unified foundational authority; the symmetry implied by the notion of constitutional pluralism is descriptively false because European nation-states are unquestionably

[59] Neil MacCormick, "The Maastricht-Urteil: Sovereignty Now," 1 European Law Journal 259, 264 (1995). The first article is Neil MacCormick, "Beyond the Sovereign State," 56 Modern Law Review 1 (1993).

[60] See Neil Walker, "The Idea of Constitutional Pluralism," 65 Modern Law Review 317 (2002); Neil MacCormick, *Questioning Sovereignty: Law, State, and Nation in the European Commonwealth* (Oxford: Oxford University Press 1999).

[61] Walker, "The Idea of Constitutional Pluralism," *supra* note 60, at 337.

dominant; neither the national high courts nor the CJEU explicitly describe the system in which they operate as constitutional pluralism; a substantial bulk of the populace do not identify with the EU but instead see themselves as citizens of the nation-states (lack of public support derailed the proposed Treaty Establishing a Constitution for Europe); existing pluralism is not normatively desirable because it creates uncertainty for individuals, businesses, courts, and officials, and creates fissures that weaken the Union.[62]

An increasingly pressing concern is that the positive aspects of constitutional pluralism identified by theorists (dialogue, flexibility, mutual accommodation) took an ominous turn when national constitutional and high courts were politically compromised by authoritarian leaders in Hungary and Poland. The Venice Commission of the Council of Europe took the extraordinary step of issuing an Opinion in January 2020 finding that recent judicial reforms in Poland undermined the independence of the courts.[63] Soon thereafter the CJEU ruled that the new disciplinary chamber in the Polish Supreme Court is a threat to judges that must be suspended—in response to which a Polish justice minister responded "that the European court had 'no power to evaluate or suspend constitutional organs of any member states.' "[64] The prospect of national refusal to abide by EU law no longer appears as functionally beneficial or benign (conducted in a cooperative spirit) as it might have initially.

Constitutional pluralism was coined at a time when the EU appeared to be evolving toward further consolidation. This process slowed in the face of public backlash, and dramatically reversed with Brexit (though the United Kingdom has all along maintained a more separatist stance). Economic trauma in the wake of the 2008 Great Recession, geopolitical stresses created by the internal migration of low-wage workers and the flood of Syrian refugees, and the COVID-19 pandemic, have re-emphasized the primacy

---

[62] See Martin Loughlin, "Constitutional Pluralism: An Oxymoron?," 3 Global Constitutionalism 9 (2014); Julio Baquero Cruz, "Another Look at Constitutional Pluralism in the European Union," 22 European Law Journal 356 (2016); R. Daniel Keleman, "On the Unsustainability of Constitutional Pluralism," 23 Maastricht Journal of European and Comparative Law 136 (2016)

[63] "Poland—Urgent Joint Opinion of the Amendments to the Law on Organization on the Common Courts, the Law on the Supreme Court, and Other Laws," January 16, 2020, Opinion No. 977/2019, Venice Commission, Council of Europe, https://www.venice.coe.int/webforms/documents/?pdf=CDL-PI(2020)002-e

[64] Joanna Berendt, "E.U. Court Rules Poland Must Suspend Disciplinary Panel for Judges," April 8, 2020, New York Times, https://www.nytimes.com/2020/04/08/world/europe/poland-judges-eu-court.html

of national interests, manifested in the rise of populism,[65] but also have highlighted the benefits of working together.

The Continuity of Legal Pluralism in US and EU Law

The EU and its relations with member states is pluralistic in multiple ways, matching the extraordinary cultural, linguistic, religious, economic, gastronomical, environmental, legal, and political heterogeneity of Europe. To expect a unified legal arrangement given this heterogeneity is to use an impossible ideal. The United States is far less heterogeneous compared with the diversity among nations in the EU, yet the earlier discussion exposed significant uncertainties and open questions about the relative powers of state and federal governments in the United States, in addition to Native American tribes. To repeat, legal arrangements are not constructed whole as organized schemes, but rather evolve historically in connection with cultural, economic, political, and power dynamics.

European jurists appear to exhibit greater concern than American jurists over significant unsettled issues. Perhaps American jurists are more pragmatic than European jurists in accepting a degree of uncertainty and less than fully articulated interrelations, or they remain blissfully unaware, beguiled by the monist image of an integrated whole. It may be that the EU, where nation-states are dominant, is a younger and more precarious union so potential conflicts over supremacy are deeply political and experienced as existential threats. Whatever the explanation for their elevated concerns, EU institutions have been highly successful overall. Given the greater heterogeneity, as well as competition among nations for tax revenues, employment, and trade, it is inevitable that clashes, inconsistencies, uncertainties, and open questions would exist even if supremacy had been clearly resolved between the EU and member states.

A factor that clouds the analysis of jurists is the ambiguous status of the EU. Recall that the monist law state image is built on a mutually reinforcing package that combines statehood, sovereignty, and law. The Montevideo Convention (1933) defines states in terms of permanent population, defined

---

[65] See Francesca Bignami, "Introduction: EU Law, Sovereignty, and Populism," in Francesca Bignami, ed., *EU Law in Populist Times: Crises and Prospects* (Cambridge: Cambridge University Press 2020).

territory, government, and capacity to enter into relations with other states. Based on these criteria the EU clearly qualifies as a state. (Tiny and weak Vatican City, Monaco, and Nauru are states.) The only element arguably missing from the EU is a coercive police force, though Europol coordinates with national police in joint enforcement actions.

The EU is in the peculiar position of looking and acting like a legally constituted state, having state political, economic, social, and legal institutions, and engaging in a full range of state actions—all the while insisting that it is *not* a state but an international organization or something (what?). It is like a duck waddling along quacking that it is not a duck to anyone who might be listening. This is politically motivated self-denial, a deliberately modest stance that presents the EU in a less-threatening guise to lessen the backlash from nationalist elements in European nations. Yet juristic discussions about the EU use state-based concepts like "constitutional pluralism," "pooled sovereignty," and so forth.

The point of these comments is *not* to insist that EU is a state, which is not my concern. Rather, drawing out a thread that weaves through this book, the point is that "state" is an abstraction, "sovereignty" has no inherent content or requirements but is filled in at any given time and place in relation to considerations of politics and power at hand (as when Bodin and Hobbes invented it), and law has no necessary connection to or relationship with state or sovereignty. Was the British East India Company a sovereign law state when it governed, collected taxes, set up courts, and enforced law across India and elsewhere? Was China a sovereign law state when extraterritorial courts were forcibly established on its territory by foreign countries? Any theorist who asserts "state sovereignty requires . . ." is writing on sand that shifts with the geopolitical tide and changing institutional arrangements.

The concepts of state and sovereignty distort our perception of legal arrangements that can be described more accurately without them. Standard legal and political theory would place the United States and the EU in different categories: the former a federal state or confederation and the latter a non-state international organization. From a ground-up perspective, however, the legal arrangements of the two are similar, along a shared continuum of legal interconnectedness rather than categorically distinct. In the United States and the EU there is a huge number of dispersed legislative, executive, and judicial legal institutions in various settings (local, municipal, regional, state, national, transnational, etc.), many differentiated by subject matter (civil, criminal, family law, juvenile justice, welfare benefits, bankruptcy, tax, immigration, labor, constitutional, etc.), operating with their own horizontal relations and vertical hierarchies, linked at various junctures to other political and legal institutions with their own vertical relations and horizontal hierarchies, connected to one another through various institutional networks, cooperating and competing for resources, power, and users.

Viewed in diachronic historical perspective, furthermore, there is an evident continuity with decentralized, overlapping legal institutions in Medieval Europe prior to the state system, from which current arrangements came about through gradually thickening institutional developments (with regular setbacks from devastating wars and realignments within and among nations). Innumerably more legal institutions and organizations exist today (along with a multitude of other types of institutions in society), to be sure, and their interconnections are thicker, more numerous, and well defined, but again the difference is one of degree rather than kind. The CJEU and ECtHR are positioned vis-à-vis nation-states today much like Imperial tribunals were through the nineteenth century, which heard cases against princes, barons, and others.

Law in the United States consists of separate bodies of municipal and state laws and courts, plus federal law and courts, plus specialized administrative law and courts, operating against a shared background common law tradition, plus civil law Louisiana and Native American tribes. Law in the EU consists of separate bodies of municipal, regional, national law, and courts, plus specialized administrative law and courts, plus EU law and courts as well as the European Declaration of Human Rights and ECtHR, operating against a shared background civil law tradition. Neither the United States nor European nations nor the EU are fully hierarchically organized, internally consistent, and unified in the monist image. Rather, they are historically evolved, dispersed, multilayered patchworks of cross-cutting, overlapping, separate as well as connected legal institutions, which generally function cohesively in the aggregate. Neil Walker was getting at this when he described constitutional pluralism in the EU as "heterarchical rather than hierarchical," though I would add that it is *both* heterarchical and hierarchical—a depiction that applies equally well to law in the United States. (A heterarchy involves networks of institutions that can exercise autonomy from, or be ranked superior to, other linked institutions in a number of different respects.)

An alternative to the monist law state image can now be concisely articulated. Modern official legal arrangements involve untold numbers of distributed legal institutions each with their own authority, powers, purposes, and resources operating within immediate hierarchies while linking in various ways and with differing degrees of institutional connections to other interacting political and legal institutions, with various means to resolve (or suppress or avoid) regular conflicts that arise between institutions. Though not the tidy unified hierarchy monism portrays, it hangs together in functionally useful and cohesive ways to manage social, economic, political, and others activities within society that law plays a role in.

Abstract Legal Pluralism of MacCormick

Before addressing global legal pluralism, we must briefly return to MacCormick's position to make a pivotal point about abstract legal pluralism that continues in coming sections and the following chapter. Set forth in "Beyond the Sovereign State" (1993), his argument was that states do not have a monopoly over law (constitutional pluralism was not mentioned). At the outset he endorses jurisprudent Roger Cotterrell's criticism of "mainstream jurisprudence for unreflectively privileging state-law over all other forms of law, as though really the only law that counts is that of the (presumably sovereign and independent) state."[66] To detach law from state law, MacCormick defines law in terms of institutionalized normative orders: "Wherever there is law, there is normative order; wherever there is normative order institutionalized, there is law."[67] Since every institutionalized normative order is law, according to his analysis, society is filled with all sorts of legal orders. Addressing jurists and theorists who unthinkingly assume that law is exclusively the product of states, he writes:

> You would tend to marginalise international law. You would tend to marginalise primitive law, you would marginalise canon law and church law. You would marginalise what is sometimes called *the 'living law' of social institutions like universities, firms or families* (all of which seem to me to work, when they do, in terms of what is at least partly institutionalized normative order).[68]

His reference to "living law" of social institutional invokes the work of legal sociologist Eugen Ehrlich,[69] about whom more will be said in the next

---

[66] MacCormick. "Beyond the Sovereign State," *supra* note 59, at 2.

[67] *Id.* at 11.

[68] *Id.* at 14 (emphasis added).

[69] Although MacCormick does not explicitly mention Ehrlich, this phrase is famously associated with Ehrlich, and the pages he refers to in Cotterrell's book, *The Sociology of Law*, discuss Ehrlich.

chapter. Two years later in a follow-up piece, MacCormick uses the same theory of law to set up his analysis of the relationship between the EU and member states: "But state law is not the only kind of law that there is. There is also law between states, international law, and law of organized associations of states such as the EC/EU, law of churches and other religious unions or communities, *laws of games and laws of national and international sporting associations*. Non-state law has also the characteristic of being institutional normative order, but not that of being physically coercive."[70] He argued that legal systems are self-referential and self-generating in the sense that they exist and interact with other systems on their own terms.[71] Recognition "of a pluralistic conception of legal systems entails acknowledging that not all legal problems can be solved legally."[72] In the interactive space of multiple legal systems conflicts are best managed by negotiation.

What MacCormick portrayed in both pieces, which were grounded in legal and sociological theory, was not the coexistence of *constitutional* orders,[73] but society filled with coexisting *legal orders*.

> Can we think of a world in which our normative existence and our practical life are anchored in, or related to, a variety of institutional systems, each of which has some validity or operation in relation to some range of concerns, none of which is absolute over all the others, and all of which, for most purposes, can operate without serious mutual conflict in areas of overlap? If this is as possible practically as it clearly is conceptually, it would involve a diffusion of political power centres as well as of legal authorities.[74]

This is abstract legal pluralism, a product of legal theorists and sociologists, as I explain shortly.

MacCormick's position subsequently morphed from a pluralism of legal orders within every society to "constitutional pluralism," and he pulled back from earlier suggestions of radical pluralism, asserting that the interaction

---

[70] MacCormick, "Maastricht-Urteil," *supra* note 59, at 261 (emphasis added).

[71] *Id.* at 272. He mentions the theory of autopoiesis of Luhmann and Teubner.

[72] *Id.* at 265.

[73] He shifted to constitutional pluralism in Neil MacCormick, *Questioning Sovereignty: Law, State, and Nation in the European Commonwealth* (Oxford: Oxford University Press 1999). Since he used the same analysis as his earlier pieces, this shift implicitly suggested that all institutionalized normative orders are constitutional, a dubious assertion. See Loughlin, *supra* note 62, at 14–19.

[74] MacCormick, "Beyond the Sovereign State," *supra* note 59, at 17.

between EU and member states was organized through international law.[75] The relevant point here is that it was unnecessary for MacCormick to engage in an abstract argument that defines non-state legal order as institutionalized normative orders. This abstraction took him in an orthogonal direction that encompasses families, universities, firms, games, sports associations (italicized above), none of which relates to his analysis of EU law. EU law, international law, and religious law, which he wants to discuss, are conventionally and officially recognized legal orders (folk law) that can be identified as such without an abstract concept of law. Abstract legal pluralism frequently is superfluous to the actual concerns of jurists, as we shall see.

Global/Transnational Legal Pluralism

An outpouring of academic writings about "global" or "transnational" legal pluralism has occurred in the past two decades. "Global legal pluralism is now recognized as an entrenched reality of the international and transnational legal order," asserts Paul Berman, a leading proponent. "Indeed, wherever one looks, there is conflict among multiple legal regimes."[76] As mentioned at the outset of this chapter, global legal pluralism highlights the contemporary profusion of international and transnational law and regulatory regimes (public, private, and hybrid) that extend between and across states dealing with such matters as trade in products and services, pollution control and environmental protection, consumer protection, labor and employment rules, terrorism, illegal migration, illicit drug trade, intellectual property rights, money flows and banking stability, securities regulations, and more. The terms global and transnational legal pluralism are used interchangeably in this literature to refer to forms of law and regulation that address matters between and across polities. This is cross-polity law.

Political scientists and legal scholars have discussed these phenomena under a number of labels, including transnational law and regulation, global regulation, global governance, transgovernmental networks, global administrative law, international economic law, and transnational commercial law,

---

[75] See Nico Krisch, "Who Is Afraid of Radical Pluralism? Legal Order and Political Stability in Postnational Space," 24 Ratio Juris 386 (2011).

[76] Paul Schiff Berman, "The Evolution of Global Legal Pluralism," in Roger Cotterrell and Maksymilian Del Mar, eds., *Authority in Transnational Legal Theory: Theorizing Across Disciplines* (Cheltenham: Edward Elgar 2016) 151.

among others.[77] Following the lead of Gunther Teubner and Boaventura de Sousa Santos in the 1980s and 1990s,[78] in the past two decades a growing number of theoretically oriented jurists, most prolifically Paul Berman, Ralf Michaels, and Peer Zumbansen, have framed these topics in terms of legal pluralism, drawing direct connections to the anthropological and sociological legal pluralist literature.[79] Proponents characterize this as the third phase of legal pluralist scholarship: first came anthropological studies of pluralistic law in postcolonial societies; next came sociological accounts of the multiplicity of law in Western societies; and now comes legal pluralism on the global or transnational level.[80]

Transnational legal pluralist works typically discuss standard legal materials, including court decisions, legislative and constitutional provisions, international law and courts, contracts and codes, regulatory regimes, private sources of regulation, and legal rights like human rights, labor rights, and so forth. Common themes in the literature include how to manage competing jurisdictions, choice of law, and conflicts of law issues, and how non-state legal or regulatory orders serve as sources of law or provide effective regulation that complements or provides alternatives to official law. The literature is filled with discussions of multitude of international law organizations, bodies of law, and tribunals (United Nations, World Trade Organization, World Health Organization, International Court of Justice, etc.); transnational economic organizations and law (International Monetary Fund, World Bank, *lex mercatoria*, etc.); transgovernmental regulatory networks (Basel Committee on Banking Supervision, etc.); non-state regulatory standard setting bodies (Codex Alimentarius Commission on food standards, Internet Corporation for Assigned Names and Numbers, etc.);[81] voluntary 'soft law' provisions like corporate codes of conduct and UNIDROIT Principles of International Commercial Contracts; as well as so-called sports law and law of the internet.

[77] See Brian Z. Tamanaha, *A Realistic Theory of Law* (Cambridge: Cambridge University Press 2017) 174–78.

[78] See Gunther Teubner, "Global Bukowina: Legal Pluralism in the World Society," in Gunther Teubner, ed., *Global Law Without a State* (Aldershot: Ashgate 1996) 3–17; Boaventura de Sousa Santos, *Toward a New Legal Common Sense: Law, Globalization, and Emancipation* (London: Butterworths 2002).

[79] For informative surveys, see Paul Schiff Berman, "The New Legal Pluralism," 5 Annual Review of Law and Social Sciences 225 (2009); Ralf Michaels, "Global Legal Pluralism," 5 Annual Review of Law and Social Sciences 243 (2009).

[80] Michaels, *supra* note 79, at 245.

[81] An excellent overview is provided in Fabrizio Cafaggi, "Transnational Private Regulation. Regulating the Regulators," in S. Cassese, ed., Research Handbook on Global Administrative Law (Cheltenham: Edward Elgar 2016).

A significant proportion of this work discusses overlapping bodies of law and regulation in the Europe Union,[82] as a transnational entity juxtaposed across multiple national law regimes.

An overflowing cornucopia of transnational law and public and private regulatory regimes is described in transnational legal pluralism, much of it generated in connection with the rise of global capitalism and its consequences, along with advances in communications technology and transportation that have rendered national borders easily and frequently traversed. States cannot manage all this acting independently, and international law is unable to fill the gap, so a great deal of regulatory work is occurring through other public and private institutions. A substantial increase in private regulatory activities has occurred domestically—private policing, private arbitration, private standard setting, etc.—as well as in international settings.

A few quick examples illustrate what is involved. The Codex Alimentarius Commission, created by the UN Food and Agriculture Association (currently with 188 member countries), produces scientifically based food standards for consumer health purposes (safe amounts of adulterants like pesticide residues, contaminants, and additives, food processing requirements, etc.) as well as labeling standards; The WTO and many countries have incorporated its standards.[83] The Basel Committee on Banking Supervision—not an international organization, but an intergovernmental group—consists of central bankers from the United States, Europe, and Japan who meet four times a year to exchange information, work out policy and banking requirements, and coordinate supervision and regulation of national and transnational banks; over 100 countries have adopted bank capital adequacy requirements they produced. Google enforces the EU's "right to be forgotten law," to date rendering judgments on over 845,000 requests, delisting 45 percent of the links (reflecting the reach of the legal mandate, it does not delist the same links outside of the EU).[84] These are legal or regulatory regimes with transnational reach; none is strictly international law or national law, though they have links with both; and Google is a private company enforcing EU law.

---

[82] See Peer Zumbansen, "Neither 'Public' nor 'Private,' 'National' nor 'International:' Transnational Corporate Governance From a Legal Pluralist Perspective," 38 Law and Society Review 50 (2011).

[83] See Codex Alimentarius: Understanding Codex, Food and Agriculture Association (2016); Eddie Kimbrell, "What Is Codex Alimentarius," 3 AgBioForum 197 (2000).

[84] See Leo Kelion, "Google Wins Landmark Right to Be Forgotten Case," September 23, 2019, Technology, BBC News, https://www.bbc.com/news/technology-49808208

A sub-theme in the literature is "international legal pluralism"[85]—also referred to as international law fragmentation.[86] This work highlights potential clashes between international tribunals and subject matter specific legal regimes: trade (WTO), health (WHO), crime (International Criminal Court), human rights (ECtHR, Inter-American Court of Human Rights), intellectual property (TRIPS), law of the sea (International Tribunal for the Law of the Sea), and more. A dispute over whether a country can provide generic drugs for its population to treat Acquired Immune Deficiency Syndrome, for example, simultaneously raises issues that fall within the jurisdiction of the WTO and the WHO, each with different norms and purposes.[87] Pluralism within international law is further exacerbated because national courts incorporate international law to different extents and with differing interpretations. There is no overarching, hierarchical international law system to create uniformity and consistency within international law.

Another sub-theme within transnational legal pluralism, discussed earlier, focuses on the invocation of human rights norms, often supported by externally funded non-governmental organizations (NGOS), by people challenging their own state laws or actions, or challenging customary or religious laws or practices recognized by the state.[88] This includes suits brought before human rights courts as well as raising human rights claims within national courts—constituting legal pluralism through the coexistence of human rights, state law, and when applicable, customary and religious law.

Transnational legal pluralists frequently hold up the new *lex mercatoria*, which Teubner crowned "the most successful example of global law without a state."[89] The medieval *lex mercatoria* consisted of tribunals staffed by merchants to resolve disputes, sitting at medieval fairs attended by merchants from across Europe, using common procedures and applying commercial usages and principles. Legal scholars have argued that a new *lex mercatoria* has emerged to handle transnational commercial transactions: a

[85] See William W. Burke-White, "International Legal Pluralism," 25 Michigan Journal of International Law 963 (2004).

[86] Marti Koskenniemi and Paivi Leinop, "Fragmentation of International Law? Postmodern Anxieties," 15 Leiden Journal of International Law 553 (2002); Joost Pauwelyn, "Bridging Fragmentation and Unity: International Law as a Universe of Interconnected Islands," 25 Michigan Journal of International Law 903 (2004)

[87] See Andreas Fischer-Lescano and Gunther Teubner, "Regime Collisions: The Vain Search for Legal Unity in the Fragmentation of Global Law," 25 Michigan Journal of International Law 999 (2004).

[88] See Sally Engle Merry, "Global Human Rights and Local Social Movements in a Legally Plural World," 12 Canadian Journal of Law and Society 247 (1997).

[89] Teubner, *supra* note 78, at 3.

private law regime constructed by European and Anglo-American lawyers for transnational commercial transactions using a combination of standard contract terms, commercial customs and practices, codes of conduct, as well as references to the UNIDROIT Principles of International Commercial Contracts, and national laws.[90] Disputes are handled through private arbitration. Parties can choose to bring their dispute to state courts, however, and they may seek state court enforcement of the arbitration decision if compliance does not follow voluntarily.

Transnational legal pluralists make descriptive, conceptual, and normative claims. They are unanimous on the *descriptive* claim that an increasing profusion of coexisting legal regimes exists on the transnational level that demand attention from jurists. There is general agreement on two conceptual aspects of legal pluralism, but less agreement on a normative claim about legal pluralism.

As a *conceptual* matter, first, they center on the interaction and hybridity of coexisting legal forms, decentering state law (while still recognizing its importance), and eschewing monistic assumptions about unity and hierarchy. A second common conceptual aspect is their focus on *non-state law* (John Griffiths, Eugen Ehrlich, Sally Falk Moore are commonly mentioned). They invoke broad concepts of law to encompass the *lex mercatoria*, private standard setting bodies, customary rules, and "soft law" provisions like corporate codes of conduct, sweeping in regulatory forms operating on the transnational level that are not generally recognized as law.[91] Paul Berman, for example, ties law to norm-generating communities: "From religious institutions, to industry standard-setting bodies to not-for-profit accreditation entities to arbitral panels to university tenure committees to codes promulgated within ethnic enclaves to self-regulation regimes in semiautonomous communities, the sites of nonstate lawmaking are truly everywhere."[92] He has also identified law within the family[93] and "in day-to-day human encounters such as interacting with strangers on a public street, waiting in lines, and communicating with subordinates or superiors."[94]

---

[90] See Ralf Michaels, "The True Lex Mercatoria: Law Beyond the State," 14 Indiana Journal of Global Legal Studies 447 (2007).

[91] See Berman, *supra* note 79, at 227–29, 232–33.

[92] Paul Berman, *Global Legal Pluralism: A Jurisprudence of Law Beyond Borders* (New York: Cambridge University Press 2012) 41-42.

[93] Berman, *supra* note 79, at 236.

[94] Paul Schiff Berman, "The Globalization of Jurisdiction," 151 University of Pennsylvania Law Review 311, 505 (2002)

Broad conceptions like this literally create a profusion of legal pluralism by drawing in all sorts of normative orders—as I explain shortly.

Several theorists of global legal pluralism also consider legal pluralism—the theoretical framework and the pluralistic situation it depicts—to be *normatively* beneficial. Berman extolls the "important systemic benefits [of accepting the inevitability of legal pluralism] by fostering dialogue among multiple constituencies, authorities, levels of government, and non-state communities."[95] He argues for "cosmopolitan pluralism," which recognizes that everyone is involved in multiple communities, each of which may generate legal orders, and judges should consider all normative orders implicated in a given dispute (community based, domestic, transnational, and international) when rendering decisions;[96] situations of legal pluralism, he suggests, should be approached with a view toward "forging provisional compromises that fully satisfy no one but may at least generate grudging acquiescence."[97] Berman elaborates pluralism within a liberal framework that recognizes the value of individuals as well as communities. Peer Zumbansen appreciates the critical potential of legal pluralism to shatter the stultifying, aggrandizing illusion of state law's exclusivity, unity, and supremacy.[98] He writes, "in the years ahead we will need to critically engage with the phenomenon of private regulatory power against the background of a far-reaching, postcolonial critique of the universalist accounts of the rise of the Westphalian international order (of sovereign nation states) and of their subsequent demise through 'privatization (Europeanization) and globalization.'"[99] Although for very different reasons, both Berman and Zumbansen portray transnational legal pluralism as a good thing that should be recognized and encouraged.

Doubts about "Global Legal Pluralism"

Transnational legal pluralist scholars have produced a number of programmatic articles setting forth their position.[100] Widely used labels like global

---

[95] Berman, *supra* note 79, at 238.

[96] See Berman, *supra* note 92, at 1–15, 262–63.

[97] *Id.* at 14.

[98] See Peer Zumbansen, "Transnational Legal Pluralism," 1 Transnational Legal Theory 141 (2010).

[99] Peer Zumbansen, "The Constitutional Itch: Transnational Private Regulatory Governance and the Woes of Legitimacy," in Michael Helfand, ed., *Negotiating State and Non-State Law: The Challenge of Global and Local Legal Pluralism* (New York: Cambridge University Press 2015) 90–91.

[100] See Berman, *supra* note 79; Michaels, *supra* note 79; Zumbansen, *supra* note 98.

regulation or transnational law, and the fragmentation of international law, cover much the same ground. So what is gained by viewing this in terms of "legal pluralism"? Ralf Michaels, a prolific author on the topic, explains:

> Legal pluralism, long a special interest within the specialist discipline of legal anthropology, has recently moved into the mainstream of legal discourse. The most likely reason is globalization. Many of the challenges that globalization poses to traditional legal thought closely resemble those formulated earlier by legal pluralists. The irreducible plurality of legal orders in the world, the coexistence of domestic state law with other legal orders, the absence of a hierarchically superior position transcending the differences— all of these topics of legal pluralism reappear on the global sphere.[101]

This passage prompts several responses and concerns.

What drew anthropological attention to legal pluralism were the stark differences between transplanted colonial state law existing alongside customary and religious laws and institutions with contrasting norms and modes of decision-making. Michaels's passage slides across two distinct connotations of pluralism: legal pluralism in postcolonial societies is about striking *diversity* between the multiple coexisting forms of law, and the manifold consequences of these contrasts; transnational legal pluralism is about the *multiplicity* of legal regimes, which might conflict on points but usually are not radically diverse. The norms and regulations mentioned in this body of work frequently are produced and utilized by legal and regulatory organizations engaging in standard lawyerly fare (writing model codes, drafting contracts, resorting to arbitration). EU legal pluralism is about *multiple* legal orders with occasional clashes, not radically *diverse* legal orders (they share a long history and civil law background); international law fragmentation is about functionally differentiated subjects with occasional clashes that arise within a common body of international law rules, doctrines, principles, and practices.

Michaels's reference to "the absence of a hierarchically superior position," although offered to show continuity, actually points to another major difference with anthropological studies of legal pluralism. Anthropologists shed light on the coexistence of state law with customary and religious law in ways that cast doubts on the monist notion of a unified, monopolistic system of

---

[101] Michaels, *supra* note 79, at 244.

state law. Pluralism gets it thrust from a contrast with monism. But law at the global level is not generally seen as unified, at least not outside a small group of European scholars who portray international law as a global constitutional order. As Michaels recognizes, "where a world state does not exist, international law is not automatically hierarchically superior to state law, and states in turn cannot claim intrinsic superiority over other states."[102] Hence there is no monistic vision of a supreme, unified, hierarchical system against which to counterpose transnational legal pluralism.

The concern that transnational legal pluralism is an untethered notion is further suggested by his phrase "irreducible plurality of legal orders in the world." This language suggests that global or transnational legal pluralism shifts the analytical frame from the state to the global level, sweeping in every existing legal system at every level within its domain. Berman confirms this extraordinary scope of global legal pluralism in his list of conflicts: when multiple nation-states assert jurisdiction over a civil or criminal matter; when nation-states and international tribunals assert jurisdiction; when federal authorities and sub-states assert jurisdiction; when states and non-state norm-generating communities claim authority.[103] All of this combined literally is *every* legal order in the world. If expanding the frame to the global level means encompassing every and all legal orders broadly defined—international, transnational, and state law, forms of private regulation, customary law and religious law, normative orders within social associations—then global legal pluralism is a vast bottomless bucket. This is tantamount to asserting that all legal orders in the world in the aggregate constitute a plurality of law. A true statement but useless.

Legal theorist William Twining, who has written extensively about globalization as well as about legal pluralism,[104] expressed skepticism about global legal pluralism: "As a concept it is not very promising."[105] In addition to difficulties with loose notions of globalization and overly broad notions of law, his concern is that "the many extensions and applications of the idea of legal pluralism to new phenomena and situations are so many and so varied that it is difficult to construct a coherent answer to the question: what is the relevance of classical studies of legal pluralism to the emerging field of 'global

---

[102] *Id.* at 253–54.

[103] *Id.* at 27–44.

[104] See William Twining, *General Jurisprudence: Understanding Law from A Global Perspective* (Cambridge: Cambridge University Press 2009).

[105] William Twining, "Normative and Legal Pluralism: A Global Perspective," 20 Duke Journal of Comparative and International Law 743, 511 (2010).

legal pluralism?' "[106] Within this body of work, he observed, a "variety of answers [have been] given to the question: plurality of what?"[107]

A separate objection is that the very effort to formulate a broad conception of law to include private and hybrid forms of regulation is unnecessary and creates irresolvable problems. One can discuss codes of conduct, private regulatory bodies, etc., and talk about their interaction and hybridity with various forms of official law, and all the rest taken up in the literature, without any loss of information by using the more general label *transnational regulatory pluralism*. Regulation and governance scholarship takes up all the same matters without bogging down in debates over what qualifies as *law* because "regulatory pluralism" encompasses the entire range of public and private regulatory forms.

More is at stake than a choice of labels. Their assertion that all of these public and private forms of regulation count as *law* (hence *legal* pluralism) leads transnational legal pluralists to proffer answers to "What is law?" This results in competing conceptualizations of law in the literature, creating disagreement and confusion. The pioneers of transnational legal pluralism, Teubner and Santos, each articulate a conception of law (described next). A single volume on pluralist jurisprudence contains three very different views of law by leading theorists of transnational legal pluralism: Roger Cotterrell proposes that law is institutionalized doctrine; Ralf Michaels articulates a relational concept of law that requires recognition from other legal orders to qualify as law; Detlef von Daniels argues that owing to empirical variability there is no single concept of law and one must look instead at various contexts of legal practices.[108] These are just five examples among others in the literature, each of which results in a different version of transnational legal pluralism.

Beyond the confusion generated by multiple concepts of law, one must question the coherence and value of each theory on its own terms. Berman purports to avoid the problem by denying the necessity to offer a concept of law. What he does, however, is presuppose an answer without specifying what it is, linking law too families, associations, and a range of normative orderings. After acknowledging that global legal pluralism is not really

---

[106] *Id.* at 512–13.

[107] *Id.* at 513.

[108] See Roger Cotterrell, "Do Lawyers Need A Concept of Law?," Ralf Michaels, "Law and Recognition—Towards a Relational Concept of Law"; and Detlef von Daniels, "A Genealogical Perspective on Pluralist Jurisprudence," in Nicole Roughan and Andrew Halpin, eds., *In Pursuit of Pluralist Jurisprudence* (Cambridge: Cambridge University Press 2017).

global in reach and not fully pluralist (because he disallows illiberal values), Berman writes: "Indeed, given the broad (and often undefined) vision of law embraced by legal pluralists, it is perhaps not properly considered 'legal' either!"[109] A leading theorist on the topic now tells us it is not really about law after all. Chapter Five explains why theorists of abstract legal pluralism repeatedly find themselves this odd position.

Global Legal Pluralism of Teubner and Santos

To obtain a concrete sense of the theoretical issues involved let us examine the views of legal sociologists Gunther Teubner and Boaventura de Sousa Santos, the early progenitors of global legal pluralism. In " 'Global Bukowina: Legal Pluralism in the World Society," Teubner highlighted a marked growth of transnational law created by private actors, citing as examples *lex mercatoria*, internal rules within transnational corporations, labor unions as lawmakers though labor agreements, technical standardization and professional self-regulation, and the law of sports leagues (*lex sportiva internationalis*).[110] Teubner's work on legal pluralism extends the theory of autopoiesis, a sociological theory originally developed in relation to society, to non-state legal forms on the transnational level.

Autopoiesis, in a nutshell, is a functionalist theory developed by Niklas Luhmann (who borrowed from biological accounts of cells), which holds that society consists of self-reproducing subsystems (economy, polity, law, science, technology, etc.) that are operationally closed networks of communication, which are open to input from other subsystems. Each functional subsystem has its own characteristic mode of discourse, while coupled with other subsystems, each incorporating input from the other subsystems on its own terms. Law, in this view, "is a self-organizing process that autonomously defines its boundaries,"[111] characterized by a binary code of legal/illegal.[112]

---

[109] Paul Schiff Berman, "Understanding Global Legal Pluralism: From Local to Global, From Descriptive to Normative," in Paul Schiff Berman, ed., *The Oxford Handbook of Global Legal Pluralism* (Oxford University Press) 62, available at https://papers.ssrn.com/sol3/papers.cfm?abstract_id=3715553

[110] Teubner, *supra* note 78.

[111] *Id.* at 11.

[112] See Teubner, *supra* note 78; Gunther Teubner, "Two Faces of Janus: Rethinking Legal Pluralism," 13 Cardozo Law Review 1143 (1991).

Teubner identifies Eugen Ehrlich's notion of living law as capturing the way in which law is created in connection with "the ongoing self-reproduction of highly technical, highly specialized, often formally organized and rather narrowly defined, global networks of an economic, cultural, academic or technological nature."[113] "Legal pluralism is then defined no longer as a set of conflicting social norms but as a multiplicity of diverse communicative processes in a given social field that observe social action under the binary code of legal/illegal."[114] *Lex mercatoria* qualifies as law, according to Teubner, because it is a self-organizing autonomous process constructed by transnational commercial lawyers involving discourse using legal/illegal. He asserts that "legal pluralism needs to shift emphasis and focus on the fragmentation of social reproduction in a multiplicity of closed discourses."[115]

Autopoiesis is a highly abstract functionalist sociological theory with devoted proponents, though it is not widely adhered to within sociology. What legal scholars find attractive is the assertion that input from other subsystems within society is incorporated within law on law's own terms. Jurists are familiar with the process in which law absorbs and translates social input into legal terminology and categories. To cite an example from the previous chapter, the state legal system enforces divorce arrangements granted by rabbinical courts under Jewish law as an arbitration decision enforceable under contract law. But this point has been made outside of autopoietic theory without the need for its dense theoretical underpinnings.

Setting aside questions about its sociological value, for the purposes of legal pluralism Teubner's autopoiesis has two main flaws: it is extremely narrow in one sense and extremely broad in another. It is extremely narrow because law is viewed entirely as a *communicative* process: law is a system of *discourse*. This isolates on just one aspect of law, apart from its coercive force, material and institutional elements, relations to power, and everything else outside the realm of communication. At the same time, it is extremely broad because it encompasses within law *all* discourse invoking the binary code of legal/illegal, including conversations between private parties. According to Teubner, an organized crime enforcer shaking down a storeowner for the monthly protection "tax" and two merchants discussing a future transaction they plan to formalize in a contract "are an integral part of legal pluralism in our semiautonomous social field insofar as they use the binary code of legal

---

[113] Teubner, *supra* note 78, at 7.
[114] *Id.* at 14.
[115] Teubner, *supra* note 112, at 1457.

communication."[116] Any and all *communication* invoking legal/illegal is law and thus part of legal pluralism under this theory.

Boaventura de Sousa Santos presents legal pluralism as "the key concept in a postmodern view of law."[117] Notoriously elusive to pin down, postmodernism is perhaps best described as a rebellious mood that revels in challenging foundationalist claims, denying universals, piercing claims of unity and systematic coherence, critiquing power and authority claims, and more. This bundle of debunking and anti-systematic orientations align with legal pluralism's challenge to monistic images of state law. About global legal pluralism he writes:

> The new international commercial contracts as well as the proliferation of charters, codes of ethics, codes of conduct or of fair practices covering the activities of multinational corporations and international economic and professional associations in fields so diverse as transfers of technology, stock markets, publicity, sales promotion, market studies, insurance, technical assistance, turn-key contracts, etc.—all these new forms of world legality create a transnational legal space which often conflicts with the national state legal space. . . .
>
> All these latent or manifest conflicts are symptoms of a tension between the geocentric legality of the nation-state and the new egocentric legality of international private economic agents.[118]

Santos defines law as "a body of regularized procedures and normative standards, considered justiciable in any given group, which contributes to the creation and prevention of disputes, and to their settlement through an argumentative discourse, coupled with the threat of force."[119] He acknowledges that under this definition society is suffused with a vast number and variety of legal orders. He trims this by focusing on six clusters: (1) *domestic law* of each household; (2) *production law* of factories, corporations, labor relations, shop floor rules, employee codes of conduct, "normative standards that rule the everyday life of wage labour relations," etc.; (3) *exchange law* of

---

[116] These examples are provided by Teubner, *supra* note 112, at 1451, 1453. "Semi-autonomous social field" is a notion developed by Sally Falk Moore, discussed in Chapter Five.

[117] Boaventura de Sousa Santos, "Law: a Map of Misreading. Toward a Postmodern Conception of Law," 14 Journal of Law and Society 279, 297 (1987)

[118] *Id.* at 293–94.

[119] Boaventura de Sousa Santos, *Toward a New Common Sense: Law, Science and Politics in the Paradigmatic* (1995) 429.

the marketplace, trade customs, relations between merchants and between merchants and consumers, etc.; (4) *community law* of "hegemonic or oppressed groups"; (5) *territorial or state law* of modern societies; and (6) *systemic law* of the world—"the sum total of rules and normative standards that organize the core/periphery hierarchy and the relations among nation states."[120] The law from each of these clusters overlaps and interpenetrates law from the other clusters—with state law in operating in all the clusters. The law of each cluster is not limited to formally stated rules, but includes informal norms as well. Domestic law, for example, includes "very informal, nonwritten, so deeply embedded in family relations that it is hardly conceivable as an autonomous dimension thereof."[121] Under this conception, a husband who physically beats his wife for putting dinner on the table later than usual is enforcing domestic law. Thus society is stuffed full of overflowing, overlapping law. In effect, Santos relabels a multitude of normative orders in society to "legal orders," immediately producing ubiquitous legal pluralism.

Santos emphasizes the dynamic interaction and "mixing of codes" in pluralistic legal spaces, as well as how people experience multiple legal orders:

> the conception of different legal spaces superimposed, interpenetrated, and mixed in our minds as much as in our actions, in occasions of qualitative leaps or sweeping crises in our life trajectories as well as in the dull routine of eventless everyday life. We live in a time of porous legality or of legal porosity, of multiple networks of legal orders forcing us to constant transitions and trespassings. Our legal life is constituted by an intersection of different legal orders, that is, by interlegality.[122]

Santos advocates an approach to legal sociology that helps emancipate people by uncovering "the latent or suppressed forms of legality in which more insidious and damaging forms of social and personal oppression frequently occur."[123]

Teubner and Santos are at opposite poles in one respect: Teubner constructs a grand sociological theory of law on which to build legal science; postmodernists like Santos reject system building in favor of debunking. What they share is a penchant for engaging in high theory. Of both theories it

---

[120] *Id.* at 429–46.
[121] *Id.* at 429.
[122] Santos, *supra* note 117, at 297–98.
[123] *Id.* at 299.

must be asked what is gained by viewing law in these complex, obscure, and expansive terms.

Theoretical Mapping

Global legal pluralists regularly cite Teubner and Santos, though many do not adopt autopoiesis and are not postmodernists. Much of this work is grounded in legal and sociological theory and amounts to exercises in theoretical mapping: analytical-descriptive work portraying the terrain of transnational law. Santos's article is entitled "A Map of Misreading." The first part of Berman's book is "Mapping a Hybrid World." The editors of a recent book on pluralist jurisprudence observe, "It is one thing to represent a reality that is indeed fuzzy, unfocused and somewhat hazy, but the theorists role is to help find, map and follow pathways through an unclear subject matter with some precision."[124]

This begs the questions: What are the purposes of these maps and who are they for? Berman focuses a great deal on national and international tribunals, analyzing jurisdictional, choice of law, and conflict of law issues, suggesting that his map is for judges. "Recognizing the 'complex and interwoven forces that govern citizens' conduct in a global society,' courts can develop a jurisprudence that reflects this cosmopolitan pluralist reality,"[125] he writes. Jurisprudent Roger Cotterrell asserts that practicing lawyers need to reorient themselves to the range of legal phenomena on the transnational level: "they need a map of law." "Providing it is a central juristic task."[126] Cotterrell sketches his own tentative map of transnational law, utilizing a concept of law as institutionalized doctrine,[127] which he believes is suited for jurists confronted with transnational legal pluralism.

The claim that judges and lawyers require, and will use, theoretical maps of law and legal pluralism is questionable, given the concrete, practical nature of their tasks, which they carry out daily in the absence of such maps. A judge or lawyer confronted with an actual problem or dispute in which multiple forms of law or multiple tribunals are potentially available

---

[124] See Nicole Roughan and Andrew Halpin, "The Promises and Pursuits of Pluralist Jurisprudence," in Roughan and Andrew Halpin, *supra* note 108, at 333.

[125] Berman, *supra* note 79, at 262.

[126] Roger Cotterrell, *Sociological Jurisprudence: Juristic Thought and Social Inquiry* (London: Routledge 2018) 106.

[127] Cotterrell, *supra* note 108, at 36–38.

will examine the various coexisting norms at hand, and render evaluations of their applicability and relative weight, and likely implications and consequences. This is a context-specific analysis, drawing upon applicable legal doctrine, conflict of law rules, jurisdictional analysis, and so forth. The weight accorded to a regulatory regime in given instances will be determined by rules of validity utilized within legal systems to address status and impact issues of this sort, referring to potentially relevant public, private, and hybrid regimes by name and institutional sources (as UNIDROIT principles, Codex Alimentarius standards, etc.). Judges and lawyers already largely follow the legal pluralist advice to pay attention to the coexisting regulatory regimes at hand and to consider their implications and interaction. Moreover, judges and lawyers can conduct their analysis without engaging in a theoretical discussion over what counts as law; if on a rare occasion the issue does arise, it is unclear how they would choose from among the many answers to this question proposed by legal theorists, though it is unlikely a court would adopt expansive theories that construe virtually every institutionalized normative ordering as law.

The context-specific nature of juridical inquiries also raises doubts about the assertion by Berman and certain other legal pluralists that legal pluralism is normatively desirable. Sometimes legal pluralism has positive benefits, but sometimes not. It all depends on the particular mix of coexisting legal orders, the consequences that follow therefrom, and desirable values and goals involved. The suggestion that judges should consider each legal order makes sense, as far as it goes, but often choices must be made that recognizes certain legal claims over others. And often that will be contested, involving different interests and values. Berman disallows illiberal values (mentioning illiberal versions of Sharia) in his embrace of pluralism, resurrecting a version of repugnancy clauses in colonial legal systems that set limits on recognition of customary and religious law. The limits he sets, his normative choices, illustrate that legal pluralism is not normatively desirable per se, but rather depends on whether the pluralist mix in a given situation plays out in ways preferred by the immediate parties involved—as well as interested scholars, development practitioners, NGOs, etc.—about which there will be disagreement.

At the conclusion of his own effort at mapping normative and legal pluralism, Twining recognizes that "mapping legal phenomena in the world is only useful up to a point—in sketching a broad context for more particular studies—and the broad concepts it involves should not be expected to do too much work at lower levels of abstraction or for more specific inquiries."[128] These maps, Twining suggests, are for scholars rather than lawyers. Theorists use the metaphor of mapping when they articulate analytical schemes and distinguish categories to clarify a given subject matter. Scholars may indeed find maps of transnational regulatory pluralism useful for grasping these complex situations, but the very same phenomena can be mapped without insisting on the additional (superfluous) assertion that codes of conduct, internet rules, etc., *are* law. Two immediate purposes are served by this claim: it rhetorically lifts the status of these forms of regulation to equivalence with law; and it enables legal theorists and legal sociologists to expand the domain of *legal* pluralism to encompass all sorts of regulatory forms and institutionalized norms. Jurists thereby apply their legal lens to portray law wherever they look.[129]

A more pointed criticism is that global legal pluralism has devolved into mapping for its own sake. International law theorist Martti Koskenniemi remarked, "The problem with legal pluralism—that is the approach that seeks to grasp all the different rationalities in the world—is the way it ceases to make demands on the world. Theorists of globalization are so enchanted by the complex interplay of the technical regimes and a positivist search for a vocabulary that would encompass all of them, losing thus the critical point of their exercise."[130] "Legal pluralism may be descriptively right," Koskenniemi states, but "So what?"[131] Fragmentation and multiplicity of law are always present, he observes, yet they are managed by legal experts with shared backgrounds, understandings, and practices who know how to deal with these contexts.[132]

The Value of "Global Legal Pluralism"

The multiplicity of regulatory phenomena addressed by transnational legal pluralists are significant and worthy of scholarly attention. Political

---

[128] Twining, *supra* note 105, at 514.

[129] See Simon Roberts, "Against Legal Pluralism: Some Reflections on the Contemporary Enlargement of the Legal Domain," 42 Journal of Legal Pluralism 92 (1998).

[130] Martti Koskenniemi, "Global Legal Pluralism: Multiple Regimes and Multiple Modes of Thought," Harvard, March 5, 2005, page 16, available at https://www.researchgate.net/profile/Martti_Koskenniemi/publication/265477439_GLOBAL_LEGAL_PLURALISM_MULTIPLE_REGIMES_AND_MULTIPLE_MODES_OF_THOUGHT/links/578eb63608aecbca4caad5f2/GLOBAL-LEGAL-PLURALISM-MULTIPLE-REGIMES-AND-MULTIPLE-MODES-OF-THOUGHT.pdf

[131] *Id.* at 16.

[132] *Id.* at 21.

scientists and legal scholars have written about them from several academic perspectives. The value of framing this in terms of "legal (or better, regulatory) pluralism" is that it centers on situations of coexisting public and private regulatory regimes and their various possible interrelations: complementary and mutually supportive, contradictory and antagonistic, competing or cooperating, and so forth. Instead of "So what?," as Koskenniemi asked, perhaps the question for global legal pluralists should be "Then what?" After telling us to center on coexisting public and private and hybrid regulatory bodies and their interaction, they have little to say beyond paying attention to the complexity and interaction, or advocating flexibility, negotiation, and other general advice with thin content. It is now abundantly clear that cross-polity law and regulation is increasing in quantity and expanding in scope and reach in the age of global capitalism. That merits highlighting. Once that lessen is absorbed, however, the import of global legal pluralism may be spent.

Five

Abstract versus Folk Legal Pluralism

Legal theorists only very recently have begun to seriously consider legal pluralism. The endemic blindness of jurisprudents to other forms of law is a testament to the powerful hold of the image of the monist law state. "In legal theory, state law is typically characterized as systemic, and claims both a kind of supremacy over any other competing normative standards and comprehensiveness in its reach to regulate any matter within its territorial boundaries."[1] Under this entrenched view state law almost by definition holds a monopoly over law. What finally opened their collective eyes to other manifestations of law is the proliferation and multiplicity of non-state law brought by globalizing factors, which does not fit theories of law grounded on the state. The "exclusive concentration on state law was, it now turns out, never justified, and is even less justified today," declared legal philosopher Joseph Raz, who has himself long depicted law in strongly monist terms.[2]

Consideration of non-state law immediately raises the classic jurisprudential question "What is law?" Legal pluralists must answer this question to specify what is encompassed within *legal* pluralism. Legal anthropologists engaged in the study of non-state law have debated the concept of law for over a century.[3] "To seek a definition of law is like the quest for the Holy Grail," wrote anthropologist Adamson Hoebel.[4] Anthropologist Paul Bohannan observed, "It is likely that more scholarship has gone into defining and explaining the concept of 'law' than any other concept still in central use in the social sciences."[5] Legal anthropologists today continue to offer answers to this question, motivated in part by the felt need to define the parameters of

---

[1] Michael Giudice, "Global Legal Pluralism: What's Law Got to Do With It?," 34 Oxford Journal of Legal Studies 589, 593 (2014).

[2] Joseph Raz, "Why the State?," in Nicole Roughan and Andrew Halpin, eds., *In Pursuit of Pluralist Jurisprudence* (Cambridge: Cambridge University Press 2017) 161.

[3] For early overviews by prominent legal anthropologists, see Sally Falk Moore, "Law and Anthropology," 6 Biennial Review of Anthropology 252 (1969); Laura Nader, "The Anthropological Study of Law," 67 American Anthropologist 3 (1965).

[4] E. Adamson Hoebel, "Law and Anthropology," 32 Virginia Law Review 835, 839 (1946).

[5] Paul Bohannan, "The Differing Realms of the Law," 67 American Anthropologist 33 (1965).

Legal Pluralism Explained. Brian Z. Tamanaha, Oxford University Press (2021). © Brian Z. Tamanaha.
DOI: 10.1093/oso/9780190861551.003.0006

their subfield.[6] Preeminent twentieth-century legal philosopher H.L.A. Hart observed, "Few questions concerning human society have been asked with such persistence and answered by serious thinkers in so many diverse, strange, and even paradoxical ways as the question, 'What is law?'"[7]

This chapter explains why attempts to build legal pluralism in terms of a concept or definition of law—what I call abstract legal pluralism—do not work. After reviewing several decades of writings on legal pluralism, jurisprudent William Twining remarked, "I have come away feeling that it is little better than a morass."[8] The source of this morass is a series of conceptual missteps committed by social scientists and legal theorists who have developed abstract legal pluralism. Abstract concepts of law, for reasons I explain, unavoidably encompass social phenomena that are usually not considered to be law. This problem (over-inclusiveness) was flagged in the 1988 essay by Sally Engle Merry that boosted the profile of legal pluralism, when she remarked, "Where do we stop speaking of law and find ourselves simply describing social life? Is it useful to call all these forms of ordering law?"[9] This objection has been raised time and again against abstract concepts of law and legal pluralism.[10] Folk legal pluralism, which looks at what people collectively identify as law, avoids the irresolvable problem of defining law, and does not suffer from over-inclusiveness.

The aim of this chapter is to clear up the theoretical morass surrounding legal pluralism and to point a way forward. Folk legal pluralism, I show, is commonsensical, theoretically sound, and works for the purposes of most theorists, scholars, and development practitioners interested in legal pluralism.

Discarding Strong versus Weak Legal Pluralism

One source of the theoretical morass is a flawed distinction between "strong" and "weak" legal pluralism implanted early on through John Griffiths's

---

[6] See Fernanda Pirie, *The Anthropology of Law* (Oxford: Clarendon Press 2013).

[7] H.L.A. Hart, *The Concept of Law* (Oxford: Clarendon Press 1961) 1.

[8] William Twining, "Normative and Legal Pluralism: A Global Perspective," 20 Duke Journal of Comparative and International Law 473, 487 (2010).

[9] Sally Engle Merry, "Legal Pluralism," 22 Law and Society Review 869, 878–79 (1988).

[10] A sophisticated recent analysis of these issues is Emmanuel Melissaris and Mariano Croce, "A Pluralism of Legal Pluralisms," Oxford Handbooks Online, April 2017, https://www.oxfordhandbooks.com/view/10.1093/oxfordhb/9780199935352.001.0001/oxfordhb-9780199935352-e-22

singularly influential article "What Is Legal Pluralism?" At the outset of the piece he targets "legal centralism": "According to what I shall call the ideology of legal centralism, law is and should be the law of the state, uniform for all persons, exclusive of all other law, and administered by a single set of state institutions."[11] This is the monistic law state image.[12] "Legal pluralism is the fact," he insisted. "Legal centralism is a myth, an ideal, a claim, an illusion."[13]

When Griffiths published his programmatic essay, legal anthropologists and jurists had used the label legal pluralism for several decades to refer to colonial and postcolonial legal systems that explicitly recognized indigenous customary law and religious law. This "weak" legal pluralism is yet another manifestation of legal centralism, he asserted, because it is a product of state recognition, which reinforces the notion that law is the product of the state. "'Legal pluralism' in the weak sense has little to do with the concept of legal pluralism which is the subject of this article,"[14] Grffiths declared. His essay put forth strong legal pluralism—"an empirical state of affairs, namely the coexistence within a social group of legal orders which do not belong to a single system."[15] Griffiths articulated a sociological conception of legal pluralism independent of state recognition that is present in *all societies*. A critical point to recognize, overlooked by many who invoke it, is that strong legal pluralism requires an abstract concept of law, as Griffiths understood.

The strong-weak distinction has since become entrenched, along with his assertion that only strong legal pluralism is genuine. "Griffiths's emphasis that the character of law should not depend on recognition by the state has been hugely influential within the literature on legal pluralism."[16] Two jurisprudence scholars recently proposed a version of his distinction (using "legal monism" in place of "legal centralism") as the basis for pluralist jurisprudence:

In these simple terms, traditional jurisprudence is municipal or state-centric jurisprudence. Even if it touches upon international law, it does so from a state-centric Westphalian perspective of viewing international law

---

[11] J. Griffiths, "What Is Legal Pluralism?," 24 *Journal of Legal Pluralism* 1, 3 (1986). I have omitted his citations to the theorists listed.

[12] *Id.* at 4.

[13] *Id.* at 4.

[14] *Id.* at 8.

[15] *Id.*

[16] Michaels, "Law and Recognition—Towards a Relational Concept of Law," in Roughan and Halpin, *supra* note 2, at 99.

through the agency or authority of states. It remains, in that sense, monist. By contrast, pluralist jurisprudence involves the recognition of non-state law in a way that is independent of both the agency and the authority of the state.[17]

The strong-weak distinction, however, is misleading and conceptually flawed. The dichotomy between state recognition (weak) versus independent forms of law (strong) leads to a distorted view of legal pluralism produced through colonization. Although colonial legal systems officially recognized customary and religious law, bodies of indigenous law had long predated the colonial state and were recognized within the community on property, marriage, child obligations, inheritance, personal injuries, debts and agreements, and other matters of everyday social intercourse. Most colonial states and their postcolonial successors lacked the capacity or need to suppress or replace indigenous law, particularly in rural areas, which functioned effectively to structure relations, maintain order, and resolve disputes for the populace. This still exists today. A recent report by the World Bank legal department observed: "In many of these countries, systems of justice seem to operate almost completely independently of the official state system."[18]

Colonial administrators and state legal officials put the best face on the matter by officially "permitting" customary and religious law to exist subject to repugnancy clauses. These forms of indigenous law likely would have continued to exist even without recognition because that is what people are familiar with and utilize in their daily affairs. As Chapter Three revealed, indigenous law in settler countries continued to exist in various forms within the community even though state legal officials denied its existence and tried to suppress it for decades. Many examples of resilient forms of community law have been provided in preceding chapters. In these situations, customary and religious forms of law exist independently through ongoing cultural processes *at the same time* that the state recognizes (or denies) them. What Griffiths dichotomized as weak and strong legal pluralism in actuality coexist and intertwine.

The conceptual flaw is that the "strong versus weak" distinction, and more specifically his strong version, depends on the formulation of a scientific or

---

[17] Halpin and Roughan, "Introduction," in Roughan and Halpin, *supra* note 2, at 3.

[18] Leila Chirayath, Caroline Sage, and Michael Woolcock, Customary Law and Policy Reform: Engaging with the Plurality of Justice Systems (World Bank Legal Department Paper 2005) 3.

philosophical conception of law, which despite many attempts has proven elusive if not unachievable. For reasons explained later, Griffiths acknowledged this when he subsequently repudiated legal pluralism.[19] Nonetheless, scholars continue to invoke Griffiths's strong-weak dichotomy, apparently unaware that he had abandoned its basis as unsound.

Differences between Abstract and Folk Legal Pluralism

The first step is to understand what legal sociologists and legal theorists have been trying to accomplish with their concepts of law and legal pluralism. Griffiths explained that without a scientific way to identify law, "It follows that the sociology of law has no distinct empirical object to study, that is, it cannot exist as a discipline."[20] Griffiths distinguished scientific from folk concepts of law:

> The first problem for the sociology of law, given the preceding assumptions, is to identify the sort of social fact it takes as its subject matter. Without clarity about that, it either lacks cohesion as a science or simply borrows its conception of its subject matter from the everyday usage of the man in the street, whose use of his folk conception of 'law' is as remote from the purposes of social science as his use of his conception of "matter" when he stubs his toe is from the concerns of particle physics.[21]

As this passage shows, Griffiths rejected folk conceptions of law because they are unscientific. "The first problem for the sociology of law," therefore, "is to identify the social fact it takes as its subject matter."[22] Legal pluralism follows from a sociological conception of law, which is why he declared it a "fact."

Producing a scientific or philosophical account of law is a common motivation behind abstract concepts of law and legal pluralism. Masaji Chiba proclaimed that "a sociology of law will be sure to be developed

---

[19] John Griffiths, "The Idea of Sociology of Law and its Relation to Law and to Sociology," in Michael Freeman, ed., *Law and Sociology* (Oxford: Oxford University Press 2006) 63–64.

[20] John Griffiths, "The Division of Labor in Social Control," in Donald Black, ed., *Toward a General Theory of Social Control*, vol. 1 (New York: Academic Press 1984) 45.

[21] *Id.*

[22] *Id.* at 39.

into a truly international sociology of law through this study of legal pluralism."[23] Ehrlich likewise offered his conception of law as the basis for the sociology of law, explaining: "legal science in the proper sense of the term is a part of the theoretical science of society, of sociology. The sociology of law is theoretical science of law."[24] Autopoiesis is a sociological theory of law, which Gunther Teubner extended to legal pluralism to account for global law: "for an adequate theory of global law, neither a political theory of law nor an institutional theory of autonomous law will do; instead a theory of legal pluralism is required."[25] Neil MacCormick articulates a theory of law as a social institution: "Law belongs to the genus 'normative order,' and is within that genus the particular species 'institutional normative order.'"[26] Joseph Raz expresses this in philosophical terms: "We talk of the 'nature of law,' or the nature of anything else, to refer to those of the law's characteristics which are of the essence of law, which make law what it is."[27]

These are very different theoretical approaches—sociological and jurisprudential, with various versions of each—that in multiple respects are at odds with one another. Griffiths was a scientific positivist who criticized theories of law produced by analytical philosophers like Hart and Raz as ideological delusions built on the monist image of state law. Notwithstanding these differences, these theories share three essentialist assumptions: (1) law is a *singular phenomenon* with (2) a particular *set of defining or essential features* that provides the basis for (3) an *objective or universal science or theory of law*. The italicized parts make three linked claims: law is one thing, that thing has defining features that make it what it is, and a science or theory of law can be constructed by centering on this thing and its features. Certain theorists maintain the first two essentialist assumptions but assume a more modest stance on the third, offering scientific or theoretical accounts of law as provisional. All of the abstract concepts of law and legal pluralism

---

[23] Masaji Chiba, "Toward a Truly International Sociology of Law through the Study of Legal Pluralism in the World," in A.J. Arnaud, ed., *Legal Culture and Everyday Life* (1989) 136.

[24] Eugen Ehrlich, *Fundamental Principles of the Sociology of Law*, translated by Walter Moll (Cambridge, MA: Harvard University Press 1936 [1913]) 25.

[25] See Gunther Teubner, "Global Bukowina: Legal Pluralism in the World Society," in Gunther Teubner, ed., *Global Law Without a State* (Aldershot: Ashgate 1996) 7.

[26] Neil MacCormick, *Institutions of Law: An Essay in Legal Theory* (Oxford: Oxford University Press 2007) 13.

[27] Joseph Raz, *Between Authority and Interpretation*, 2nd ed. (Oxford: Oxford University Press 2009) 24.

conveyed in this chapter make the first two claims, and a number also make the third.

Folk law legal pluralism denies all three essentialist assumptions.[28] Law is not a singular phenomenon—it is whatever people collectively view as law within social communities. Since people have viewed more than one social phenomenon as law—customary law, religious law, state law, international law, transnational law, etc.—multiple kinds of law have been identified with their own features, which vary and change over time. Although it is possible that common features within each kind of law and across all types of types of law can be identified, these are not essential or necessary features, but rather typical and overlapping features that can be absent or deviated from in particular instances of collectively identified law.[29] There is no universal science or theory of law. The best we can do is produce theoretical frameworks (always partial) that advance our understanding of law for given purposes; although, as I show, this approach enables important insights about law past and present.

The second step in understanding the differences between abstract and folk legal pluralism is in how they identify and conceptualize law. There are numerous versions of abstract legal pluralism, but every such theory formulates a concept or definition of law with a particular set of characteristic features. Whatever has these features *is* law, and whatever lacks these features *is not* law. Thus, abstract legal pluralism results in a *multiplicity of a single form of law* identified by the theoretical concept of law. To produce a concept or definition of law, a theorist starts by positing what she considers the paradigm of law, strips away what appears to be contingent features, and formulates in basic terms the essential features of law that provide the standard for what qualifies as law. The process of devising a theory of law is circular: the theorist must presuppose what law is to begin the analysis, which then determines the theory of law produced at the completion of the analysis. Different concepts of law exist because theorists posit different paradigms of law at the first step, and/or at the second step they reduce law in different ways, and/or they consider different features to be essential.

---

[28] For the pragmatist theoretical underpinnings of this position, see Brian Z. Tamanaha, "Pragmatic Reconstruction in Jurisprudence: Features of a Realistic Theory of Law," Canadian Journal of Law and Jurisprudence, forthcoming 2021.

[29] This view is often attributed to Wittgenstein's famous notion of "family resemblances." See Pirie, *supra* note 6, at 8.

Nearly all concepts of law within legal pluralist literature can be placed in one of two broad categories: (1) the inner ordering of associations or groups, or (2) institutionalized rule systems. John Griffiths's conception falls in the first category, conjoining the living law of Eugene Ehrlich with the semi-autonomous social field of Sally Falk Moore. This conception of law—which traces back to nineteenth-century historian-theorist Otto von Gierke—encompasses normative ordering within social groups generally. Legal sociologist Marc Galanter's conception of legal pluralism, which he bases on Hart's concept of law, falls in the second category, and similar versions have been articulated by legal theorists Neil MacCormick and Joseph Raz, among others. This approach encompasses institutionalized rule systems generally. After describing each stream in upcoming sections, I explain why irresolvable problems of over- and under-inclusiveness arise.

Folk legal pluralism identifies law in a different fashion and produces a wholly different account of legal pluralism. It does not formulate a scientific or philosophical concept or definition of law. Since law is ultimately a folk concept, folk legal pluralism identifies law by asking what people in a given social arena collectively recognize and treat through their social practices as law (*recht, droit, lex, ius, diritto, prawo,* etc.). This approach does not assume law has a single set of defining features, but instead accepts that conventionally recognized manifestations of law vary and change over time in connection with surrounding social, cultural, economic, political, techno-logical, and ecological circumstances. Sharia takes a different form in an Islamic theocracy than it does in liberal democracies, and local versions of Sharia vary greatly because they are infused with surrounding cultural notions and practices (Sharia in Afghanistan is very different from Sharia in Indonesia).

In contrast to abstract legal pluralism, which centers on a multiplicity of a single phenomenon theoretically defined as law, folk legal pluralism is about *a multiplicity of different forms of law collectively recognized by people within society* (state law, customary law, religious law, etc.), as well as *a multiplicity of the same kind of law.* It is pluralistic along two axes, not one. This approach, for instance, includes state courts at different levels or jurisdictions applying law; bodies of transnational law within and beyond the state; religious tribunals applying religious law, as well as informal village tribunals carrying out unwritten customary law; all of which are collectively recognized as law within many societies, sometimes with very different features, and often multiple manifestations of one or more may coexist. Legal pluralism understood in these terms is far more realistic, nuanced, and useful than abstract legal pluralism. Its application has already been demonstrated: the first four chapters of this book discussed many historical and contemporary examples of legal pluralism without defining law and without suffering from over- or under-inclusiveness.

Although these approaches are conceptually distinct, theorists can easily overlook their differences. In a recent essay Joseph Raz lists both types without marking their separation:

> I mean laws that are uncontroversially normative. They include international law, or the law of organizations like the European Union, but also Canon Law, Sharia law, Scottish law, the law of native nations, *the rules and regulations governing the activities of voluntary associations, or those of legally recognized corporations, and more, including very transient phenomena, like neighborhood gangs.*[30] (italics added)

The non-italicized forms of law Raz lists are examples of collectively recognized law (folk law), whereas the italicized examples are law constructed in abstract theoretical terms as institutionalized rule systems (abstract law). Neil MacCormick did the same: "You would tend to marginalise international law. You would tend to marginalise primitive law, you would marginalise canon law and church law. You would marginalise what is sometimes called *the 'living law' of social institutions like universities, firms or families* (all of which seem to me to work, when they do, in terms of what is at least partly institutionalized normative order)."[31] Like Raz, MacCormick mentions examples of folk and abstract law without distinction. Listing serially these alternatives sows confusion because they are derived in contrasting ways and have very different implications.

This chapter draws out the differences between these two perspectives and the superior coherence and use value of folk legal pluralism. The analysis progressively unpeels abstract concepts of law within legal pluralism, identifying their problems. We begin with the first category of abstract legal pluralism: law as the normative order of social associations.

---

[30] Raz, "Why the State?," in Roughan and Halpin, *supra* note 2, at 138.
[31] Neil MacCormick, "Beyond the Sovereign State," 56 Modern Law Review 1, 14 (1993) (emphasis added).

Ehrlich's "Living Law"

Eugen Ehrlich is widely identified in legal pluralist works as the original pioneer of the field. He holds this pride of place thanks to Griffiths's anointment of Ehrlich in "What Is Legal Pluralism?" The conception of law Griffiths adopts melds Ehrlich with Sally Falk Moore's notion of the semi-autonomous social field calling it "the 'living law' of 'semi-autonomous social fields.'"[32] Many legal pluralist theorists have credited Ehrlich. Jurisprudent Roger Cotterrell, for example, asserts that Ehrlich's "enduring contribution lies in his advocacy of a legal pluralist perspective that refuses to be confined by the scope of what lawyers and state officials recognize as law."[33]

Ehrlich taught law in undeveloped, multiethnic Bukovina in the waning days of the Austro-Hungarian Empire, with a mixed population of Ukrainians, Germans, Poles, Rumanians, Armenians, Jews, and Gypsies.[34] The empire accepted sub-communities with their own languages, customs, and customary laws, and Ehrlich witnessed firsthand that the Austrian Civil Code did not always match law followed within the community. Roscoe Pound remarked that "Ehrlich lived and taught in a place where modern law and primitive law came together and a modern complex industrial society jostled with groups of much older types."[35] It was evident to Ehrlich that many communities followed their own bodies of law in their daily affairs, particularly on family law matters, which were not consistent with the official Code.

He was sharply critical of jurists of the day for their exclusive focus on official codes, legislation, and judicial decisions. "As law is essentially a form of social life, it cannot be explained scientifically otherwise than by the workings of social forces."[36] Ehrlich summarized:

> The rule of law [of the state] does not proceed directly from society, it is devised by legislators and jurists. Society itself fashions only the legal order

---

[32] *Id.* at 36.

[33] Roger Cotterrell, "Ehrlich at the Edge of Empire: Centers and Peripheries in Legal Studies," in Marc Hertogh, ed., *Living Law: Reconsidering Eugen Ehrlich* (Oxford: Hart Publishers 2009) 87.

[34] See *id.* at 79–83. For an informative piece on Ehrlich's background, see Monica Eppinger, "Governing in the Vernacular: Eugen Ehrlich and Late Hapsburg Ethnography," in Hertogh, *supra* note 33, at 21–48.

[35] Roscoe Pound, "Introduction to 'The Sociology of Law,'" 36 Harvard Law Review 130, 130 (1922).

[36] Eugene Ehrlich, "Montesquieu and Sociological Jurisprudence," 29 Harvard Law Review 582, 584 (1916).

of the fundamental social institutions, the order of the clan, family, village, community, property, contract, inheritance. The ruling of this legal order, without any trace of the rule of law properly so called, constitutes the only law which may be found in primitive tribes or lower stages of civilization, and even in our own time a great deal of law still consists only in the legal order of social institutions. From this primary legal order the rule of law is derived by jurists and legislators by very intricate processes which I have endeavored to expound in the Sociology of Law. The rule of law cannot be understood sociologically without considering the legal order from which it arises.[37]

"The mass of law arises immediately in society itself in the form of a spontaneous ordering of social relations," he maintained.[38]

Law regulates relations within social associations, he asserted, "whether they are organized or unorganized, and whether they are called country, home, residence, religious communion, family, circle of friends, social life, political party, industrial association, or good will of a business."[39] These "numberless" associations exercise regulatory influence on members "much more forcibly than the state."[40] Ehrlich famously labeled this "living law," which he urged jurists to pay attention to:

> The *living* law is the law which dominates life itself even though it has not been posited in legal propositions [by legislatures or courts]. The source of your knowledge of this law is, first, the modern legal document; secondly, direct observation of life, of commerce, of customs and usages, and of all associations, not only of those that [state] law has recognized but also of those that it has overlooked and passed by, indeed even of those that it has disapproved.[41]

"In order to understand the actual state of the law we must institute an investigation as to the contribution that is being made by society itself as well as by state law, and also as to the actual influence of the state upon social law."[42]

---

[37] *Id.* at 584.
[38] Eugen Ehrlich, "The Sociology of Law," 36 Harvard Law Review 130, 136 (1922).
[39] Ehrlich, *supra* note 24, at 63.
[40] *Id.* at 64.
[41] *Id.* at 493.
[42] *Id.* at 504.

The living law, Ehrlich emphasized, is lived social ordering that does not necessarily take the same institutionalized form as state law:

> It is not an essential element of the concept of law that it be created by the state, nor that it constitute the basis for the decisions of the courts or other tribunals, nor that it be the basis of a legal compulsion consequent upon such a decision. A fourth element remains, and that will have to be the point of departure, i.e. the law is an ordering.[43]

These arguments were part of Ehrlich's more general point that law is interconnected within society, subject to ceaseless social, cultural, economic, political, and technological changes that continuously throw up new needs and conditions for law. "For the social order is not fixed and unchangeable, capable at most of being refashioned from time to time by legislation. It is in a constant flux. Old institutions disappear, new ones come into existence, and those which remain change their content continuously. . . . New conditions, moreover, mean also new conflicts of interest, new types of dispute, which call for new decisions and new Legal Provisions."[44] The bulk of legal development comes through the creative work of lawyers and judges, who steadily alter the law when keeping up with surrounding social changes by constructing new interpretations, legal documents, and legal fictions to "put a new picture into an old frame."[45] Ehrlich memorably declared, "The center of gravity of legal development therefore from time immemorial has not lain in the state but in society in itself, and must be sought there at the present time."[46]

Ehrlich's ideas about social and legal change are commonplace among law and society scholars today, but were novel for jurists at the time. His views were enthusiastically embraced by American sociological jurisprudents and the legal realists. Roscoe Pound declared, "I think it is the best thing that has been written lately."[47] He praised Ehrlich for showing "that it is not enough to be conscious that the law is living and growing, we must rather be conscious that it is a part of human life. It is not merely that it should look upon nothing human as foreign to it, in a sense everything human is a part of it."[48]

---

[43] *Id.* at 24.

[44] Ehrlich, *supra* note 38, at 139–40.

[45] Ehrlich, *supra* note 24, at 397.

[46] *Id.* at 390.

[47] Quoted in N.E.H. Hull, Roscoe Pound, and Karl Llewellyn: Searching for an American Jurisprudence (Chicago: University of Chicago Press 1997) 110.

[48] *Id.* at 108–109.

Notwithstanding this praise, jurists at the time widely rejected Ehrlich's notion of "living law" within social associations—the aspect of his work incorporated by contemporary legal pluralists. Ehrlich attributed this notion to Otto von Gierke:

> It is the deathless merit of Gierke that he discovered this characteristic of law in the bodies which he called associations (*Genossenschaften*), and among which he numbered the state, and that he gave an account of it in a detailed study. As a result of his labors, we may consider it established that, within the scope of the concept of the association, the law is an organization, that is to say, a rule which assigns to each and every member of the association his position in the community . . . and his duties.[49]

Law exists within associations "chiefly for the purpose of deciding controversies that arise out of communal relations."[50] "The inner order of the associations is determined by legal norms."[51]

The most common criticism voiced by jurists was that his notion of law is fuzzy and encompasses much of social life. Ehrlich made several efforts to clarify what is law. Social associations, he wrote, consist of "a plurality of human beings who, in their relations with one another, recognize certain rules of conduct as binding, and, generally at least, actually regulating their conduct according to them."[52] But these statements apply to all normative orderings, so law tied to social associations must be more narrowly defined.

Ehrlich suggests two ways to distinguish which kinds of normative orders are legal and which are not. The first way focuses on what he called the "workshop of law" within associations reflected in "usage, domination, possession, and declaration of will." Citing the family, his examples involve regularity, power over others, economic relations to things, and contracts and testaments.[53] Recognizing that this still does not suffice, however, Ehrlich proposes a final test for law: "Peculiar to the legal norm is the reaction for which the jurists of the Continental common law have coined the term *opinio necessitatis*. This is the characteristic feature which enables one to identify the legal norms."[54] This test points to subjective perceptions of

---

[49] Ehrlich, *supra* note 24, at 24.
[50] *Id.*
[51] *Id.* at 38.
[52] *Id.* at 39.
[53] *Id.* at 85, 118.
[54] *Id.* at 165.

fundamental gravity by people subject to the rules. "Compare the feeling of revolt that follows a violation of law with the indignation at a violation of a law of morality, with the feeling of disgust occasioned by an indecency, with the disapproval of tactlessness, the ridiculousness of an offense against etiquette."[55] "The legal norm regulates a matter which, at least in the opinion of the group within which it has its origin, is of great importance, of basic significance."[56] "Matters of lesser significance are left to other social norms," Ehrlich asserts.[57]

His criteria for law are too vague and too broad. Legal philosopher Morris Cohen wrote at the time, "Ehrlich's book suffers from the fact that it draws no clear account of what he means by law and how he distinguishes it from customs and morals."[58] Jurisprudent Felix Cohen objected that "under Ehrlich's terminology, law itself merges with religion, ethical custom, morality, decorum, tact, fashion, and etiquette."[59] This is the problem of overinclusiveness. Even John Griffiths concluded that Ehrlich's "theory therefore lacks an independent criterion of 'the legal.' He seems to take it as obvious which sorts of rules of conduct are legal in character."[60]

Law of Social Associations

The notion that law exists in the ordering of social associations shows up in a surprising number of sociological and juridical theories of law. Seldom mentioned by legal pluralists, Otto von Gierke is the original progenitor of this version of abstract legal pluralism, as Ehrlich acknowledged. Examining how he derived this idea will reveal the critical move that took his analysis down a path that multiple theorists have followed to the same dead end.

Gierke was a leading nineteenth-century proponent of historical jurisprudence who accepted Friedrich Savigny's view that law is an emanation of the collective people (*Volk*). Gierke criticized the proposed German Civil Code for its reliance on foreign Roman law concepts, which failed to reflect

---

[55] *Id.* at 165.

[56] *Id.* at 167–68.

[57] *Id.* at 168.

[58] Morris R. Cohen, "Recent Philosophical Literature: Legal Literature in French, German, and Italian," 26 International Journal of Ethics 528, 537 (1916).

[59] Felix Cohen, "Book Review: Fundamental Principles of the Sociology of Law," 31 Illinois Law Review 1128, 1130 (1937).

[60] Griffiths, *supra* note 11, at 27.

homegrown German legal concepts tied to social associations.[61] Social associations manifest our nature as social beings, he claimed, and constitute group-persons, organic unities, each with their own legal orders. The historical prototypes for his account were medieval guilds, towns, and churches, which were legally self-regulating groups with a common purpose; modern counterparts identified by Gierke include labor unions, corporations, social and economic clubs and associations, and others, including the state itself.[62]

"The systematic foundation of law, the form and content of its most important ideas, and the resolution of many very practical questions, are dependent upon the construction of the personality of association," Gierke observed.[63] The law of associations, or "social law," as he labels it, is involved in the formation and organization of associations, the inner unity of the group, and the relations between individuals and the group.[64] "The inner organization of an association is a legal organization," he wrote; "principles of law govern the relation of the one to the many in an organic whole."[65] Social groups large and small—from the family to local community to vocational groups to churches to the state—are social associations with attendant social law. Social law also addresses relations between groups, including the highest association—the state.

Gierke's polemical purpose was to invoke traditional Germanic associations to challenge the Roman law conceptualization of law in dualistic terms of absolutist states and individualism. His identification of bonds within social associations as "law" raised their status to one of equivalence. A jurist as well as historian, Gierke supported this argument by invoking medieval forms of law, which he studied as a scholar. The pivotal theoretical move he made was to *abstract from medieval forms of law to social associations generally.* Through this process of abstraction, he went from a specific historical complex of institutions collectively recognized as legal during the medieval period (manifestations of folk law at the time) to claims about modern social

---

[61] See Michael F. John, "The Politics of Legal Unity in Germany, 1870–1896," 28 The Historical Journal 341 (1985).

[62] For a summary of his theory, see John D. Lewis, "The Genossenschaft-Theory of Otto von Gierke," 25 Wisconsin Studies in the Social Sciences and History 1 (1935).

[63] Otto Gierke, The Nature of Human Associations, quoted in George Heiman, *Otto Gierke, Associations and Law: The Classical and Early Christian Stages* (Toronto: University of Toronto Press 1977) 10. See also Otto van Gierke, "The Social Role of Private Law" (translated by Ewen MacGaughey) 19 German Law Review 1017, 1110 (2018).

[64] Heiman, *supra* note 63, at 10–15. My account of Gierke's social law is substantially indebted to Heiman.

[65] Otto Gierke, Basic Concepts of State Law and the Most Recent State Law Theories, 25 University of Wisconsin Studies in the Social Sciences and History 158, 182 (1935).

associations of all sorts, including social clubs, economic clubs, unions, and many more.

However, two factors made this analytical move irreparably flawed. First, following the consolidation of law in the state, formerly recognized forms of law, like guilds, were no longer collectively recognized as law—social views evolved to consider them private rule systems. Second, the medieval forms of law he identified addressed fundamental rules of social intercourse (property, personal injuries, agreements and transactions, marriage, etc.) or were examples of ruling regimes, whereas the overwhelming majority of social associations today are not about these body of rules, but about the specific purposes of the organization. His abstraction to social associations, consequently, went in an orthogonal direction that pointed away from law addressing core elements of social intercourse or polities toward social ordering of groups generally, thereby extending beyond what are usually seen as law.

A few examples of abstract legal pluralism grounded on the ordering of social associations—directly or indirectly traceable to Gierke—exposes their inability to delimit law and as well as their over-inclusiveness. We have already seen this flaw in Ehrlich. A legal sociologist who took this position to an extreme is Georges Gurvitch. A scientific positivist with a penchant for categorization, Gurvitch (discussing Gierke and Ehrlich) identified a profusion of group-based "social law" operating within families, churches, trade unions, "classes, professions, producers, consumers, political parties; learned societies and welfare organizations; clubs, sports teams, tourist associations; and so on, without end."[66] Gurvitch's identification of multiple layers and kinds of law "would give not less than 162 (27 x 6) kinds of law which clash and balance with varying degrees of intensity and actuality inside every framework of law corresponding to each group, to each real collective unit."[67] Sociologist Alan Hunt critically remarked that Gurvitch's definition of law in terms of the inner ordering of social groups "is so broad that it runs the danger of redundancy through excessive indeterminacy." "In his usage, 'law' often appears interchangeable with the term social."[68] Legal sociologist Nicolas Timasheff identified the same flaw: "It is evident that numerous customary rules, for instance, rules of politeness and the rules pertaining to the

---

[66] Georges Gurvitch, *Sociology of Law* (New Brunswick, NJ: Transaction Press 2001) 232.

[67] *Id.* at 230. An informative explanation of Gurvitch's legal sociology is Pauline McDonald, "The Legal Sociology of Georges Gurvitch," 6 British Journal of Law and Society 24 (1979).

[68] Alan Hunt, "Introduction to the Transaction Edition," in Gurvitch, *supra* note 66, at xxxiv.

dueling custom, are covered by Gurvitch's conception of law. . . . [W]hat is being isolated is not law."[69]

A prominent mid-twentieth-century legal anthropologist, Leopold Pospisil, developed an elaborate version of abstract legal pluralism in the 1960s,[70] two decades before Griffiths. He incorporated Gierke's and Ehrlich's identification of law within social associations, asserting that "every functioning subgroup of society has its own legal system."[71] Law, according to Pospisil, is a combination of four necessary features: (1) legal decisions are made by a third-party leader with authority; (2) they are meant to apply to similar situations going forward (intention of universal application); (3) they define the rights of one party and duties of the other in a dispute (*obligatio*); and (4) they are enforced by psychological or physical sanctions.[72] "Law, which is characterized by these four criteria, is present in all societies— indeed, in every functioning group or subgroup of people," operating at multiple levels of inclusiveness.[73] The very existence of subgroups substantially depends on legal regulation of the behavior of members.[74] "Consequently and ultimately, even a small grouping such as the American family has a legal system administered by the husband, or wife, or both, as the case may be."[75] Since people are members of different subgroups, he continued, they are simultaneously subjected to different forms of law at the same level as well as at different levels of inclusiveness, including potentially contradictory laws.[76] Lower levels of law, in his analysis, were progressively encompassed within higher levels, constituting a hierarchical complex of legal arrangements. Yet another example of theoretical mapping of legal pluralism, Pospisil presents an account of multiple levels containing innumerable legal orders within society.

---

[69] Nicolas TImasheff, "Fundamental Problems of the Sociology of Law," 2 American Catholic Sociological Review 233, 240–41 (1941).

[70] See Leopold Pospisil, "Legal Levels and Multiplicity of Legal Systems in Human Societies," 11 Journal of Conflict Resolution 2 (1967). An earlier brief account is Leopold Pospisil, "Multiplicity of Legal Systems in Primitive Societies," 12 Bulletin of the Philadelphia Anthropological Society 1 (1959).

[71] Pospisil, "Legal Levels and Multiplicity of Legal Systems," *supra* note 70, at 9. He criticized Gierke for seeing groups as real organisms, and Ehrlich for identifying law with actual behavior rather with the articulation and enforcement of norms, but otherwise took on their view of law within social groups.

[72] *Id.* at 8–9, 24.

[73] Leopold Pospisil, *Anthropology of Law: A Comparative Theory* (New York: Harper and Row 1971) 8.

[74] Pospisil, *supra* note 70, at 13, 17.

[75] *Id.* at 13.

[76] *Id.* at 9, 24.

Few scholars outside of anthropology paid much attention to Pospisil's map of legal pluralism, and even within legal anthropology his ideas about the plurality of law spawned few followers (though his cases studies were informative).[77] Legal anthropologist Sally Falk Moore objected that Pospisil "applies the term 'law' to virtually every form of rule pertaining to an organized group in any society;" "but to call it all law, particularly speaking of complex societies, may be to risk confusion."[78]

Theorists who took this approach never convincingly justified the assertion that the inner ordering of associations *is law*. Ehrlich offered several scattered justifications: medieval social associations predated the state in serving the same legal functions; some of these institutions serve these functions even when state law is present; rules followed within social associations provide sources of law drawn on by legislators, judges, and lawyers; and state law is often less effective than rules followed within social associations.[79] These are reasons to identify these bodies of norms as predecessors to state law, functional equivalents of state law, and sources of law, but to say they *are law* requires more, particularly when it generates over-inclusiveness. Ehrlich could have made all the same observations about how lived social norms influence the operation of state law without making the additional claim that these social norms—relations within families, among business partners, within clubs, and much more—*are law*.

Folk legal pluralism was manifestly apparent in Ehrlich's Bukovina, a normal and unremarkable condition at the time (he did not actually speak about legal pluralism as such). In addition to multiple divisions within official law, ethnic and religious communities within the Austro-Hungarian Empire followed their own bodies of law, a common practice in empires throughout history, as Chapter One conveys. Ehrlich could have depicted legal pluralism in terms of collectively recognized forms of law (in terms of folk law). But his goal was to build a science of law on top of a sociological conception of law, the goal also pursued by Griffiths, Gurvitch, Pospisil, and others. In pursuit of a scientific theory of law, they rejected folk identifications of law, instead formulating abstract concepts that equated law with normative ordering of groups—which collapses out of sheer excess.

---

[77] An appreciative look at Pospisil's work, and why its impact on the field was limited, is Mark Ryan Goodale, "Leopold Pospisil—A Critical Reappraisal," 40 Journal of Legal Pluralism 123 (1998).

[78] Sally Falk Moore, *Law as Process: An Anthropological Approach* (London: Routledge and Kegan Paul 1978) 17.

[79] Ehrlich, *supra* note 24, at 2–24.

Repudiation by Moore and Griffiths

Griffiths used Moore's notion of the semi-autonomous social field (SASF) to solve Ehrlich's inability to delimit law, and following his lead, her idea is cited in many legal pluralist works as the locus of law. Griffiths acknowledged that Moore purposefully declined to use the label law for the norms within the SASF, but he dismissed her decision as a "last minute lapse into legal centralism."[80] Over her objections, he declared "law is the self-regulation of a semi-autonomous social field."[81] And he proceeded to assert: "'law' is present in every 'semi-autonomous social field,' and since every society contains many such fields, legal pluralism is a universal feature of social organization."[82]

Griffiths understood that his conception of law encompasses a broad continuum of normative ordering, from informal to institutionalized. The reason this occurs is that the normative ordering of social associations and groups— clubs, families, reading groups, neighborhood associations, partnerships, corporations, universities, sports leagues, governmental offices, etc.—are maintained by a range of types of normative mechanisms. Accepting this implication, Griffiths asserted "all social control is more or less legal."[83] Another leading early legal pluralist, Gordon Woodman, held the same: "The conclusion," he asserted, "must be that law covers a continuum which runs from the clearest form of state law through to the vaguest forms of social control."[84]

Unable to identify law as one form of social control among others, this version of abstract legal pluralism asserts all social control is law, conflating the two. A more sensible alternative position, in contrast, would hold that social control involves a broad category of normative mechanisms, one of which is law. But if Griffiths adopted the latter view he would be forced to drop the claim that living law of SASFs is law, for much of that involves informal norms.

To explain Moore's position, I must first say a few words about Bronislaw Malinowski's concept of law. Malinowski's *Crime and Custom in Savage Society* (1926) provides a classic account of non-state law. Trobriand Islanders, he showed, were not mindless followers of custom, but people in

---

[80] Griffiths, *supra* note 11, at 38.
[81] *Id.* at 38.
[82] *Id.* at 38.
[83] *Id.* at 39 n. 3.
[84] Gordon R. Woodman, "Ideological Combat and Social Observation: Recent Debate About Legal Pluralism," 42 Journal of Legal Pluralism 21, 45 (1998).

generally ordered societies punctuated by regular conflict who follow rules as well as try to utilize, manipulate, and avoid rules to achieve their objectives ("exactly as a civilized businessman would do"[85]). Common to many small-scale societies, the Trobriand did not have "central authority, codes, courts, and constables";[86] nonetheless, their society had "unquestionably rules of binding law" (albeit "elastic and adjustable")[87] addressing property, economic exchanges, killings, marriage and sexual intercourse, authority of chiefs, and a few other matters. These are the "rules of a Melanesian community which correspond to our civil law."[88]

Since the Trobriand lacked institutionalized coercion, Malinowski had to identify other reasons why people generally abide by the law. "The binding forces of Melanesian civil law are to be found in the concatenation of the obligations, in the fact that they are arranged into chains of mutual services, a give and take extending over long periods of time and covering wide aspects of interest and activity."[89] People follow the law mainly owing to shared normative agreement and positive inducement, a loss of future benefits, mutual dependence, and a sense of reciprocal obligations woven into relationships, not to fear of force-based coercion.[90] Law does not "consist in any independent institutions. Law represents rather an aspect of their tribal life, one side of their structure, than any independent, self-contained social arrangement."[91]

Ehrlich's and Malinowski's conceptions of law are similar in core respects.[92] Both identify law through observation of "concrete usages," with law consisting of what "the parties actually observe in life" (Ehrlich[93])— discernable by attention to how "they function in actual life" (Malinowski[94]). Both denied that law requires courts or police or institutionalized enforcement. Both point to reciprocity, positive incentives, and social obligations as primary forces behind binding law, while denying that physical coercion is necessary to law. As Ehrlich put it, "A man therefore conducts

---

[85] Bronislaw Malinowski, Crime and Custom in Savage Society (Totowa, NJ: Rowman and Allenheld 1982 [1926]) 30.

[86] *Id.* at 14.

[87] *Id.* at 31.

[88] *Id.* at 66.

[89] *Id.* at 67.

[90] *Id.* at 55.

[91] *Id.* at 59.

[92] Pospisil also sees their approaches as similar, though for different reasons from the ones I mention. Pospisil, *supra* note 73, at 29.

[93] Ehrlich, *supra* note 24, at 493.

[94] Malinowski, *supra* note 85, at 125.

himself according to law, chiefly because this is made imperative by his social relations";[95] as Malinowski put it, owing to "the concatenation of the obligations."[96] Although they approached from different directions, both saw law in terms of lived social ordering.

Malinowski's conception of law, like Ehrlich's, was widely criticized for failing to distinguish law from other aspects of social life—for being overinclusive. "The conception of law that Malinowski propounded was so broad that it was virtually indistinguishable from a study of the obligatory aspect of all social relationships," objected Sally Falk Moore. "Law is not distinguished from social control in general."[97] Simon Roberts likewise remarked, "Although Malinowski uses the term 'law' here, he seems to employ it so widely as to embrace all modes of social control."[98] Anthropologist Ian Schapera concluded that the inability to distinguish law from other social rules is why "with a few exceptions . . . jurists and sociologists are unwilling to accept his general conception of law."[99]

Moore's SASF builds on Malinowski's argument while avoiding what she identified as his error. Through anthropological studies of the Chagga in Africa and garment industry in New York City, Moore exposed how the efficacy of state laws and regulations are significantly affected by social obligations people experience as more immediately compelling in their local contexts of interaction.[100] Reviving Malinowski's argument, she showed that these binding obligations are maintained through relations of interdependency and reciprocity, enforced by social sanctions like loss of economic benefits or ostracism. Arenas of interaction are thick with rule-bound relationships of this sort, which significantly influence, impede, temper, and alter the actual impact of state laws that bear on their conduct. To frame these situations, she coined the "semi-autonomous social field," which is defined by "the fact that it can generate rules and coerce or induce compliance to them."[101] What makes these fields "semi-autonomous" is that, while their

<hr>

[95] Ehrlich, *supra* note 24, at 75, 77.

[96] Malinowski, *supra* note 85, at 67.

[97] Sally Falk Moore, "Law and Anthropology," 6 Biennial Review of Anthropology 252, 258 (1969).

[98] Simon Roberts, "Law and the Study of Social Control in Small-Scale Societies," 39 Modern Law Review 663, 674 (1976).

[99] Ian Schapera, "Malinowski's Theories of Law," in R. Firth, ed., *Man and Culture: An Evaluation of the Work of Malinowski* (London: Routledge and Kegan Paul 1957) 151.

[100] Sally Falk Moore, "Law and Social Change: The Semi-Autonomous Social Field as an Appropriate Subject of Study," 7 Law and Society Review 719 (1973).

[101] *Id.* at 722.

binding rules are effective, state law also matters in various ways as well in shaping and affecting contexts of social interaction.

Moore brilliantly conveys through these case studies that people are subject to multiple forms of normative ordering that influence them in ways that can lead to outcomes different from those dictated by state law. Remember that she had previously criticized Malinowski and Pospisil for confusingly broad concepts of law that encompassed much of social life. She rejected calling the rules within SASF "law" for the same reason. The norms and sanctions she identified in the semi-autonomous social fields of the Chagga and New York City garment industry involved phenomena like gift giving, future deals or benefits (or loss thereof), social ostracism, and a range of informal social norms well as official laws and regulations. Rather than use the label "law" for the normative ordering within SASFs, Moore proposed the term "reglementation," meaning regulation, which is literally correct, though unwieldly.

In a 2001 retrospective on the last half-century of legal anthropology, Moore laid out Griffiths's account of legal pluralism, omitting to mention that he had adopted her SASF to identify law. Then she issued this criticism:

> Following Griffiths, some writers now take legal pluralism to refer to the whole aggregate of government and non-government norms of social control, without any distinction drawn as to their source. However, for many purposes this agglomeration has to be disaggregated. For reasons of both analysis and policy, distinctions must be made that identify the provenance of rules and controls. To deny that the state can and should be distinguished from other rule-making entities for many practical purposes is to turn away from the obvious. And if one wants to initiate or track change, it is not only analytically useful but a practical necessity to emphasize the particular sites from which norms and mandatory rules emanate. To make such distinctions is not necessarily to adopt a 'legal centralist' view.[102]

In the next paragraph Moore identifies several social phenomena highlighted by legal pluralism, including "the way in which the state is interdigitated (internally and externally) with non-governmental, semi-autonomous social fields which generate their own (*non-legal*) obligatory norms to which they

---

[102] Sally Falk Moore, "Certainties Undone: Fifty Turbulent Years of Legal Anthropology, 1949–1999," 7 Royal Anthropological Institute 95, 106–107 (2001).

can induce or coerce compliance."[103] Recall that under Griffiths's theory, the norms of the SASF *are* law. By purposefully injecting "non-legal" after her reference to SASF, Moore firmly disagrees. Although politely delivered, her repudiation of Griffiths's use of her concept to identify law is unmistakable.

After two decades of promoting legal pluralism, the unresolvable problem of over-inclusiveness finally convinced Griffiths to concede that it does not work:

> In the intervening years, further reflection on the concept of law has led me to the conclusion that the word 'law' could be better abandoned altogether for the purposes of theory formation in sociology of law. . . . It also follows from the above considerations that the expression "legal pluralism" can and should be reconceptualized as "normative pluralism" or "pluralism in social control."[104]

This is a stunning reversal for Griffiths, a belated confirmation of Moore's refusal to use the term law for the rules of semi-autonomous social fields. He was the most outspoken champion of abstract legal pluralism for several decades. Abandoning a position that brought him scholarly renown, this turnaround is a testament to his inestimable intellectual integrity.

This repudiation also wipes away his widely cited distinction between strong and weak legal pluralism. To reiterate, he asserted that postcolonial state legal systems that recognize indigenous law are "weak" legal pluralism, which is just another variation of legal centralism. Strong legal pluralism is a multiplicity of legal orders entirely independent of state law. Earlier I argued that his strong-weak dichotomy does not map on to actual contexts of legal pluralism because official state recognition is not the basis for the existence of customary and religious law, often both independent provenance and official recognition are simultaneously present, and the bodies of law are intertwined in various ways. Here the objection is more fundamental: once he concludes that a scientific concept of law is not viable, strong legal pluralism falls by the wayside as well because it presupposes a scientific concept of law.

While the bulk of the preceding analysis has focused on legal sociologists and anthropologists, jurisprudents have articulated positions

---

[103] *Id.* at 107.
[104] Griffiths, *supra* note 19, at 63–64.

that succumb to over-inclusiveness. Jurisprudent Emmanuel Melissaris, the author of a book and several articles on legal pluralism, presents a vague, provisional conception of law based on normative discourses that "are institutionalized in that they create generalized expectations that are confirmed by a third party by being either enforced of confirmed and re-established in cases of their having been disappointed."[105] This includes "instances of legality ranging from the rules set by nightclubs and applied by their bouncers to the more intricate rules of associations or corporations."[106] Global legal pluralism theorist Paul Berman asserts there is no need to define law, as mentioned earlier, but he implicitly draws on a conception of law that echoes Gierke and Ehrlich,[107] identifying law with normative ordering within the multitude of communities within society, including families and people waiting in line.[108] And Berman recently acknowledged, "Indeed, given the broad (and often undefined) vision of law embraced by legal pluralists, it is perhaps not properly considered 'legal' either!"[109] These are variations of Griffiths's now-abandoned position that all forms of social control are law.

The view that law exists within the inner ordering of associations has captivated many theorists since Gierke first made this claim by abstracting from law in medieval manors, guilds, churches, etc., to law in social associations generally. Ehrlich's notion of living law, based thereon, has enjoyed a resurgence of popularity in legal pluralist works thanks to Griffiths. A century of repeated criticisms that this notion is incapable of delimiting law and is over-inclusive has not halted its use. Many legal pluralist works cite Moore's semi-autonomous social field as the locus of non-state law, against Moore's firm and repeated objections. Most remarkable of all, Griffiths concluded fifteen years ago that this approach does not work, though scholars continue to invoke it. Any legal pluralist who follows this path has been forewarned.

---

[105] Emmanuel Melissaris, "The More the Merrier? A New Take on Legal Pluralism," 13 Social & Legal Studies 57, 74 (2004).

[106] *Id.* at 74.

[107] Paul Schiff Berman, "The New Legal Pluralism," 5 Annual Review of Law and Social Science 225, 228 (2009).

[108] See Paul Berman, Global Legal Pluralism: A Jurisprudence of Law Beyond Borders (New York: Cambridge University Press 2012) 11–15, 262–63.

[109] Paul Schiff Berman, "Understanding Global Legal Pluralism: From Local to Global, From Descriptive to Normative," in Paul Schiff Berman, ed., *The Oxford Handbook of Global Legal Pluralism* (Oxford University Press) 62, available at https://papers.ssrn.com/sol3/papers.cfm?abstract_id=3715553.

Institutionalized Norm Enforcement

The second category of legal pluralism is based on law defined as institutionalized norm enforcement. Theorists who produce this concept of law posit state law as their model. They strip away surface trappings to conclude that a legal system, reduced to its essential features, consists of institutions that recognize, apply, and enforce legal norms. H.L.A. Hart engaged in this process when he centered on state law (what "most educated people see as law"[110]) and pared it down to a union of primary rules obligatory for social actors, and secondary rules used by legal officials to recognize, change, and apply the primary rules.[111] The combination of primary and secondary rules comprises the institutional structure of the legal system. When only primary rules of social obligation exist without secondary rules, which Hart identifies with primitive law and international law, it is pre-legal rather than law.[112]

"Many, if not all, legal philosophers have been agreed that one of the defining features of law is that it is an institutional normative system," Joseph Raz tells us.[113] Accordingly, many conceptions of law, particularly those produced by jurists, are based on institutionalized norm enforcement. There are multiple versions in this category—some formulated as institutionalized dispute resolution, some incorporating justice or legitimate authority, some adding a public or governmental element, or something else—but at bottom they focus on an institutionalized system of norms for the purposes of social order. Sociologist Max Weber, who was trained in law, asserted: "The term 'guaranteed law' shall be understood to mean that there exists a 'coercive apparatus,' i.e., that there are one or more persons whose special task is to hold themselves ready to apply specially provided means of coercion (legal coercion) for the purpose of norm enforcement."[114] (The coercive apparatus with the special task of enforcement is the institutional component.) Coercion could be "of a physical or psychological kind."[115] Although the modern state characteristically claims a monopoly over law, Weber denied that the state is the exclusive form of law and he recognized that multiple legal systems can coexist, which he was acquainted with as a scholar of medieval law.

---

[110] Hart, *supra* note 7, at 2, 3.

[111] *Id.* at Chapter 5.

[112] *Id.* at 91.

[113] Joseph Raz, *The Authority of Law*, 2nd ed. (Oxford: Oxford University Press 1979) 105.

[114] Max Weber, *Max Weber on Law in Society and Economy*, edited by Max Rheinstein (New York: Simon and Schuster 1954) 13.

[115] *Id.* at 17.

Another definition that garnered support was put forth by legal anthropologist Paul Bohannan. He held that law consists of two kinds of rules: customary rules on basic matters of social intercourse, and rules "that govern the activities of the legal institution itself (called 'adjectival' law by Austin and procedure by most modern lawyers)."[116]

> Customs are norms or rules (more or less strict, and with greater or less support of moral, ethical, or even physical coercion) about the ways in which people must behave if social institutions are to perform their tasks and society is to endure. . . . Some customs, in some societies, are *re*institutionalized at another level: they are restated for the more precise purposes of legal institutions. When this happens, therefore, law may be regarded as a custom that has been restated in order to make it amenable to the activities of the legal institutions. In this sense, it is one of the most characteristic attributes of legal institutions that some of these "laws" are about the legal institutions themselves, although most are about the other institutions of society—the familial, economic, political, ritual, or whatever.[117]

This conception closely resembles Hart's account of law as a union of primary and secondary rules.

An influential early work on legal pluralism, Marc Galanter's "Justice in Many Rooms: Courts, Private Ordering, and Indigenous Law" (1981), adopted this approach. Published a few years apart in the *Journal of Legal Pluralism*, this was a companion piece with Griffiths's "What Is Legal Pluralism?"; the latter had been circulating since 1979, and both essays favorably cite the other. Like Griffiths, Galanter observed that the "legal centralist model is deficient," and he offered an understanding of law with greater "descriptive adequacy."[118]

Galanter has produced a series of leading sociological studies of law and the legal profession. This article draws from a range of studies to show that society is thick with normative orders. Galanter emphasizes several points: the overwhelming majority of disputes in society are not resolved in state courts; a substantial amount of social regulation in society occurs within private rule

---

[116] Bohannan, *supra* note 5, at 33, 35.
[117] *Id.* at 36.
[118] Marc Galanter, "Justice in Many Rooms: Courts, Private Ordering, and Indigenous Law," 19 Journal of Legal Pluralism 1, 2 (1981).

systems like workplaces and schools; state law has a limited capacity to penetrate social arenas; and often state law is less efficacious than private regulation. Since they exercise regulatory functions equivalent to law, he argued, these private rule systems are "indigenous law." "By indigenous law I refer not to some diffuse folk consciousness," Galanter explained, "but to concrete patterns of social ordering to be found in a variety of institutional settings—in universities, sports leagues, housing developments, hospitals, etc."[119]

Galanter recognized that there are multiple forms of social ordering that exist on a continuum. "How then can we distinguish 'indigenous law' from social life generally?,"[120] he asked. The demarcation for law, he offered, is "the organization and differentiation of norms and sanctions. The differentiation is the introduction of a second layer of control—of norms about the application of norms—along the lines of Hart's (1961) identification of law with the union of primary and secondary rules and Bohannan's (1965) identification of law with the reinstitutionalization of norms."[121] Recognition of indigenous law helps convey the "recurrent rediscovery that law in modern society is plural rather than monolithic, that it is private as well as public in character and that the national (public, official) legal system is often a secondary rather than a primary locus of regulation."[122]

This version of legal pluralism also suffers from over-inclusiveness. The clue that signals this problem is the often repeated assertion that law exists in "universities, sports leagues, housing developments, hospitals, etc.," as Galanter observed. Legal theorist Neil MacCormick also identified law as institutional normative orders, concluding that law exists in "the 'living law' of social institutions like universities, firms or families";[123] as well as "laws of games and laws of national and international sporting associations."[124] Joseph Raz identifies law in "the rules and regulations governing the activities of voluntary associations, or those of legally recognized corporations, and more, including many very transient phenomena, like neighborhood gangs."[125] The legal institutions he has in mind, Raz elaborates, "are themselves rule-governed, ultimately governed by practice-based rules that

---

[119] *Id.* at 17–18.

[120] *Id.* at 18 n. 26.

[121] *Id.* at 19 n. 19.

[122] *Id.* at 20.

[123] MacCormick, *supra* note 31, at 1, 14 (1993).

[124] Neil MacCormick, "The Maastricht-Urteil: Sovereignty Now," 1 European Law Journal 259, 261 (1995).

[125] Joseph Raz, "Why the State?," in Roughan and Halpin, *supra* note 2, at 138.

determine if not all at least the most important aspects of their constitution, powers, and mode of operation. Perhaps the most elementary legal powers institutions have are enforcement and adjudication."[126] "In this sense," he continues, "both the rules of the Roman Republic and those of the University of Wales (disbanded 2011), just as the rules of the United States and of Columbia University, *are legal systems*."[127]

A century ago Italian jurist Santi Romano articulated a theory of legal pluralism that takes this line of thinking to its utmost extension, asserting that every institution is a legal order and every legal order is an institution.[128] An institution in his theory has four characteristics: a concrete objective existence, a social entity, borders that render it individual, and a permanent unity with continuity.[129] Legal orders, in this view, include states, municipalities, corporations, factories, political parties, a prison, a church, a family, a criminal gang, and much more.[130] The state is not the exclusive source of law, but just one species of the *genus* law.[131] Romano acknowledges that his view of law is close to Gierke's,[132] though he shifts the locus of law from social associations to institutions.[133]

What this version does, in effect, is simply relabel "institutional rule systems" as "law." Since every society is overflowing with a multitude of institutionalized rule systems—universities, sports leagues, etc.—society is suffused with a multiplicity of law. But *why* is this *law*? It makes more sense to assert that society is filled with a multitude of institutionalized rule systems, some of which are law. Legal pluralist Boaventura de Sousa Santos responded to this objection with a question:

It may be asked: why should these competing or complementary forms of social ordering be designated as law and nor rather as 'rule systems', 'private governments', and so on? Posed in these terms, this question can only be answered by another question: Why not?[134]

[126] *Id.* at 142.

[127] *Id.* at 143 (emphasis added).

[128] See Santi Romano, *The Legal Order* (Abingdon: Routledge 2018).

[129] *Id.* at 17–19.

[130] For a concise description of Romano's account of law, see Lars Vinx, "Santi-Romani Against the State?," 11 Ethics and Global Politics 25, 27–29 (2018).

[131] See Aldo Sandulli, "Santi Romano and the Perception of the Public Law Complexity," 1 Italian Journal of Public Law 1, 23 (2015).

[132] For the connection and similarity, see Anna di Robilant, "Genealogies of Soft-Law," 54 American Journal of Comparative Law 499, 539–43 (2006).

[133] Romano, *supra* note 128, at 68.

[134] Boaventura de Sousa Santos, Toward a New Common Sense: Law, Science and Politics in the Paradigmatic (1995) 115.

The short answer is that it is confusing, counterintuitive, and allows less refined analysis of differences among rule systems. Postmodernists like Santos might not care, as long as their objective of debunking settled understandings of law is served, but most theorists who take this position are not postmodernists and they seek theoretical coherence. The commonplace sociological assertion that innumerable institutionalized rule systems exist in society is transformed by these theorists into the puzzling assertion that all of them *are law*. Nor is this claim necessary to the analysis—the insights Galanter conveyed about the ubiquity and influence of rule systems in society remain valid without the separate claim that they constitute "indigenous law." It was labeled "law" by analogy and for rhetorical reasons, not based on theoretical justifications.

Institutionalized rule systems are ubiquitous because that is a highly effective way to create and enforce bodies of rules in a variety of settings. These features are not unique to law but are aspects of social institutions generally.[135] The reconstructed chain of reasoning applied by these theorists goes as follows: (1) state law, when abstracted to its fundamental features, is an institutionalized rule system that enforces norms; (2) all institutionalized rule systems enforcing norms are law; (3) universities and corporations have institutionalized rule systems enforcing norms so they *are* legal systems. The problem lies in the second proposition. This assertion must be justified as analytically sound. The slide from one to the next is evident in MacCormick's assertion: "Wherever there is law, there is normative order; wherever there is normative order institutionalized, there is law."[136] The second proposition does not follow from the first.

Over- and Under-Inclusiveness of Functional Analysis

Let me briefly explain why over- and under-inclusiveness of abstract concepts of law are unavoidable. To produce a concept or definition of law, as mentioned earlier, theorists typically begin with (presuppose or posit) a paradigm of law and produce abstractions based on *function* and *form*.

---

[135] For a fuller explanation, see Brian Z. Tamanaha, A Realistic Theory of Law (New York: Cambridge University Press 2017) 48–54.
[136] MacCormick, *supra* note 31, at 11.

The first category ties law to the normative ordering of social associations. The origins of this idea, as indicated, lies in the move made by Gierke that abstracted from law of medieval associations like guilds to law in the ordering of social associations generally. However, many social associations today—family, book club, neighborhood committee, bowling league, etc.— are bound together by customs, morals, habits, informal agreements, shared rules, legal contracts, etc. The internal normative ordering of social groups is maintained by a range of normative mechanisms. In sociology this is known as "functional equivalents" or "functional alternatives," which recognizes that many social functions can be satisfied in more than one way. When law is defined in terms of the inner ordering of associations, all functional equivalents—everything that contributes to normative ordering within groups—are encompassed as law. That is why the concepts of law as social ordering presented by Ehrlich, Malinowski, Gurvitch, Pospisil, and others, elicited the same criticism: they encompass all of social life (customs, morals, habits, etc.). This approach unavoidably leads to the assertion that all social control is law.

The second category, law as institutionalized norm enforcement, trims the pool of normative ordering by adding the structural requirement that law is an institutionalized normative system. This institutional component is derived through an abstract reduction of the institutionalized structure of state law. Applying this standard to identify law eliminates custom, morals, habits, etc., which typically are not enforced by standing institutions. Law is now conceived in terms of a combination of form (institutionalized) and function (norm enforcement to maintain social order). However, the problem of over-inclusiveness again arises because a multitude of rule-based social institutions have the same combination of form and function. This involves the repetition of effective functional arrangements in multiple settings. Institutionalized norm enforcement is a common arrangement in society because many social organizations utilize systems to declare, enforce, and apply rules, including universities, corporations, sports leagues, etc., which Galanter, MacCormick, Raz, Romano, and others assert *are law*. Under this approach, all institutionalized norm enforcement is law.

Form and function concepts of law abstracted from state law, it should be noted, are also *under*-inclusive, that is, they exclude recognized forms of law. Law collectively recognized by communities that lack the institutionalized form of state law—like informal village gatherings carrying out customary law—are disqualified as law under these concepts. Many collectively recognized manifestations of law are excluded by the formulation of law as institutionalized norm enforcement, including customary and versions of transnational law. The absence of an organized system of secondary rules is why Hart concluded that under his concept of law primitive law and international law are not fully fledged law, but "pre-legal."

Over- and under-inclusiveness of concepts of law result in peculiar assertions. Theorists who hold that law is institutionalized norm enforcement assert that corporations and universities *are legal systems*, although people working in corporations and universities typically do not see them as legal systems. The same theorists assert that manifestations of customary law that lack institutions *are not law*, although people in these communities see them as law. In both instances the formulation of law produced by theorists is at odds with the understandings of people involved. The theorists are left to respond that people are mistaken about what they identify as law, even though law is ultimately a folk concept.

One might think that these problems can be solved by somehow combining the concepts of law in the two categories. But they cannot be joined together because each directly contradictions the other. Theorists who see law in terms of normative ordering of groups, like Ehrlich and Malinowski, explicitly deny that law requires institutions; while theorists who see law in terms of institutionalized norm enforcement insist that normative orders without such institutions are not law. This impasse cannot be overcome because each side starts from a different paradigm of law as the basis of their respective abstract concepts of law. The former assert that law exists in all societies, whereas the latter conclude that societies without legal institutions do not have law.

An instructive theory of law by anthropologist Adamson Hoebel encompasses both customary law and state law, but still does not overcome this problem. "A social norm is legal if its neglect or infraction is regularly met, in threat or in fact, by the application of physical force by an individual or group possessing the socially recognized privilege of so acting,"[137] he declared. This captures the intuition that the regular application of physical coercion for violations of norms distinguishes law from morality, custom, and other social norms; and what distinguishes legal force from revenge or retribution is prior social authorization of the imposition of the sanction.

---

[137] Adamson Hoebel, *The Law of Primitive Man* (Cambridge, MA: Harvard University Press 1954) 28.

When the victim's kin carries out the punishment, as was often the case in small-scale societies, this is law under Hoebel's formulation when community approval is required (via chiefs or elders or the community as a whole). But his formulation does not meet a standard of law that requires institutionalized norm enforcement. Law can exist for Hoebel although "there are no courts and no specialized law-enforcing agents."[138] As anthropologist Simon Roberts observed, "in small scale societies, the mechanisms for maintaining continuity and handling disputes tend to be almost universally directly embedded in everyday life, unsupported by a differentiated legal system."[139] If one is committed to the proposition that law exists in small-scale societies, then law cannot be defined in terms of an institutionalized normative system.

The lesson of these many unsuccessful attempts is clear: any concept of law based solely on function and form cannot avoid over- and under-inclusiveness. That is why abstract legal pluralism fails. To distinguish law from non-law we must rely on the collective identification of law, that is, on folk law.

Several seminal insights conveyed in these theories, I should emphasize, remain valid even if we discard assertions that they constitute law. One point is that actually followed normative orders within social groups are maintained in a range of ways that do not necessarily involve institutionalized sanctions. Shared understandings, shared norms, mutual interest, relationships of reciprocity, and informal sanctions like ostracism or loss of future benefits often are effective. This does not necessarily involve state law and indeed may be contrary to what state law officially requires. That is what Moore emphasized. Another point is that people in society are directly subject to many different rule-based institutionalized systems, not just state law. That is what Galanter emphasized. These points are timeless reminders that state law frequently is influenced by, interacts with, and is secondary in impact to other sources of normative order and other rule systems circulating within society—as Moore, Galanter, and Ehrlich emphasized. Legal sociologists and anthropologists have long made these points. Many jurists have come to accept them as well, persuaded by Robert Ellickson's

---

[138] E. Adamson Hoebel, "Fundamental Legal Concepts as Applied in the Study of Primitive Law," 51 Yale Law Journal 951, 956–57 (1942).

[139] Simon Roberts, "Law and the Study of Social Control in Small-Scale Societies," 39 Modern Law Review 663, 667 (1976).

Order Without Law,[140] studies of extralegal contractual relations among merchants,[141] and other such studies, going back a half-century to Stewart Macauley's celebrated "Non-Contractual Relations in Business."[142] These insights stand undiminished even if one rejects claims that all social groups have law, or that all social ordering is more or less legal, or that all institutionalized rule systems *are* law. Griffiths's enduring contribution is the rhetorical sledgehammer he wielded to shake prevailing assumptions about the monist law state, helping pave the way for broader recognition that multiple manifestations of law coexist in society.

Postmodern Legal Pluralism

Only a few words can be said about postmodern legal pluralism, put forth by various proponents. Postmodern legal pluralists and critical legal pluralists (overlapping groups) reject scientific and analytical concerns about defining or conceptualizing law. For these theorists, legal pluralism should be crafted in whatever ways that further the political agendas of debunking state law, challenging its hegemonic claims, advancing the interests of the oppressed or marginalized. Pluralistic thinking in general, not just legal pluralism, has an affinity with the postmodernist challenge to universalistic, objectivistic claims of whatever kind.[143] All aspects of law and legal discourse should be deconstructed, in their view, including puncturing claims about law within the social sciences and jurisprudence. Concepts of law are constructs that can be dispensed with entirely or provisional concepts can be utilized in particular contexts without making any broader claims.

The picture conveyed by postmodern legal pluralism is a thick overlapping of legal orders (epitomized by Santos's map, described in the preceding chapter). One version of critical legal pluralism eschews the usual focus on society and groups, proposing instead to center on individuals (citizens and

---

[140] Robert C. Ellickson, *Order Without Law: How Neighbors Settle Disputes* (Cambridge, MA: Harvard University Press 1994).

[141] Lisa Bernstein, "Opting Out of the Legal System: Extralegal Contractual Relations in the Diamond Industry," 21 Journal of Legal Studies 115 (1992).

[142] Stewart Macauley, "Non-Contractual Relations in Business: A Preliminary Study," 28 American Sociological Review 25 (1963).

[143] Gregor McLenan, *Pluralism* (Minneapolis: University of Minnesota Press 1995) 9–24.

legal officials) at the intersection of multiple (pluralistic) narratives about law,[144] showing how law is constituted by drawing on coexisting sources.[145]

Consistent with its anti-grand theory posture, postmodern legal pluralism resists generalization; critical theory challenges elite hegemony and structures of domination through legal ideology and power. Beyond these ideas, it is difficult to characterize postmodernism legal pluralism, as each instance is unique and goes its own way. Still, one may question whether the postmodern approach furthers their announced critical goals. Every conception of legal pluralism creates a framework to help make sense of a messy presence of coexisting legal orders. To the extent that knowledge is empowering, formulating a consistent way to grasp these situations across contexts may have emancipatory potential.

Folk Law in Social-Historical Terms Tied to Social Complexity

A social-historical theory of law that focuses on folk law and tracks changes tied to social complexity provides a framework for understanding many manifestations of law and legal pluralism across history and today. Social complexity, to put it concisely, is linked to population size and density; the degree and quantity of differentiated institutions to organize social action for various purposes; and the extent of networks and channels of interaction between and among people, groups, entities, and institutions. Collectively recognized forms of folk law can be grouped in the three categories I have used throughout this book[146]—community law, regime law, and cross-polity law—now understood in relation to social complexity.

Once again, Malinowski points the way. What Malinowski posited as paradigmatic of law among the Trobriand are fundamental rules of social intercourse that exist in all societies, primitive and modern. "Under civil law in a native society," he wrote, "we can understand the set of rules regulating all

---

[144] See Martha-Marie Kleinhans and Roderick A. Macdonald, "What Is Critical Legal Pluralism?," 12 Canadian Journal of Law and Society 25 (1997). This position was presaged in Jaques Vanderlinden, "Return to Legal Pluralism: Twenty Years Later," 28 Journal of Legal Pluralism 156 (1989).

[145] See Margaret Davies, "Plural Pluralities of Law," in Roughan and Halpin, *supra* note 2, at 238–60.

[146] Other forms of collectively recognized law may exist that do not fit in these three categories. The most significant example is natural law, which is a long-standing tradition that differs from these three.

the normal relations between persons, as kinship, marriage, economic co-operation and distribution, trading, etc.; and between persons and things, property inheritance, etc."[147] Ehrlich likewise recognized that these fundamental rules exist in all societies, "uncivilized and half-civilized": "All these matters, marriage, family, possession, contracts, succession, are legal affairs unthinkable without a law."[148] His examples of living law relate to these matters, though, led astray by Gierke, he went in an orthogonal direction when abstracting from this corpus to social associations generally.

The fundamental rules of social intercourse address the basic conditions of social relations within societies.[149] Anthropological and psychological research have confirmed a number of human universals, albeit with a great deal of cultural variation in their expressions.[150] Among these common traits (group living, shelter, tools, music, aesthetic standards, reciprocal gift giving, cosmology, etc.), those specifically related to law include property rights, prohibitions against murder, redress for violent injuries, debts and agreements, marriage, inheritance, sexual restrictions, rights and obligations related to statuses, binding decisions, and punishments for infractions.[151] These are the same matters that decentralized medieval law took up, that empires throughout history left in place as local community law, that colonial legal systems recognized as indigenous customary and religious law, and that operate across the Global South today, as earlier chapters described. These are the rules that people live by and arrange their daily social interaction through. This basic set of rules of social intercourse has been collectively recognized as "law" (and its translation) in many societies past and present. This is what I call *community law*.

Sally Falk Moore declared "No society is without law."[152] Her assertion is correct with respect to community law: no society is without the fundamental

---

[147] Malinowski quoted, in Schapera, *supra* note 99, at 140.

[148] Ehrlich, *supra* note 38, at 131.

[149] See Bronislaw Malinowski, "A New Instrument for the Interpretation of Law—Especially Primitive Law," 51 Yale Law Journal 1237 (1942).

[150] See Donald E. Brown, *Human Universals* (New York: McGraw Hill 1991).

[151] On evidence for the naturalistic basis for these basic rules of social intercourse, see Daniel Sznyer and Carlton Patrick, "The Origins of Criminal Law," Nature Human Behavior 506 (2020); Brown, *supra* note 150, at 136–40; Kent Flannery and Joyce Marcus, *The Creation of Inequality: How our Prehistoric Ancestor Set the Stage for Monarchy, Slavery, and Empire* (Cambridge, MA: Harvard University Press 2012) Chapter 4; Edward Wilson, *The Social Conquest of Earth* (New York: Liveright Publishing 2012) 192–93; Tamanaha, *supra* note 135, at 82–84. See also Robert M. Sapolsky, *Behave: The Biology of Humans at Our Best and Worst* (New York: Penguin Press 2017); This is a different version of what Hart called the minimum content of natural law. See Hart, *supra* note 7, at 188.

[152] Moore, *supra* note 78, at 215.

rules of social intercourse. Though the content of the rules varies greatly and changes over time, some version of these rules always exist because natural human traits and the requirements of everyday social life give rise to these rules. While these rules help maintain cohesion within small- and large-scale societies, under the folk law approach, law is not *defined* in terms of the function of maintaining social cohesion. Rather, law is what people collectively recognize as law (hence folk law)—and this category is derived inductively, empirically based on a corpus of rules collectively recognized as law across many societies.

In larger populations, divisions of labor develop whereby specialized institutions carry out regularized activities, including governing, commercial activities, food and water procurement and distribution, sanitation, etc., the tasks all large societies much manage. Legal institutions—staffs of people who create, enforce, and apply legal rules—emerge in larger groups as a part of the general process of social differentiation. As Malinowski put it, "Evolution consists in a constantly increasing institutional crystallization of such specific activities as those related to economic production, distribution, and consumption; the administration of law and justice; education and politics; practices of religious cult; the cultivation of science, literature, art and music; and the pursuit of sport and recreation."[153]

In chiefdoms and early states, coercive legal institutions maintain political domination and internal control, defense from outsiders, and enforce social and economic hierarchy.[154] This is law of the ruling polity governing a population. Rulers, priests, administrators, and judges were typically drawn from a hereditary aristocracy that controlled landed wealth, using commoners, serfs, and slaves to work the land under property and labor arrangements enforced by law.[155] Legal systems provide the enforcement muscle that backs ruling polities as they secure their control within society. This is what I call *regime law*—law attached to the polity (centers of governance)—a second major category of folk law. Ruling regimes—including chiefdoms, sub-states, states, empires, and other forms—can coexist in various relationships with subordinate or superior regimes, nested or cross-cutting or at parallel levels.

---

[153] Malinowski, *supra* note 149, at 1237, 1240.

[154] An excellent overview is Robert L. Carneiro, "The Chiefdom: Precursor of the State," in Grant D. Jones and Robert R. Kautz, eds., *The Transition to Statehood in the New World* (Cambridge: Cambridge University Press 1981) 37–75; See Gil J. Stein, "Heterogeneity, Power, and Political Economy: Some Current Research Issues in the Archaeology of Old World Complex Societies," 6 Journal of Archaeological Research 1 (1998). See Tamanaha, *supra* note 135, at 84–89.

[155] Flannery and Marcus, *supra* note 151, at 478–81, 500–502.

Regime law may include within its ambit the creation and enforcement of fundamental rules of social intercourse (community law), which is typically how contemporary state legal systems are constructed, but that is not necessary. Empires throughout history left local community laws and institutions intact, and a version of this, the legacy of European colonization, still exists in areas across the Global South.

Legal anthropologist Simon Roberts, a critic of legal pluralism,[156] argued that our notion of law is tied to centralized governmental control: law involves institutionalized governance by power-holders. "Law is a concomitant of centralizing processes, processes that, at a certain point, resulted in the formation of the nation state."[157] This is what I mean by regime law. Roberts did not insist that small-scale societies did not have law, only that "it has proved very difficult, despite sustained attempts to do so, to talk confidently about law in the case of the acephalous orders of pre-state/non-state world or about local level orderings within centralized polities."[158] He is correct. However, previous efforts have defined law through abstractions based on form and function, which do not work for the reasons explained. The fundamental rules of social intercourse that exist in all societies (community law) allow us to draw direct parallels between law in small-scale societies and in large-scale societies, the difference being that the latter also have institutionalized regime law. Manifestations of both community law and regime law have been collectively identified as law so both *are* law—now understood in relation to evolving social complexity.

Along with the increasingly explosive growth of human populations and the development of technology, societies have undergone the consolidation of state law in territorial terms (regime law), while also witnessing a growth and proliferation of law between and across polities to deal with a range of activities and consequences that cross borders, particularly transnational commerce. A significant subset of this today is collectively recognized as "law," including international law and transnational law. This is *cross-polity law*—a third category of folk law. The literature on global legal pluralism highlights these forms of law, though this literature also includes private regulation and

---

[156] See Simon Roberts, "Against Legal Pluralism: Some Reflections on the Contemporary Enlargement of the Legal Domain," 42 Journal of Legal Pluralism 95 (1998).

[157] Simon Roberts, "After Government: On Representing Law without the State," 68 Modern Law Review 1, 13 (2005).

[158] *Id.* at 17.

other regulatory and governance mechanisms that are not collectively recognized as "law," which does not diminish their significance.

These categories are generalizations inductively derived from grouping common historical and contemporary manifestations of folk law. Community, regime, and cross-polity law have coexisted in the past and all exist today, though their relative volume has changed over time. Community law today largely addresses the same matters as in the past (though again, the content of the rules varies greatly). Regime law has grown enormously in the last two centuries with the vast expansion of government bureaucracies and instrumental lawmaking; and lately cross-polity law has multiplied to deal with global capitalism and modern cross-border transportation and communication.[159] Legal pluralism involves the coexistence and juxtaposition of multiple instantiations of community, regime, and cross-polity law in given social arenas.

Folk law understood in social-historical terms is the most coherent way to capture legal pluralism. It builds on and tracks folk conceptions of law, and makes theoretical generalizations based on folk conceptions of law without veering away through abstraction. (Family, clubs, universities, corporations, sports leagues, etc., and institutionalized rule systems generally, are not law because they are not collectively considered law.) It picks up the basic variations present in situations of legal pluralism: multiple coexisting bodies of community law; divergences between regime law and community law; multiple bodies of regime laws with various realms of authority; multiple bodies of cross-polity law; and other variations. The social-historical approach helps capture another important element of legal pluralism: forms of community law that survive over time (Romani, Jewish, Islamic, Indigenous, etc.), which transform in relation to surrounding social changes and attitudes of the governing regime and populace (whether friendly, hostile, indifferent).

Several objections have been raised against the folk law approach. To repeat, law is identified not with an abstract concept of definition but through collective (conventionalist) recognition of law within communities: law is whatever people identify and treat through their social practices as "law" (or *droit, recht,* etc.).[160] Yapese customary law, New York state law, international law, Halakhah, Sharia, and countless other manifestations are collectively recognized as "law." Several theorists have asked: "but why choose *droit* and

---

[159] See Tamanaha, *supra* note 135, Chapters 5 and 6.
[160] For a fuller elaboration, see *id.* at 73–77; Brian Z. Tamanaha, *A General Jurisprudence of Law and Society* (Oxford: Oxford University Press 2001) 166, 194.

Recht, rather than *loi* and *Gesetz*?";[161] "some languages have not one word for 'law' but two: they track the Latin vocabulary of *ius* and *lex*. Should both be attended to?"[162] The answer is that if multiple terms in a given vernacular are translated as "law" then, yes, they all count as collectively recognized forms of law. Jurisprudent John Gardner notes that the conventionalist approach is "mysterious"; "what Tamanaha wants us to search for . . . are various indigenous ideas (aka concepts) of law." He objects: "How can we possibly identify them as concepts of law before we know what counts as law?"[163] But there is nothing mysterious about this: the cluster of ideas the term law represents has been translated from classical languages to contemporary languages across the globe. Translations inevitably face ambiguities and indeterminacies, which does not prevent their achievement.

Theorists might worry that under a conventionalist approach, anything can be deemed law if it secures collective recognition within a community. While it is true that conventionalism is open to this possibility, in actual social practices the term law (and translations thereof) is not easily attached to all kinds of phenomena because it is laden with content and connotations that limit its usage. The overwhelming bulk of phenomena collectively identified as law within societies past and present are versions of what I have identified as community law, regime law, or cross polity law.

Another objection against centering on folk law is that it gives up the goal of constructing a science or philosophy of law based on an account of the essential features of law. That objection is correct. Social scientists and legal theorists are free to pursue this goal, though the problems elaborated in this chapter raise significant doubts about whether it can be achieved.[164] Meanwhile, for people grappling with or striving to understand situations of legal pluralism, it makes little sense to insist that legal pluralism must be constructed on an answer to a puzzle that legions of sophisticated theorists over centuries of attempts have been unable to satisfactorily resolve. Moreover, since theorists devise different theoretical concepts of law, what results is multiple versions of legal pluralism, generating disagreement, and confusion.

---

[161] Pirie, *supra* note 6, at 44.

[162] Gregorie Webber, "Asking Why in the Study of Human Affairs," 60 American Journal of Jurisprudence 51, 61 (2015).

[163] John Gardner, *Law as a Leap of Faith* (Oxford: Oxford University Press 2012) 298.

[164] See Brian Z. Tamanaha, "Reconstruction in Jurisprudence: Features of a Realistic Theory of Law," Canadian Journal of Law and Jurisprudence, forthcoming 2021.

More to the point, the objective itself is flawed. As I have argued, collectively recognized law has assumed different forms and functions in connection with developing social complexity (community, regime, and cross-polity), which do not all share the same features. The classic question "What is law?"—framed in the singular *is*—misleadingly suggests that there is one true law with a single set of essential features, which is mistaken. Multiple forms of law have been collectively recognized, which have different features that cannot be captured by one definition or conception.

Using folk law as the basis for understanding legal pluralism does not entail giving up on social scientific and theoretical inquires. What I articulate is a mid-range theory built on paying attention to the historical development of law, the social circumstances of law, collective understandings of law, actions in connection with law, and the social consequences of law. A great deal can be learned about law through this approach.

Conclusion
Legal Pluralism Explained

Legal pluralism in relation to state law falls on two sides of a permeable and shifting divide: (1) multiple forms of collectively recognized law coexist within social arenas (external pluralism), and (2) manifestations of law are internally pluralistic (internal pluralism). Systems of state law face coexisting external forms of collectively recognized law and are internally pluralistic. The divide is permeable and shifting because one of the factors contributing to internal pluralism is interaction with, influences from, and efforts to absorb or control other coexisting forms of law like customary and religious law and international law. An array of legal norms and institutions exist in society: outside, inside, and intertwined with state legal systems.

This social reality challenges two core elements of the image of the monist law state: that state law is supreme and holds a monopoly over law within the territory; and that state law is a unified, hierarchically organized whole. No state legal system has stamped out all other forms of law collectively recognized by communities. No state legal system has stamped out internal divergences, competing claims of power and authority at the same level and different levels, and so forth. Contemporary state legal systems consist of numerous legal institutions dispersed throughout society in ways that are not tightly bound together within monopolistic, unified hierarchies of supreme law. Existing legal arrangements evolved in the course of history subject to contingencies, compromises, politics, power, and a variety of other factors—not drawn up as integrated wholes. The ultimate source and fuel of external and internal pluralism is social, cultural, economic, and political heterogeneity that exists in every society.

From a monist perspective this appears defective, but there are at least three significant benefits of having distributed state legal institutions operating with separate horizontal and vertical relations and hierarchies loosely connected to in the aggregate: it allows significant regional variations to be reflected in law in ways that match the values of local communities, which is harder to

Legal Pluralism Explained. Brian Z. Tamanaha, Oxford University Press (2021). © Brian Z. Tamanaha.
DOI: 10.1093/oso/9780190861551.003.0007

accommodate with uniform law; it creates multiple pathways for different positions to secure legal recognition, opening up state legal institutions to alternative views and legal change; and widely dispersed institutions of law creation, enforcement, and application not contained within a single hierarchy are harder to capture and be directed in a totalitarian fashion.

This study exposes the interaction between and among community law, regime law, and cross-polity law. Community law, the fundamental rules of social intercourse that exist in all societies (property, personal injuries, marriage, family obligations, inheritance, debts, labor obligations, and a few more), has proven to be extraordinarily resilient in many contexts because it constitutes the framework within which people interact with one another—it is what they know and take for granted as aspects of their life-world. The main dynamic underlying legal pluralism today involves the relationship between regime law (state law in particular) and community law, with cross-polity law intersecting and interacting with both.

Regime law has undergone a long-term arc of increasing institutionalization (in the modern period becoming entrenched bureaucratic organizations) at multiple levels of geographical scale—local community, municipality, county, district, state, national, and lately transnational. In the course of this arc, state legal systems crystallized to govern significant territorial groupings, securing the primary role as centralizing regimes that encompass locally distributed governing units in institutional networks collectively linked through legal and financial arrangements. This ranges today from confederations to unitary states, though in the past city states were also important polities. Territorial groupings that exist today were drawn for contingent historical reasons and many encompass multiple distinct cultural, ethnic, religious and other communities.

As long as governing regimes have existed, cross-polity legal arrangements have addressed matters between and across polities. Formal understandings between polities extend back four millennia, addressing such matters as which king has jurisdiction over particular cities, rights of foreign merchants, guarantees against robbery and confiscation of trading goods, taxation of foreign citizens, protection of emissaries, and other matters.[1] Cross-polity law is part of the mix of law operating within societies along with regime law and community law.

---

[1] See Brian Z. Tamanaha, *A Realistic Theory of Law* (Cambridge: Cambridge University Press 2017) 168.

The distinction between regime law and cross-polity law is fluid. The Holy Roman Empire, the British Empire, and the European Union, to name just a few of many examples, can be seen from one angle as instances of regime law or from another angle as cross-polity law. The previously proposed Treaty Establishing a Constitution for Europe captures this duality in its title. Beginning as a construct of cross-polity law, the European Union has developed institutionally to become a solid surface manifestation of regime law—and where it goes from here time will tell.

In locations where regime law and community law coevolved together over many centuries—where the governing polity absorbed and incorporated the fundamental rules of social intercourse—the populace largely arrange their affairs in connection with state legal rules. This has occurred in Western societies. Even in these situations, however, pockets of law recognized within distinct sub-communities have continued to exist, whether officially recognized by the ruling regime or suppressed or ignored or accommodated (as has occurred with indigenous law, Romani law, Jewish law, and Islamic law, among others). Social heterogeneity thus generates external and internal legal pluralism for state law.

When immigrants move to a very different society in significant numbers, or when people migrate from rural to urban areas, they often re-create aspects of their own community law. This occurred with German tribes that migrated through the Roman Empire, merchant diasporas across the Mediterranean, European colonial administrators and settlers, Chinese and Indian immigrant laborers in many areas during European colonization, and the migration to Europe of large numbers of Muslims in recent decades. Throughout human history multitudes of people have forcibly or voluntarily migrated and re-created communities following aspects of their own law in their new lands. This too gives rise to external or internal legal pluralism or both for state legal systems.

When a single polity covers expanses of territory with multiple distinct sub-polities and communities, external and internal legal pluralism exists owing to sub-regimes, as well as communities following their own law in daily social intercourse. This was the situation in the Balkans and *millet* system during the Ottoman Empire, Bukovina during Ehrlich's day, the former Soviet Union, China, and African countries where territorial boundaries were drawn by European powers with little attention to the groupings of ethnic and religious communities. The larger the territorial scale encompassed by a given regime, the greater the heterogeneity, increasing the likelihood that multiple sub-regimes and communities with their own law will be encompassed. This inevitably gives rise to external and internal legal pluralism.

A major source of legal pluralism occurs when state law is transplanted from one society to another with wholly different social, cultural, economic, political, and legal arrangements. This occurred through colonization, creating not only a multiplicity of legal orders external and internal to the state law regime, but also stark contrasts between state law and the way of life of many people within the community. It has occurred through imposition or voluntary borrowing on many occasions and continues today through the implementation of Western-derived economic laws in countries around the world in connection with economic globalization as well as the spread of human rights. Transplanted legal regimes inevitably work differently (often ineffectively) when implanted to a completely different milieu because the law originally worked in connection with supportive surrounding cultural, economic, and political factors that are not present in the new location.

Given the lengthy history traced in the course of this book, there is little reason to believe that states will soon evolve to match the monist law state image in either its external or internal aspects—securing a supreme monopoly over law and total internal hierarchical unity. External and internal legal pluralism can be eliminated only through total social homogeneity. Dystopian sameness to this extent is not remotely possible as far as one can foresee.

What the relations between community law, regime law, and cross-polity law will look like a millennium hence is impossible to know—but for everyone living today, and for many generations that follow, legal pluralism undoubtedly will continue to exist and will have consequences along the lines set forth in this book. Legal pluralism is present in the lives of many people and societies around the world.

There is no universal formula for dealing with external and internal legal pluralism, for each situation is unique. No generalizations can be made about whether legal pluralism always is good or bad, socially desirable or problematic, for the answer depends on the circumstances at hand. Legal pluralism creates legal uncertainty for people but it also allows them to utilize law they understand and identify with, and it provides them with alternatives; it creates potential competition among coexisting fora, which can be debilitating to the functioning of each, but it can produce cooperation and prompt institutional improvements.

Perhaps the only advice useful for all contexts of legal pluralism is that to properly understand the situation and to devise strategies for achieving objectives, one must discard the assumptions of the monist law state, a false vision that continues to shape and distort the views of many. This powerful image has enchanted jurists for over three centuries, but it is normatively questionable, theoretically unjustified, and has never been descriptively accurate. The normal condition of law across societies past and present is external and internal legal pluralism in various ways and to differing extents. Absorbing this lesson is necessary to a sound understanding of law and society.

Index

For the benefit of digital users, indexed terms that span two pages (e.g., 52–53) may, on occasion, appear on only one of those pages.